Clinical Hypnosis Textbook

A GUIDE FOR PRACTICAL INTERVENTION

Second Edition

URSULA JAMES

Honorary Lecturer, Barts and The London School of Medicine and Dentistry
Visiting Teaching Fellow, Oxford University Medical School
and Chair of the Medical School Hypnosis Association

Forewords by

DR MARK FELDMAN

and

SHEELAGH HEUGH

Radcliffe Publishing
Oxford • New York

Radcliffe Publishing Ltd
18 Marcham Road
Abingdon
Oxon OX14 1AA
United Kingdom

www.radcliffe-oxford.com
Electronic catalogue and worldwide online ordering facility.

British Library Cataloguing in Publication Data

100 615 7142

A catalogue record for this book is available from the British Library.

ISBN-13: 978 184619 420 7

The paper used for the text pages of this book
is FSC certified. FSC (The Forest Stewardship
Council) is an international network to promote
responsible management of the world's forests.

Mixed Sources
Product group from well-managed
forests and other controlled sources
www.fsc.org Cert no. SGS-COC-2482
© 1996 Forest Stewardship Council

Typeset by Pindar NZ, Auckland, New Zealand
Printed and bound by TJI Digital, Padstow, Cornwall, UK

Contents

Foreword

It only happens rarely, perhaps three or four times in a lifetime of attending lectures – the hairs stand up on the back of your neck, and you experience a sense of wonder and a sudden need to discover more about the subject that is almost a physical craving.

This is what I felt when I first heard Ursula James lecture on the introductory course for clinical hypnosis. Ursula is a natural teacher, and she has distilled the essence of clinical hypnosis into this new text. However, theory is all very well, but it carries little weight if practical skills are lacking. It is in this aspect of the work that she excels. When discussing a hypnotherapeutic puzzle with her, there is a sense that, instead of merely looking at the patient and finding an option for treatment, she walks around the problem viewing it from all angles to arrive almost magically at the best solution.

I remember vividly one case that I referred to her, of a young woman at a business meeting far from home who had awoken to find a stranger in her hotel bedroom. She talked to him for six hours before he finally left her. During this time she was in constant fear of physical attack.

I first saw her three weeks later when she was still unable to talk without crying, and could barely leave home. I referred her to Ursula, and after one session she was back at work – the trauma behind her. She had no further problems. I am convinced that conventional counselling or medication could not have accomplished this almost miraculous transformation.

Of course it was not a miracle, but the application of hypnotherapeutic techniques by a master practitioner, Ursula James.

This wide-ranging primer covers the theory, practice and history of the subject, as well as including very useful links to further information.

This fascinating subject is made accessible by Ursula's clearly structured approach, and everyone who reads it, from novices to experienced hypnotherapists, is sure to gain new insights from the book.

In this latest edition several new topics have been included, namely hypnotic diagnostics, weight control and obstetrics. Ursula also introduces us to the Medical School Hypnosis Association (MSHA), an important new organisation dedicated to the ideal of ensuring that hypnosis is accepted as the scientific discipline which it is rapidly becoming.

The main body of the text has been extensively revised and updated, ensuring that this book remains at the forefront of literature on learning and understanding hypnosis and hypnotherapy. Once again it gives me great pleasure to recommend this text unreservedly.

Dr Mark Feldman
President
British Association of Medical Hypnosis
October 2009

Foreword

In 2007, Ursula James approached the School of Life Sciences at London Metropolitan University to host the newly created Medical School Hypnosis Association (MSHA). Its purpose, she informed me, was to bring together medical students, clinical hypnosis practitioners, medics and researchers in order to move clinical hypnosis and its perceived role in medicine out of the fringes and into the mainstream. Already she had three active projects under way, and the interest level for this within the profession was very encouraging.

As I learned more about Ursula James, I discovered that she had brought clinical hypnosis education to medical students at 11 medical schools in the UK, including Oxford and Cambridge. Her methods of training interested me and, as a biomedical scientist, I quickly became interested in the potential for identifying biomedical changes resulting from the hypnotherapeutic process.

Ursula James' passion to see clinical hypnosis become part of mainstream medicine has led her down two paths to that destination, namely education leading to professional regulation, and sound scientifically-based clinical research. Both of these were identified in a report of the House of Lords Select Committee (published in 2001) on complementary therapies in medicine requiring a more professional approach before the medical practice as a whole would be prepared to accept clinical hypnosis as a profession that can legitimately ally itself with mainstream medicine. Her scientific approach to this topic interested me sufficiently for me to take her on as a PhD student, and to become involved in her drive to produce valid and replicable research in this field.

The MSHA itself is rapidly growing in stature, and now has the patronage of both Professor Whorwell, whose research on irritable bowel syndrome and hypnosis is world renowned, and Dr David Spiegel, one of the most famous names in clinical hypnosis research. If you are interested in research into clinical hypnosis, I would encourage you to join the MSHA (membership is free) and become part of a rapidly growing worldwide network of professionals who are conducting research into this fascinating field, making it more accessible to the general public, and for medical practitioners to refer the patients who will benefit from this fascinating and useful tool. For further information about the MSHA, visit www.msha.org.uk or email msha@londonmet.ac.uk

Sheelagh Heugh BSc PGCE MSc FIBMS BBTS
London Metropolitan University
School of Life Sciences
October 2009

Preface

Clinical hypnosis is a useful personal tool for stress management, goal setting and relaxation. It can also be an excellent addition to the range of professional techniques available to anyone working within the caring professions. Hypnosis creates a relaxation state, the therapeutic component allows the patient to access positive states, and it can also be used as a stress reduction mechanism, as well as enhancing the patient's responsiveness to change. These are some of the benefits over and above its use within a formal protocol. One area that is often overlooked and which is elemental in clinical hypnosis is the use of stylised language techniques. These can be utilised in patient evaluation, to enhance diagnostic skills, and also to improve general communication.

This book gives an overview of the subject of clinical hypnosis, and sets out to introduce the reader to the potential for its application within the medical setting. In addition, it teaches individuals how to experience self-hypnosis and induce it in others. It further explores the framework of a session, and breaks down the individual components and how they are constructed to create a unique therapeutic protocol using specific language patterns. Lastly, this volume provides an overview of the historical context of clinical hypnosis and the current variations in and schools of thought on its application, together with a glossary of terms and a list of useful contacts and websites.

The book can be used as an introduction to the subject, or for the experienced practitioner to gain a deeper understanding of the ways in which sessions are constructed. The use of specific language in patient communication and therapeutic evaluation is discussed at some length, and this can be used outside the framework of a formal clinical hypnosis session whenever patient evaluation skills are required. Specific techniques for the more common conditions where clinical hypnosis can be effective are also covered in some detail at the end of the volume.

Ursula James
October 2009

Acknowledgements

I wish to thank Dr Lyn Williamson for giving me the opportunity to design and present the first clinical hypnosis course at Oxford University Medical School.

I am also grateful to Sheelagh Heugh, for her willingness to share knowledge and her endless patience under fire.

Finally, I would like to thank Thomas Connelly, Secretary of the British Society of Clinical Hypnosis, for creating the glossary of terms and the list of useful website addresses, and allowing it to be replicated in this volume.

This book is dedicated to:

My family – for always believing in me.

Phil Benjamin – for changing my mind.

Dr Mark Feldman – for his boundless enthusiasm.

CHAPTER 1

What is hypnosis?

The term 'hypnosis' was derived originally from the Greek god of sleep, Hypnos, who was the father of Morpheus, the god of dreams. In the 1800s, James Braid coined the term 'neurypnosis', which he believed to be a form of paralysis of the central nervous system that occurred during a sleep-like state. The term was subsequently shortened to 'hypnosis'. There have been many changes in the definitions of hypnosis since then, from theories that suggest it is a form of mind control, or a symptom of hysteria, through to the current, more practical definition which identifies it as a structured therapeutic tool. The subject of clinical hypnosis, although it has been around for many years on the periphery of medical application, is now experiencing a renaissance thanks to advances in fMRI and CAT scanning. Hypnosis is now being systematically researched as a viable medical intervention that is free from any known side-effects, and which is cost-effective and time-efficient.

The first thing to be aware of is that a hypnotic experience is a conscious experience. The individual is aware and in control throughout. It is a usually a pleasant experience, often involving relaxation, and there will be times during the process when the individual feels less aware of their surroundings and more aware of internal events. After the experience, the individual will often notice time distortion, with a feeling that the perceived time was much shorter than clock time. Rather than being unfamiliar, hypnosis can be defined as an extension, or amplification, of normal states of awareness.

The experience that each person has will be unique, and will depend on a number of factors, including their previous experience, expectations and motivation, to name just a few. Hypnosis can be difficult to define even when you have experienced it. This is for two reasons. First, it takes place in the internal environment, and we therefore do not have the language to communicate it fully. It is the same when you try to describe your dreams to another person – the telling is a pale reflection of what happened to you. Secondly, hypnosis is hard to describe because each patient's encounter with it is different, depending on that person. However, it is not sleep.

Hypnosis is often defined by what it is *not*. It is not sleep, it is not like a general anaesthetic and it is not unlike some other familiar states of awareness. One of the first things that occur during a clinical hypnosis session is that the practitioner will ask the patient what they know about hypnosis. Once the practitioner has a clear picture of the patient's current understanding of hypnosis, the practitioner will then select a model to describe the experience to the patient in a way that will best help them to experience it. Models are frequently used in clinical hypnosis sessions as ways of providing a framework for the patient to feel comfortable, or become more receptive to suggestions. Models will take what the patient previously understood about the process and re-interpret it in a way that will allow them to obtain the maximum benefit from the event.

The attitudes of the medical profession towards hypnosis are changing, with an increasing awareness that the hypnotherapeutic model may have a role in modern medicine (Eslinger, 2000). In this volume I shall discuss the practical ways in which hypnosis can be used as both an adjunct and an alternative to mainstream medical practice. In addition, the importance of specific language and the influence of suggestions given in hypnosis and how these create changes in both psychological and organic-based conditions will be described and explained.

The *Encarta Dictionary* defines 'hypnosis' as follows:

> hypnosis
> *noun*
> **1. artificially induced condition**: a condition that can be artificially induced in people, in which they can respond to questions and are very susceptible to suggestions from the hypnotist
>
> **2. induction of hypnosis**: the technique or practice of inducing a state of hypnosis in people

The term 'hypnotherapy' is defined as follows:

> hypnotherapy
> *noun*
> **treating illness with hypnosis**: the use of hypnosis in treating illness, for example, in dealing with physical pain or psychological problems.

The term 'clinical hypnosis' is now more commonly used to denote a specific treatment protocol. It is the use of hypnosis or the hypnotic state, in a medical framework, for the alleviation of physical, psychological or behavioural problems. Clinical hypnosis employs a protocol whereby the technique selected correlates directly with information collected from the case history. This lends itself more readily to research and, in theory, is replicable regardless of practitioner.

- *Hypnosis* is a physical and mental state of highly focused concentration.
- *Hypnotherapy* is the process of inducing hypnosis and making suggestions to a patient for a therapeutic purpose.
- *Clinical hypnosis* incorporates a range of defined and replicable methodologies within the hypnotic state, including physical relaxation and a state of mental focus and receptiveness to assist the patient to take control of their condition and effect a change.

This volume will use the term 'hypnosis' when referring to the state, the term 'hypnotherapy' when referring to the process, and the term 'clinical hypnosis' when referring to therapeutic application or the use of a specific protocol.

A NATURAL PHENOMENON

The state of hypnosis can be simply explained as a naturally occurring phenomenon during which the body remains relaxed while the mind goes into a highly focused state (Kirsch, 2001). In the course of an ordinary day we may enter hypnotic-like states many times, and for varying reasons. When we are bored or not fully engaged with our current surroundings, our system has a way of distracting us by daydreaming about things that we would like to do in our future, or going into a state of reverie to re-experience pleasant events from our past. If we are in physical pain, or traumatised by an event, we can also shift our awareness. This ability to dissociate is a protective mechanism and, as with daydreams and reverie, it is a completely natural process. Whichever way, we become disconnected from our immediate surroundings and can shift our current mood, or ability to interact with our surroundings. The protocols of clinical hypnosis engage and enhance an individual's ability to relax and alter their current state. Clinical hypnosis takes processes and events which are already part of the individual's experience of the world, and utilises them to create positive change. In hypnosis the individual becomes focused and receptive to positive suggestions. Generally, the attention is directed towards pre-experiencing or re-experiencing positive states and outcomes. As a result, individuals begin to feel more optimistic, and start to direct their attention towards potential change. There are some therapeutic protocols which actively promote the re- or pre-experiencing of unpleasant or anxiety-inducing states. Even with these protocols, the therapeutic emphasis remains on the individual's capacity to experience something different from this – that is, something more positive and beneficial (McNeilly, 1994).

In addition to the passive states of daydream and reverie, there are learned activities, such as driving a car, which become automatic. Driving on 'auto-pilot' is sometimes known as 'highway hypnosis' (Cerezuela *et al.*, 2004), and it usually occurs when a route is so familiar that we do not need to 'think' about where we are going. On occasion it appears as if our body is carrying out the behaviour while our mind is elsewhere. It is the ability of the body (or some would term it the unconscious mind) to carry out functions without conscious processing of information, and it is a very useful capacity. The individual's ability to store and retrieve information when required is very useful with regard to habits and learned behaviours. However, it does make it more difficult if the individual wishes to change that unconscious pattern (Taggart *et al.*, 2005).

This capacity for automatic activity (that is, without conscious or deliberate thought) occurs most commonly when we are in familiar surroundings or easily recognised moods. This explains the higher incidence of accidents close to or even within the home. As individuals feel comfortable and do not need to 'think' about their surroundings, they are not on alert when a change occurs – hence the increased response time, and the higher rate of accidents. When individuals are hypnotised they are encouraged to focus on the familiar events of the hypnotic state so they will recognise them and feel comfortable, therefore activating the state of low conscious activity, or automatic processing. Patients will often state on awakening that they 'did not feel as if they were hypnotised' precisely because the state is already a familiar one, and they often expect something very different. In clinical hypnosis, this capacity to be relaxed in familiar surroundings is used to encourage patients to access their unconscious capabilities.

The third component of clinical hypnosis, which again is a naturally occurring event, is the capacity of hypnosis to enhance the mind's ability to access emotional variations by use of memory or prediction. This natural capacity to add emotion to events can have a positive or negative effect. Mark Twain once remarked, 'I have known many troubles in my life, and most of them never happened.' This highlights the way in which individuals have a tendency to predict, and often with a negative outcome if they feel lacking in confidence. Once emotion has been added to a memory, that memory becomes much stronger and more intense (Kensinger and Schacter, 2007). If the emotion associated with a memory subsides, the capacity to recall that memory will be reduced.

In summary, the hypnotic state helps the patient to access the following:

➤ the passive events of daydreaming and reverie
➤ an increased focus of attention on unconscious activity
➤ influencing the future by accessing positive memory associations.

In turn, the occurrence of these three natural events is enhanced by hypnotic suggestion. This in turn increases the patient's capacity to:

➤ pre-experience or re-experience an event
➤ utilise their unconscious functionality to stay calm and relaxed
➤ produce a positive emotion or response.

> **Clinical hypnosis uses naturally occurring states and behaviours and amplifies them.**

HYPNOTIC SUGGESTIONS

The first element of hypnotic suggestions that needs to be understood is that these are suggestions based only on the discussion between the patient and the practitioner before formal induction of hypnosis takes place. Suggestions are refined, clarified and agreed by the patient. If a practitioner decided to add suggestions that were not previously agreed with the patient, they would automatically pull themselves out of the hypnoidal state. Hypnotic suggestions are therefore unique to the interaction between patient, condition and symptoms or effects, and must be created with attention to detail to ensure that they will be accessible and acceptable to the person receiving them. The use of specific language is a very important factor in making suggestions acceptable and accessible to the patient.

Once the hypnotic state has been induced, it can then be used for positive suggestions to be introduced to the patient. Suggestions must be made with a single objective in mind, and whenever possible should be given to the patient using positive vocabulary. This is discussed in more depth in Chapter 8. These types of suggestions are known as post-hypnotic suggestions, and they are the suggestions which the patient is instructed to carry out after termination of the session. These form the hypnotherapeutic component of a hypnosis session.

Hypnosis cannot turn a patient into something which they are not, nor can it give anyone the ability to do something that they could not do before. There are (as yet unsubstantiated) claims of individuals undergoing hypnosis to display the capacity to communicate spontaneously in a language of which they had no prior knowledge (known as 'xenoglossy'). Under examination these cases have often demonstrated that the patient is speaking the words but has little or no understanding of what they are saying. In some instances the individual has later recalled having seen these words written down, or heard them spoken in a context which they had previously forgotten.

However, clinical hypnosis does provide five fundamentals that then increase the patient's capacity to enhance what is already present. It can do the following:

Amplify abilities

The relaxed and focused state of awareness that is experienced in hypnosis allows patients to remember positive events and successful memories, therefore reminding them what they are already capable of doing once they put their mind to it – that is, once they focus.

Focus attention on whatever task is in hand in order to achieve it more easily

As the hypnotic state is one of concentrated attention, where distractions are reduced, and a relaxed and focused state is suggested, individuals can direct all of their attention towards achieving their objective. The installation of positive suggestions in hypnosis reduces individuals' capacity to talk themselves out of their objective by giving conflicting auto-suggestions.

Help to create a specific goal so that the mind can work towards it

The pre-induction talk between patient and practitioner will refine the objective of therapy. Other, potentially conflicting objectives are compartmentalised in order to reduce distraction. Objectives are subjected to SMART principles in order to reduce loopholes.

Reduce stress or anxiety

Poor stress coping strategies or over-anxiety will often result in a mental paralysis, which in turn holds the patient back from gaining a therapeutic benefit. As a result of being taught self-hypnosis, the patient can learn to manage stress better, learn how to relax and reduce unnecessary nervous tension or anxiety (Anbar, 2003).

Stimulate autonomic functions

In order to be prepared for a future event, the autonomic nervous system will become activated in advance, as in the fight or flight response to stress, or salivation when imagining a feast. Through the intense physical experiences associated with clinical hypnosis, individuals can be prepared for a future event and, as they are preparing in a focused and relaxed state, will be able to optimise their experience of the event when it happens.

The form and content that suggestions will take come from the pre-induction talk between the practitioner and the patient. Only one suggestion at a time can be processed fully, so time is taken to clarify the patient's objective in each session. The patient will only accept suggestions of a positive nature. Milton Erickson commented on this phenomenon and concluded that if inappropriate suggestions were made to a patient, the patient would discriminate, fail to respond, and even construct methods of retaliation for the breach of trust.

If suggestions are made *not* to do something, this can often produce a reversed effect. An example of this would be to try not to think of a white horse. Immediately this produces the effect of thinking about a white horse. This is a direct result of the way in which the brain functions. In order not to think of something, that thing has to be thought of first. This event is fundamental to the way in which suggestions are delivered in clinical hypnosis. In hypnosis the suggestions relate to what the patient wants, not what they don't want. Clear and direct instructions are given to focus the patient's attention away from their problem, or the patient's experience of a positive state is used to create a different approach to their problem. The practitioner will direct the patient to think differently about their problem, based on strategies that the patient may have employed previously, and by doing so will encourage them to behave and respond in a more appropriate manner.

There are occasions when negative states are recalled in hypnosis as a way of reminding the patient that they only know they are in pain if they have a memory of what having relief from pain means to them. There are times when these useful (that is, non-pain-based) memories may have been made inaccessible, and hypnotherapeutic techniques can be used to work on stimulating those memories to produce a healthier response or more control over the pain state (De Pascalis *et al.*, 2008).

There is another form of suggestion given in hypnosis, known as 'ego-strengthening' suggestions. These will be included in most sessions. Once again, this type of suggestion works because it is an extension of everyday life. It is natural to feel better when we are told that we are looking well or particularly trim today. Conversely, when we are told that we do not look well, the focus of attention shifts towards noticing every ache and pain. Ego-strengthening suggestions encourage the patient to look for positives around and within them, and generally enhance their capacity to experience positive states. The suggestions will also move the emphasis away from self-monitoring and on to an appreciation of what is going on around them as a way of encouraging the patient to take their mind off their symptoms.

Therapeutic suggestions take one of two forms.

Post-hypnotic suggestions

These relate specifically to the presenting condition, and will direct the patient's attention on to specific thoughts, feelings or actions. Post-hypnotic suggestions will be created by the clinical hypnosis practitioner, and will be based on the language patterns and past successes of the patient and the specific objective of the process.

Ego-strengthening suggestions

These are included in most clinical hypnosis sessions except where contraindicated by the condition. The purpose of ego-strengthening suggestions is to remind the patient of events and successes where they have achieved their objectives. One purpose of this is to remind them what they are capable of. However, the primary purpose of these suggestions is to act as a motivational tool with regard to their condition, and encourage the patient to recall positive states so that they will feel better generally.

HOW DOES CLINICAL HYPNOSIS WORK?

At the moment no one fully comprehends how clinical hypnosis works. This is partly attributed to an attitude held by some practitioners, who maintain a firm belief that standard protocols cannot be created, and that most of the work which is done in a consulting room is unique to the individual practising it. This attitude does not lend itself to double-blind trials, and therefore there is a dearth of *good* research on the subject. This is the main reason why I became involved in creating the Medical School Hypnosis Association (MSHA), as a way of creating, informing and coordinating good research into hypnosis and its medical application. Medical practice will not fully accept a procedure for general application that cannot prove itself to be a reliable approach with a predictable outcome. The other reason for the lack of definitive evidence on how clinical hypnosis works has been the result of the ways in which success has been evaluated. Much of the research that has been done has relied on subjective evaluation by the patient. This is necessarily open to interpretation. However, this situation is changing with a shift towards objective testing of variables such as basal skin temperature, heart rate and, most significantly, brain function during the hypnotic state. It appears that the breakthroughs in technology with fMRI scanning and brain mapping will finally put clinical hypnosis on the neurological map and, it is hoped, move it towards the mainstream of medical application. The cost of collecting biomedical data has also come down with the use of saliva testing, and this will necessarily have implications in producing more robust research data.

In terms of the events that take place during the session, an important part of a clinical hypnosis session will include describing to the patient a model of the way in which clinical hypnosis will work. The key point to be aware of here is that the process can be explained and described in a number of ways. The significance of explaining it to the patient lies in creating a model of the event that will best help them to experience the benefits of the process. One of the models most commonly used describes the differing areas of the brain and its functionality. Patients will often complain that they do not understand how hypnosis can do something that they cannot do for themselves. This model describes the event of hypnosis as an opening up of the neurological pathways between conscious thought processing and unconscious activity and function. The result of this is that the individual can then gain access to the information they need to successfully make the changes they require.

Using the functionality model gives the patient an explanation of why hypnosis will work and, just as significantly, why they have not been able to make the changes for themselves before. Although this is still a model in so far as it cannot yet be fully endorsed by the facts, it does appear to be one of the more accurate explanations of how hypnosis operates on the brain, and it seems that medical science is starting to back up this model as the mapping of brain function continues to enhance our knowledge and understanding of different brain events (Grant and Rainville, 2005). There are a number of other models which can be used to describe hypnosis to the patient, depending on the mindset of the patient and the nature of the condition. The question of which model can best be used really depends on the character of the patient, the nature of the condition and the expectations of the process. How to select the appropriate model is discussed at length later in this book.

Explaining the events of hypnosis and the potential applications of clinical hypnosis is only one element of how it works. Another key element in the modern use of clinical hypnosis in a medical setting is the concept of the therapeutic partnership. To put this concept into context it is worth looking at some of the history of hypnosis. To understand where it exists today, clinical hypnosis needs to be viewed as a product of the society within which it is conducted.

Before the First World War, some physicians considered hypnosis to be an event that was a side-effect of hysteria, and as only women were thought to be capable of suffering from hysteria, only women were thought to be capable of experiencing hypnosis. This view changed when soldiers returned from the trenches after the First World War with symptoms of hysteria. Hysterical symptoms were reclassified, and hypnotherapeutic techniques were then used to help soldiers suffering from what would later become known as post-traumatic stress disorder.

In Freud's day, when he observed Pierre Janet using hypnotic techniques with patients, hypnosis involved the patient being told what to do and carrying out the suggestion unquestioningly. In contrast, Milton Erickson, the most well-known exponent of clinical hypnosis in modern times, would hold what seemed like a gentle, rambling monologue with his patients while he made indirect suggestions to direct the patient's attention to various aspects of their condition. He believed that 'confusion was the gateway to learning', and by helping the patient to produce questions, they would then be able to come to their own conclusions about how best to help themselves.

From these examples we can observe that one of the factors in how clinical hypnosis operates relates to the interaction between the practitioner and the patient. This is at least partly based on expectation and a clearly defined relationship between the two parties. In modern clinical hypnosis, the practitioner defines the process as one in which both the practitioner and the patient are active participants in the event and in deciding on a therapeutic outcome. We live in more rapidly moving times than ever before, and clinical hypnosis is moving towards defining itself as a brief strategic therapy, whereby the patient will only attend for a small number of sessions (interspersed in some instances with homework done by the patient). Clinical hypnosis is now much more clear and streamlined, as the therapeutic partnership defines specific parameters that are required to produce changes in the patient's state and perception of events. These parameters are discussed in more depth in Chapter 8, 'Creating the hypnotherapeutic protocol'. This development lends itself to clearly defined protocols, which can then be submitted to research. Further information about this can be obtained by visiting www.msha.org.uk. There will always be practitioners out there who believe that the work which they do is unique to their talents as an individual. To a greater or lesser extent this might be true, as the more competent and confident practitioners will create a greater degree of trust and rapport with their patients. Without it, the initial induction of hypnosis does not easily occur, and therapeutic suggestions will not be readily received.

With regard to the process of hypnosis itself, this works by the more easily observable processes of physical relaxation allied with mental focus. In this state the patient will be relaxed and focused, and can therefore more easily access capabilities of which they were previously unaware, or thought to be outside their conscious control (for example, the control of tremors associated with Parkinson's disease) (Buell and Biehl, 1949; Wain *et al.*, 1990). Induction of hypnosis is done by means of specific suggestions relating to focus (for example, by instructing the patient to pay attention to their breathing), and is enhanced by suggestions of relaxation and focused attention. The practitioner may make suggestions for the patient to notice their breathing becoming deeper, or to become less aware of noises around them. Once a patient is observed to be in a relaxed and focused state, their altered awareness is enhanced by a process known as 'deepening', whereby any observable phenomena are commented upon and amplified by the practitioner, by use of verbal cues or suggestions, or by changing their own breathing patterns. The patient will then reach a level of hypnosis where they feel comfortable and relaxed, and suggestions for changes in thought, activity or emotional states can be made. Although the process is usually a linear one, with the hypnotic suggestions for change following suggestions made for inducing and deepening the hypnotic state, there are some techniques in which suggestions are interspersed.

The procedure for clinical hypnosis takes into account the following:

> ➤ the patient's personality
> ➤ the patient's personal history
> ➤ the history of the presenting condition
> ➤ the specific objective for the session.

A treatment appropriate to the patient can then be formulated by using the above criteria. Each session is different and personal, and it is vital that patients experiencing the clinical hypnosis are aware that this process will take them to the positive limits of their potential, physically, mentally or emotionally, whichever combination of personal characteristics they need to use to fulfil their goals. How this is achieved is discussed in more detail in later chapters.

Another model that is used to describe the process of hypnosis is a very simplistic one. It describes hypnosis as a state of focused concentration with associated physical relaxation. As this is such a familiar state, and the suggestions that are made can seem obvious, patients may be curious as to how the hypnotic experience differs from, for example, making these suggestions in the form of affirmations. To amplify this model, the practitioner may then go on to explain hypnosis in terms of where the brain experiences various events. The cerebrum (which in this model is equated with conscious or logical thought) already knows what the patient needs to do to make a required change. However, the cerebellum (here equated with memory storage and the autonomic nervous system) stores memories of habits and unconscious processes. Hypnosis can be described (as in the previous model) as a mediator between these two areas of the brain, allowing the conscious process to rest whilst the unconscious areas receive and interpret the information, allowing changes to take place. Quite simply, the hypnosis acts as a conduit to take what the patient already knows (which is stored in the cerebrum) and move it to the part of their brain which can act to make changes take place unconsciously (the cerebellum).

With regard to the specifics of how hypnosis works with any one patient, as yet there has been insufficient research into the topic, and we shall only get a clearer picture when we have an increased understanding of the neurological processing.

> ➤ Clinical hypnosis is an extension of natural states of awareness.
> ➤ It cannot make anyone do or be something that they are not already capable of, although it can help to focus on developing skills and resources that are already present.
> ➤ Suggestions that are made in hypnosis will only be taken on board by the patient if they feel safe and comfortable.

CHAPTER 2

Self-hypnosis

There are some theories of hypnosis which state that all hypnosis is self-hypnosis. To a certain degree there is accuracy in this, as no person can be hypnotised against their will, so one element of the process is complicity or agreement in undergoing hypnosis. However, there is a reported difference between the experiences of self-hypnosis as opposed to hetero-hypnosis, which is done by one individual (an operator) to another (the subject) (Johnson *et al.*, 1983; Moss and Magaro, 1989). When individuals undergo self-hypnosis, they take themselves into a focused state by using their awareness as the operator. They then make suggestions to influence or access their own unconscious processes and events, such as memories, effectively hypnotising their unconscious mind as the subject, while still remaining conscious and able to make suggestions as the operator. Individuals who have experienced both hetero- and self-hypnosis will often describe the self-hypnosis as less intense, or they find it more difficult to relax as fully as if they were experiencing the same suggestions made by another person. The advantage of self-hypnosis over hetero-hypnosis is that the individual may feel more able to fully control the experience, and can also practise it and gain benefit whenever they need to. They can also improve their ability to experience the phenomena of hypnosis, and will therefore respond more fully when hypnotised by another person.

The best way to learn self-hypnosis is to be taught it while in a hypnotic state. This way the individual learns the process both on a cognitive level, so they can repeat the procedure, and on a physical level, where they experience the event as it is being described to them. The subject will then be able to both control the event and recognise the phenomena which indicate that they are hypnotised when they later come to practise for themselves.

Teaching a patient self-hypnosis has a number of benefits. It gives the patient a new and potentially more appropriate coping strategy for dealing with their condition, it is a method of relaxation for patients who say they do not know how to relax, and it is a framework for continuing therapeutic and beneficial suggestions which patients themselves can control. In addition, the number of formal sessions required can be reduced by incorporating suggestions made by the patient in self-hypnosis.

By learning self-hypnosis, patients can benefit in terms of their general health and well-being, as well as in terms of their presenting symptoms. In addition, the more frequently patients experience hypnoidal states, the more comfortable they become with them. Although there is no known direct correlation between the depth of hypnotic state experienced by patients and their capacity to benefit from the therapy, it is appropriate to suggest that when a patient is at their most relaxed, they are more inclined to take on board suggestions which they might otherwise reject by analysing them in more detail.

This chapter contains the script of the companion audio track (*see* www.radcliffe-oxford.com/clinicalhypnosis). If you wish, you can use this as a template to teach patients self-hypnosis. You can read from the script, modulating your voice in a similar way to that on the audio track, while using the pauses (denoted by the ellipsis [. . .] between phrases) to observe the patient. If you are intending to do this, it is important that you read the whole volume first, as the script is only one component in a hypnotherapeutic session. If your intention is purely to teach self-hypnosis to your patient, you will still need to observe the six stages of the hypnosis session described elsewhere in this book. Attempting to hypnotise a patient 'cold' will rarely work.

If you do intend to teach patients self-hypnosis, you will need to make them aware of the benefits below. The practitioner does not need to discuss all of them with the patient, only the ones which are most relevant. If you try to hypnotise a patient without fully explaining the potential benefits for them, their motivation levels will be much lower than if you do explain the benefits. In this way we are also introducing the concept of suggestions and motivation for change even before beginning the formal hypnosis process. This element is explored in more depth in Chapter 3, 'The structure of a clinical hypnosis session.'

WHAT ARE THE BENEFITS TO THE PATIENT?

The most effective method of motivating the patient to do self-hypnosis is to sell the benefits.

Stress management

When an individual responds to a stress-inducing situation, the body will activate the autonomic nervous system. This consists of the sympathetic and parasympathetic systems. The sympathetic nervous system is responsible for producing biochemical and physiological changes to prepare the individual to respond to the stressor. This is known as the 'fight or flight' response (Goligorsky, 2001). Once this response has been discharged, the parasympathetic nervous system kicks in to reset the biochemistry and physiology back to resting mode. This circuit is known as the 'stress cycle.' Individuals who have started to respond poorly to stress will find that their ability to activate the parasympathetic nervous system is reduced. The result of this is a system which remains on high alert. Self-hypnosis promotes the parasympathetic nervous system responses. Self-hypnosis is a relaxed state, and is therefore also an excellent way of reducing stress, allowing the patient to complete the stress cycle safely and promote more effective ways of responding to stress (Whitehouse *et al.*, 1996).

Distraction technique

As with many of the techniques used most effectively in hypnosis, the use of self-hypnosis as a distraction technique is an extension of a naturally occurring process. If you look at the faces of people who are travelling on a train, for example, you will see that they absorb themselves in music, reading or watching the landscape passing by. Within this framework, self-hypnosis is used as a state of absorption to take the individual away from their immediate surroundings. The benefit of using self-hypnosis is once again its accessibility, and the fact that while in hypnosis the individual is able to experience hallucinatory states whereby they can alter their perception of the event around them.

This ability to alter the sensory experience is especially useful for patients who are in physical pain or undergoing surgical procedures (Shenefelt, 2003). In these situations, self-hypnosis can be used as a method of distracting attention away from the immediate environment, while producing specific alterations in perception to reduce awareness of pain, or to change it into a different sensory experience. Once pain management has been taught by a practitioner, the patient will be encouraged to reinforce this state on a regular basis (Kohen and Zajac, 2007). Studies have been undertaken which suggest that if hypnoanaesthesia is induced by a practitioner and then reinforced by the patient every four hours during a normal day, for a three-day period, the efficacy of the anaesthetic effect will be twice that found in those who only had the initial session (Buchser *et al.*, 1994).

Personal enhancement tool

In the self-hypnosis script, the patient is encouraged to focus on positive events. Patients with low self-esteem are more focused on the negative aspects of any presenting condition, so are encouraged to use the self-hypnosis to give themselves positive suggestions. They can only make and receive positive suggestions in this state, and will take them on board at a safe and appropriate level. Assurances of this kind also help the patient to begin to be more aware of auto-suggestions of a negative nature, which they may have already been making in relation to their condition – for example, 'I don't think I will get better.' The direct suggestions in the self-hypnosis script instruct the patient to start thinking more positively. This concept is known as 'ego strengthening', and is a characteristic of most hypnosis scripts except where contraindicated by the condition – for example, depression.

Improved control

One of the elements of patient care that it is important to be aware of is the aspect of perceived loss of control resulting from the presenting condition, medication or medical procedures. This is particularly relevant for chronic conditions. Self-hypnosis is completely structured and controlled by the patient.

Patients cannot overdose on self-hypnosis, and they can self-medicate, so are thus able to choose when, where and how much benefit they can gain. This is why it is so vital to fully explain what hypnosis is, and what benefits patients might reasonably expect from its use.

In addition to an explanation of the benefits, if you are intending to teach patients self-hypnosis you would still need to take them through the six stages of the hypnosis session. As there is no specific condition mentioned in this self-hypnosis track, the emphasis in the session will be placed on the benefits of learning self-hypnosis and on personal ego strengthening. These benefits then become the therapeutic outcome component of the session. When teaching a patient self-hypnosis within a session, the practitioner should always help to identify a specific benefit. That benefit may be as simple as better sleep or improved control generally. This serves to focus the patient's attention in a positive way, and also helps to motivate them and to increase their confidence in the process when they notice the benefits of the self-hypnosis. The six stages of the hypnosis session are discussed comprehensively in a later chapter.

The practitioner would need to explain to the patient how to prepare for self-hypnosis, including the significance of setting a time limit. This way, when patients do enter hypnosis, they are setting themselves up for a positive experience of the event.

PREPARING FOR SELF-HYPNOSIS

Before undertaking self-hypnosis, certain preparations are necessary. The practitioner will instruct the patient to go through the following process before starting to make suggestions to enter a hypnotic state.

Set a time

Decide how long to spend in the hypnotic state, even when doing this just before waking or sleeping. It is better to start with around 10 minutes, and then increase the time. Aim for approximately 20 minutes as an optimum. The time is to be set internally, rather than with an external alarm. This encourages the patient to start trusting their capacity to control internal states.

The accuracy with which they achieve this time can be a useful calibrating device. If the patient is easily able to assess the time they have set for their self-hypnosis, it can be judged that they are generally functioning healthily. If they wake before the time they have set, this is often an indicator of stress. Conversely, when the patient's assessment of the time in the hypnotic state is longer, this can be an indicator of lack of motivation, or lethargy. It is possible that when an individual is in a hypnotic state they unconsciously use their heart rate as a device for calculating time. If they are stressed, the heart is beating faster and therefore their concept of time will be that it is faster than real time. If the patient is dejected or lethargic, this effect is reversed.

It is useful to get the patient to practise their self-hypnosis first thing in the morning and last thing at night, as they will already be in a physical space where they can do it, and also the hypnogogic and hypnopompic states lend themselves well to moving into self-hypnosis easily. I encourage patients to use the session in the morning to prepare themselves for the day, and to use the session at night to let go of any of the stressors or tensions that would otherwise disturb their sleep. This works well and encourages the patient to view self-hypnosis as a natural and easy method of mental preparation as well as stress management. If self-hypnosis is done in the morning before rising, I encourage the patient to include suggestions of feeling energised and positive when they count themselves to full awareness, and to get out of bed as soon as they have completed the self-hypnosis count-up.

Find a time and place to be undisturbed

It is important that the practitioner explains that if there is a need for the patient to become fully alert because their attention is required elsewhere, they will be able to immediately bring themselves back to a fully alert state.

Sit down or lie down

If the self-hypnosis is done during the day, it is generally recommended that the patient does it in a comfortable reclined chair rather than prone. This is because there is an association of sleep with lying down. If the self-hypnosis is to be done immediately before sleep, the patient will obviously be lying down and then fall into a natural sleep, from which they will wake at the appropriate time.

Assume a neutral position

The patient is then instructed to arrange their body in a neutral posture, with their arms resting on their lap or at their side, and their feet uncrossed. This is demonstrated as the posture that patients are in when being hypnotised to learn self-hypnosis. A neutral posture is preferable to ensure that no distractions are caused by paraesthesia. In addition, other postures, such as crossed arms and legs, can be counter-productive as they may be associated with tension or stress, or even sleep.

Close the eyes

The patient is then instructed to close their eyes to start the self-hypnosis suggestions. Eye closure alone becomes an auto-suggestion to become more internally aware, and to begin to pay more attention to thoughts and, in this case, suggestions. The patient should also be informed that if they wish or need to open their eyes at any point during the process, they will be able to do so.

DURING THE PROCESS

The patient is directed to be aware that sounds and sensations will be perceived throughout. These should not distract them, and they can treat them as background to their auto-suggestions. If a sound or sensation requires the patient's immediate attention, they can deal with it, and, should full alertness be necessary, the self-hypnosis will end immediately and they will be fully aware.

POSITIVE SUGGESTIONS

People will often have more than one objective for self-hypnosis. Unless the self-hypnosis has been taught so that the patient can supplement suggestions made during a formal hypnotherapeutic session, it is best to keep the suggestions as individual concepts, positively phrased. The most important aspect is that only suggestions of one kind should be made at any one time (McNeilly, 1994). Examples of useful suggestions for self-hypnosis are suggestions of focus, relaxation, confidence or motivation. The suggestions need to be phrased by the patient to refer to the near future, rather than the present. The rationale behind this is explained in greater depth in a later chapter. The patient is encouraged to continue to make these suggestions in self-hypnosis until they have achieved the objective and they can then change the tense of their suggestions to the present rather than the future (e.g. *'I am confident . . .'* as opposed to *'I will be more confident . . .'*). Only then is it appropriate to start on new suggestions. The aim of this is to build up a conditioned response to the suggestions in order to begin to respond unconsciously to them.

WAKING UP

The self-hypnosis script gives instructions on how to wake from the hypnotic state. If sleep results from the self-hypnosis, that is natural, and the patient needs to be assured that if this happens, they will wake from their sleep as normal.

THE HYPNOTIC VOICE

When inducing a hypnotic state, the practitioner will modulate their voice to be appropriate to the words spoken. You can listen to the audio track to identify how the voice changes depending on what is being said, and at what stage of the script. When delivering a hypnotic script, the voice is used to maintain the interest of the subject, and to place particular emphasis on certain instructions or concepts.

DELIVERING A SCRIPT

The instructions from this stage to the hypnosis script itself are relevant to most types of hypnotherapeutic sessions. Variations are discussed more fully in Chapter 8, 'Creating the hypnotherapeutic protocol', as is the construction of therapeutic suggestions.

Phase of hypnosis: Induction and deepener

Change in voice quality: slow, gentle, quiet

The purpose of the voice slowing down, and becoming quieter and increasingly gentle, is for the patient to begin to focus their attention on what is being said. The quality of the voice needs to be sufficiently interesting for the subject to begin to tune in to the spoken words. If the subject needs almost to strain to hear, they will pay closer attention, whereas if the voice is dull or kept at a normal sound level, the subject may allow their attention to wander.

Phase of hypnosis: Therapeutic suggestions

Change in voice quality: dependent on therapeutic approach and condition

If the approach is authoritarian, the voice may be raised slightly when making suggestions. When making permissive suggestions the voice remains gentle, but is made more persuasive in tone. There may be times when suggestions are made more rapidly. This is useful with individuals who are analytical or who have secondary gains in relation to letting go of a problem. These individuals often attempt to deconstruct the suggestions. The change in pace reduces their capacity to analyse all of the suggestions, so some of them will slip past their analytical guard and be taken on board.

Phase of hypnosis: Ego strengthening

Change in voice quality: motivational, directive

These suggestions are sometimes interspersed throughout a script. In this instance, the way in which the suggestions are delivered will be congruent with the stage of the script in which they are delivered. In formal hypnotherapeutic scripts, the ego-strengthening suggestions come just before the awakening suggestions, and their purpose is to remind the patient of positive states and to encourage them to stay focused. The direct suggestions can be emphasised with a change in tone, pitch and volume of the voice accordingly.

Phase of hypnosis: Awakening

Change in voice quality: louder, faster, more directive

The voice in hypnosis is soothing, and modulation should be gradual. Care must be taken to ensure that the voice has a non-sexual quality. Keeping the words spoken precise and clear, especially when at the state of therapeutic suggestions, ensures this. The speed, pitch and volume of the voice by the end of the awakening process should be almost that of normal speech. It should never be louder, as the aim is to bring the patient back to a state of normal alertness at a natural pace so that when they are fully reoriented they will then feel normal.

USE OF THE PAUSE

In scripts there are pre-set pauses, usually denoted by '. . .' In these pauses, the practitioner needs to observe the patient and take note of the following.

➤ Has the patient followed any instruction made?
➤ Is the patient showing any signs of distress, such as speeding up of breathing rate?
➤ Are any of the suggestions being particularly well received?

The practitioner can then vary the script by either repeating an instruction, in the first instance, or by modifying the forms of suggestion to alleviate the distress, in the second instance.

In the introduction, deepening, therapeutic suggestion and ego-strengthening stages of the script, the pauses can be timed by silently and mentally repeating the phrase just spoken – twice. By doing this the practitioner will have sufficient time to observe the patient, while giving the patient time to process the suggestions given.

When awakening the patient, the pause can be reduced to one silent repetition of the phrase just spoken. As the practitioner becomes more proficient at delivering hypnotic suggestions, pacing with the patient's breathing pattern will become more natural.

DELIVERY OF SUGGESTIONS

The practitioner may wish to deliver specific ego-strengthening suggestions to the patient when teaching them self-hypnosis. Suggestions are most effectively delivered once the patient has been told that they will soon be awakened. It is considered that at this point the patient will go more deeply into hypnosis as their confidence of experiencing the state is at its height. Suggestions can be delivered as follows:

> 'in a few moments' time . . . I am going to wake you . . . but *before* I wake you . . . I am going to make a few simple, positive suggestions . . . suggestions which will be able to help you . . .'

At this point, deliver the suggestions discussed with the patient during the pre-induction talk. Always use positive language, suggesting to the patient something they wish to work towards rather than away from – for example, suggestions to 'sleep deeply and well' rather than 'not stay awake worrying all night.' As you can see, explicit in the latter statement is the very suggestion that the patient wishes to avoid (stay awake all night and worry).

USE OF SELF-HYPNOSIS FOR THE PRACTITIONER

Battle fatigue or burnout can be a common factor with any individual who works in a one-on-one scenario with individuals who have problems. Self-hypnosis is a useful method of dealing with this potential problem. In addition to this, a calm, relaxed practitioner of clinical hypnosis will inspire more confidence and be able to build rapport more quickly than one who is tense and anxious. Self-hypnosis is recommended as a tool for practitioners to use on a regular basis to reduce their own stress levels. When seeing patients on a regular basis, self-hypnosis can be used as a way of releasing any tension induced by the sessions themselves. It can also be used as a way of preparing for future sessions. It really comes into its own as a stress management tool when practitioners are in a situation where they do not have anyone with whom they can offload. In the self-hypnosis, the practitioner can access a healthy mindset for working with each patient and ensure that any issues relating to them can be filed safely, and then processed unconsciously. As with the recommendations for patients, I suggest a morning session to prepare for the day, and a session just before sleep to let go of stress or irritations from the day that has just ended.

SCRIPT FOR USE WITH PATIENTS

The accompanying audio track (*see* www.radcliffe-oxford.com/clinicalhypnosis) contains an audio recording of this script. Listen to the track first before attempting to deliver the script yourself.

Induce hypnosis

. . . make yourself comfortable . . .

(*if patient is sitting*)
. . . place your feet flat on the ground . . . and . . . let your hands rest comfortably on your thighs . . . rest your head back . . . you can relax now . . .

(*if patient is lying down*)
lie flat on your back . . . and let your arms rest comfortably by your sides . . . place your feet together . . . side by side . . . and then start to allow your body to relax . . .

and just close your eyes . . . let them close . . . and . . . you can relax your eyes now . . . so comfortably relax them . . . that they won't bother to open at all . . . they will remain . . . comfortably closed . . . comfortably closed throughout . . . and . . .

Deepening the state

I would like you to focus in on your breathing . . . take three deep . . . relaxing breaths . . . let them out in your own time . . . that's right . . . and as you do . . . I would like you to notice that your breathing has become deep and even . . . and . . . in a few moments' time . . . I would like you to take control of the process . . . and you will start this by deciding how relaxed you choose to go . . . you can go deep enough to access any information which will help you to make the changes you want in your life . . . deeply relaxed . . . you are in control . . . so ready . . . continue to pay attention to your breathing . . . and as soon as you wish you can take control of the process you can begin a countdown . . . silently and mentally . . . using your out breath to time the numbers . . . you can start when you wish . . . with the number 100 . . . and with each breath out you count down to the next number . . . and with each descending number between 100 and zero . . . you go deeper and deeper into hypnosis . . . more and more in control . . . ever closer to the memories which can help you today . . . you are in control . . . completely in control . . . and as you count . . . you may wish to see the numbers written on the screen of your mind's eye . . . some people hear their own inner voice repeating the word . . . it is entirely up to you . . . you can allow yourself to experience this process in any way you wish . . . because you are in control . . . and I want you to know that the more control you take of the process . . . the more you will relax . . . and the more you relax the more easily you can access the part of your mind which will help you . . . it is time for you to take control . . . complete control of the process . . . and you will find . . . that when you do . . . there may be times when you focus so hard on counting . . . that you forget to listen hard to the words that I say . . . and there may be times when you forget to count . . . and that will be fine . . . just fine . . . you will pick up at the next number which occurs to you . . . or not at all . . . it really doesn't matter . . . what does matter is that you will hear and remember everything of importance for you to hear and remember . . . whether this is your own inner voice . . . or the sound of my voice relaxing you . . . you are in control . . . and as you count ever deeper and deeper . . . going more and more relaxed . . . you may even notice that the sensations in your body are changing . . . there may be times when you notice that you feel as if you are drifting or floating . . . but that will be fine . . . it is a very pleasant experience . . . similar to the moments between waking and sleeping . . . your body warm and comfortable . . . completely at peace.

Give the following post-hypnotic suggestions:
and . . . now you are deeply relaxed . . . I am going to teach you how to take yourself into this fully relaxed state . . . whenever you need it . . . whenever you want to take time out . . . and . . . you will find that the more you practise . . . the better you become . . . the better you become . . . the more deeply you can go . . . it is very simple . . . all you have to do . . . is find a time and a space where you can make yourself comfortable . . . a place where you can make sure that there is nothing which can disturb you while you practise . . . but I want you to know . . . that if . . . for any reason you need to be immediately alert and aware . . . you will be . . . you are completely in control . . . so for now . . . you can relax . . . knowing that you are able to go as deep as you like . . . when you do this for yourself . . . first of all . . . decide how long you want to be in hypnosis . . . five minutes . . . ten minutes . . . fifteen . . . it is entirely up to you . . . your internal clock will tell you when it is time for you to wake yourself up . . . then . . . all you have to do . . . is sit down or lie down . . . and close your eyes . . . take three deep breaths . . . and . . . on the last one . . . hold your breath for a count of three . . . and . . . let that breath go . . . and . . . as you do . . . allow every muscle of your body to relax . . . continue to pay attention to your breathing . . . noticing your chest rising and falling . . . and be aware that any sounds or sensations around you can just fade into the background . . . just as they do when you drift off to sleep . . . you can now notice your thoughts . . . and let your thoughts connect themselves to your breathing . . . so you can start to allow your thoughts to fade in . . . and out . . . as if connected to your breathing . . . and . . . you will soon notice . . . that some of those thoughts fade away completely . . . while others take a while . . . but it doesn't matter either way . . . as you are going into a state of self-hypnosis . . . you are controlling it . . . and . . . you can now begin to count yourself deeper into this state . . . by using the numbers between ten and one . . . count on your out breath . . . this will help

you to relax ever more deeply . . . more and more relaxed . . . and . . . as you count down . . . any tension in your body fades away . . . any feelings you want to release . . . you can count down to letting them go completely . . . so by the time you reach the number one you will find that you have let go of any stress or tension . . . and can just relax . . . relax and think clearly . . .

Pause for 5 seconds
and . . . once you reach the number one . . . you can use this time to give yourself a positive suggestion . . . something simple . . . something that will come in useful for the next 24 hours . . . you may wish to focus . . . or to be more motivated . . . or to have some extra confidence . . . keep it simple . . . you can do this now if you want . . .

Pause for 5 seconds
. . . then just let your mind drift . . . enjoy the peace . . . enjoy being relaxed and focused . . . after a little while . . . your internal clock will tell you it is time to wake . . . and . . . to wake yourself up . . . all you need to do is count slowly up from one to ten . . . and . . . with each number you become more aware of your surroundings . . . and feel more alert . . . you will wake refreshed and relaxed . . . and . . . these benefits will increase . . . the more often you take time to do your self-hypnosis . . .

. . . and . . . so it is easy for you to fit this into your day . . . you can do it just before you go to sleep at night . . . you can give yourself suggestions to let go of any tension or frustration from the day . . . so that you can fall asleep and sleep deeply and well . . . taking all the benefit from your sleep that you need . . .

. . . and . . . if you want to . . . you can do it in the morning . . . just before you are fully awake . . . to give yourself positive suggestions for the day . . . suggestions on how you are going to be confident . . . energised and in control . . . you can even walk yourself through a situation which you know you have to deal with that day . . . and imagine yourself as completely in control . . . confident and at ease with yourself and your surroundings . . .

. . . you can do your self-hypnosis whenever you need it . . . to give yourself a rest . . . a boost . . . or positive suggestions . . . and the more you practise . . . the better you get at it . . . the more you improve . . . the more easily you will take on board the positive suggestions for change . . .

General ego strengthening
and . . . before I wake you . . . I would like you to know that when you wake you will be able to notice how much better you feel . . . you will feel more relaxed . . . more focused . . . and more at ease with yourself and the world around you . . . you will be aware that you feel stronger . . . and clearer in your mind . . . more

able to make decisions . . . more capable too . . . and . . . you will find that these positive feelings continue to grow . . . as the days go by . . . and . . . from now on . . . just before you sleep . . . you will be able to allow your unconscious mind to work through any of your problems as you sleep . . . so that you can . . . and you will . . . sleep deeply and well . . . and wake feeling refreshed and more positive . . . so positive that you will find that you can feel in control throughout the day . . . helping you to cope better . . . to be stronger and more able to deal with anything . . . anybody . . . any situation . . . and . . . as a result of this you will feel more motivated . . . to make the changes suggested to you today . . . more focused . . . more confident too . . . confident that you can change . . . you can take control . . . you can feel and be different . . . altogether more positive too . . .

Awakening
. . . in a few moments in time I am going to slowly count up from one to ten . . . and . . . as I count . . . you will become more aware of your surroundings . . . more aware of the sensations in your body too . . . all healthy . . . appropriate and normal sensations will return to your body . . . and every healthy . . . normal . . . and appropriate part of you will be back here in the present . . . and at the count of eight your eyes will gently start to open . . . and you can start to stretch your body . . . and at the count of ten you will be fully awake . . . feeling alert and focused . . . your body relaxed . . . your mind refreshed . . . so ready . . . one . . . two . . . three . . . becoming more aware now . . . four . . . five . . . six . . . more alert . . . seven . . . eight . . . open your eyes now . . . starting to stretch . . . nine and ten . . . fully awake . . . alert . . . feeling refreshed and relaxed . . .

CHAPTER 3

The structure of a clinical hypnosis session

There are six stages to a clinical hypnosis session: introduction, induction, deepening, therapeutic suggestions (post-hypnotic suggestions), the awakening stage and finally post-hypnosis, which consists of feedback and debriefing the patient.

INTRODUCTION

The introduction session takes the form of a discussion between patient and practitioner. It is a structured discussion that includes a number of components, each with a specific objective. It is important to remember that the patient needs to be clear about each of these components before they will be secure enough to enter a hypnotic state. It is also worth noting that failure to incorporate each of these components before taking the patient into hypnosis can often adversely affect their experience of the state, and of the therapeutic objective.

The stages within the introduction section can be equated to the five-stage Calgary–Cambridge model of the medical consultation. Within this familiar structure, the specific use of language described in this volume takes the concept one step further. These skills then become transferable to any diagnostic setting where the emphasis of the communication is on accuracy and speed.

Patients also need time to look around the room, to accommodate the sounds and sights or even unaccustomed smells of the room in which the hypnosis is going to take place. On the subject of smells, it is best to keep the room where the hypnotherapeutic session will be conducted as odourless as possible. Smells are very evocative of memories, and can often be distracting for the patient. If they are disturbed when in hypnosis yet have had time to become accustomed to their surroundings, they will be more comfortable about staying in the hypnotic state.

There is no hypnosis as such during this stage, but the elements of the hypnotic state can be introduced at this time. The patient will become more relaxed, more focused and progressively directed towards solutions and positive states – just as will happen when they experience the hypnosis. If done properly, this section is a precursor to the hypnotic state, as well as an opportunity to reassure the patient and collect sufficient information for them to have a positive experience of hypnosis, as well as a successful therapeutic outcome.

INFORMATION GATHERING

In the introduction to this stage the practitioner will follow a fixed sequence of questioning. First, the presenting condition is pinpointed briefly. This is kept to a minimum. Once the patient is more comfortable, later on in the session, the following specifics of the condition are then discussed:

➤ what it is
➤ how it developed
➤ the symptoms
➤ the physical and psychological impact
➤ ways in which hypnosis may help.

Information about the patient as an individual is next requested. This is then used in hypnotic script formation, and will include details such as personality or resource states, current anxieties or potential stressors, any future anxieties of the patient with regard to potential change, and sensory future projection which can be incorporated into visualisations.

More time and emphasis are placed on the patient than on the condition in order to initiate perceptual changes. It is said that a good physician will tell patients many things about them that are functioning correctly before moving on to the problem, so that the emphasis is on the positive.

A clear and realistic outcome for treatment is then established. This is a vital component of the effective use of clinical hypnosis. Once a clear and realistic outcome can be established, the practical methodology of using clinical hypnosis to achieve this outcome can be constructed by both the patient and the practitioner.

CASE HISTORY

A full history of the condition and a description of the symptoms are then taken. The purposes of this information-gathering stage are manifold. It emphasises to the patient that they are not the problem, and that the condition does not occur all the time, and that often there was a time before the condition occurred, or at least before it affected them so severely. This process begins to deconstruct the problem both qualitatively and quantitatively (that is, it does not happen all the time, and there are times when the symptoms are less pronounced, and even possibly a time when the condition did not exist). A comprehensive description of the type of questions necessary to establish an appropriate case history can be found in Chapter 8, 'Creating the hypnotherapeutic protocol.'

It is important to be aware that the case history is not intended as a comprehensive medical or personal history.

It is essential that information requested from the patient is of specific value to the session. If the patient feels that they are being asked for information which they do not feel is relevant, rapport will be lost and, in the worst-case scenario, this will generate anxiety. It is important to remember that one of the fears of hypnosis which patients might have is that of being compelled to reveal information about themselves. It is therefore vital for the practitioner to know why they are asking the questions, so that they can respond appropriately if asked by the patient to justify the need for certain information.

The requirement for information requested during the case history section of the session comes under one or more of the following groupings. Each of these will be discussed to ensure that the practitioner knows why they are asking the questions. This will allow each practitioner to achieve flexibility with their questioning technique, so long as the required information is collected. The information provided by the patient will then be used in the following.

Creating the hypnotic script

The way in which patients talk about how they experience themselves, the world around them and their interaction with the problem will give the practitioner indicators of the type of language to use and suggestions to make during the script.

First, this will personalise the hypnotic experience to the patient's current experience of the world. Secondly, it will allow the practitioner to use the patient's language, cognition and behavioural patterns – the way they talk, think and act – as an indicator of how the suggestions can best be delivered.

Allowing the patient to gain a greater understanding of their potential

One of the underlying themes of clinical hypnosis as a therapeutic tool is that patients who have created a problem for themselves will necessarily know how to solve that problem, even if they are not consciously aware of that solution. At its most simplistic level, this may involve directing the patient to an awareness that there was a time before they had the problem. This can be done in the case history, or it can be done as part of the hypnotherapeutic suggestions.

Appropriate questions in the case history will be phrased in such a way as to lead the patient to think about their solutions, rather than their problem. Questions are therefore best phrased in positive language and will be solution-focused.

Discovering how the patient developed the condition

The practitioner will ask questions relating to the history of the condition – that is, when it started, when it developed from being a condition to being problematic for that person, and what was going on in their life at that time. A timeline of the condition can then be established, and any times at which the condition was more or less manageable can be identified. If the patient believes that the condition has been present for all of their life, this will also be an indicator of possible courses of action for treatment.

Analysing how the patient currently manages the condition

Questions about how the condition currently affects the patient are asked during this section, so symptoms are described, and the patient is encouraged to give as full a description of the event as possible. This series of questions will be used to identify what, if anything, currently helps them to manage the condition. This information will also give the practitioner an indication of whether the patient is currently motivated.

Understanding the interaction between the patient and their environment as a result of the condition

The present ego state of the patient is assessed in this sequence of questions in order to identify whether the patient is ready for the implications of change, and also whether they have thought through the ways in which this change will affect their life. If any secondary gains from the symptom are present, it will become evident at this point when the patient begins to justify their current behaviour and moves the focus of the process away from making changes.

Creating a safe environment for the patient to express their concerns

The case history needs to be more than a question-and-answer session – it is an opportunity for the patient to become more comfortable with the practitioner, to assess the practitioner's level of skills, and to start to feel that the practitioner is gaining a clear picture of them and their problem. The case history is also an opportunity for the practitioner to begin to lead the patient, with open-ended questions, to come to their own conclusions about what is most appropriate for them in terms of therapeutic objectives.

Producing a safe and realistic outcome

By the end of the case history component, the practitioner and the patient will have agreed on an appropriate course of action for the patient to take with regard to their condition. It may seem like a very obvious point to raise at this stage, but patients frequently come for hypnotherapy knowing what they do *not* want (that is, their condition), but have not thought through what they *do* want (that is, their objective). The outcome must be described in clear terms by the practitioner, and agreed upon by the patient at this stage. The potential number of sessions required to achieve this outcome is then clarified. It is important to note that in the modern use of clinical hypnosis the objective is to have as few sessions as possible, supplemented if necessary with homework by the patient.

RAPPORT

Establishing rapport is a vital component of the introduction section. Without it the patient will not be able to enter a state of hypnosis. One of the easiest ways to establish rapport is by encouraging the patient to talk about him- or herself rather than the problem. Within this structure, the following information is also identified by questioning:

➤ What do you do to relax?
➤ What do you enjoy/did you enjoy doing?
➤ What would you like to enjoy doing?

➤ What will you be doing when you no longer have the problem?
➤ What do you want specifically in relation to the problem?

DISCUSS THE HYPNOSIS STATE

Identify any previous experience

It is important to be aware of whether the patient has had previous experience of hypnosis and to discover what, if anything, they found useful about the process. The methods used, if well received by the patient at the time, can be replicated. If, on the other hand, the patient did not like a particular method, this should be avoided.

Allay fears and misconceptions based on previous experience

If a patient has been hypnotised before, it is always useful for the practitioner to ask questions about their experience of the phenomena of hypnosis. If they did not 'feel' hypnotised, this is often because a misconception was not discussed in sufficient depth. For example, if a patient states that they did not feel hypnotised because they could hear everything that was said to them, the practitioner can then explain that hearing everything in hypnosis is to be expected, and in fact it is important that the patient does so.

Patients with no previous experience of hypnosis

In this situation, this fact will need to be considered when discussing the hypnotic state, so that any of the patient's concerns can be addressed appropriately. Often a fear of dominance or loss of control will be a concern of the patient who is new to hypnotic experiences, or whose preconceptions are based purely on impressions drawn from the media.

In summary, the practitioner should:

➤ include what the patient expects of the experience
➤ include an explanation and description of the events of hypnosis
➤ incorporate any fears or misconceptions that are expressed at this stage.

BACK TO THE PROBLEM

By this time the patient will feel considerably more relaxed and will be more comfortable discussing their condition. There are rare occasions when the patient will change direction at this point and tell the practitioner that they would rather deal with some other problem, rather than the condition with which they originally presented. If this is the case, the patient is demonstrating that they have thought through their condition and also that they feel the practitioner has understood them and they feel sufficiently comfortable to deal with a different matter which the patient has decided will be of more value to them.

The patient will do most of the talking during this section, with the practitioner directing them to remain focused on the aspects of the condition that are relevant when creating the hypnotic script, and evaluating the most appropriate objective, protocol and treatment plan.

ANY QUESTIONS BEFORE WE START THE CLINICAL HYPNOSIS?

At this point, if the previous sections have been covered comprehensively, the patient should have no questions, because the practitioner should have already gone through all of the relevant information. However, asking the patient whether they have any questions gives them time to consider anything that may have occurred to them during the introduction session, and to prepare mentally. The patient is given a specific opportunity to ask questions at this stage because they will now be more comfortable than at any previous point in the session. If this question is asked at the beginning of the session, it is unlikely to provoke any response, as patients are usually still feeling too anxious, or are too polite or have not yet thought of any questions about the session. Once this question has been asked, and all responses dealt with, the patient should then be able to enter hypnosis with a positive and motivated mindset. Patients' questions are covered in Chapter 4, 'Questions patients ask', which gives an indication of the wide range of questions that may be asked and the types of answers that are appropriate.

A PRACTICAL POINT

Before commencing hypnosis, and after the introduction session, the patient should be asked whether they wish to use the toilet. Nothing distracts a patient more than a full bladder!

Before taking the patient into an induction, the practitioner will lead with statements to encourage the patient into hypnosis. An example of this could be as follows: 'When you are ready to let go of this problem, you can . . . start to relax . . .'

Suggestions for induction of hypnosis will follow from this point. Once again, specific phraseology is used to encourage the patient into hypnosis, with their focus on positive events in the future. This phraseology is created from an amalgam of the language that the patient uses, together with solution-focused phrases which direct the patient towards their therapeutic objective. The other aspect of this phraseology comes from the patient's interaction with their condition.

Finally, the patient is asked at this point whether they have any physical problems which might distract them during the hypnosis, such as pain or discomfort. Suggestions can then be incorporated into the script to move the focus away from the pain, or to reduce it with suggestions of warmth or relaxation. The patient is also reminded that, should they need to do so, they can move during the session to make themselves more comfortable. Check whether they need to use the toilet before the hypnosis commences, and if they are wearing glasses, mention that they can now take them off. Also check whether the patient is wearing contact lenses and, if so, whether they will be comfortable wearing them while their eyes are closed. By asking these questions at the end of the case history, the practitioner is gently leading the patient to a realisation that the hypnosis session is about to start.

The introduction part of the session can take anything up to 45 minutes.

INDUCTION

This is the part of the session in which the practitioner usually asks the patient to close their eyes in order to concentrate their attention on sound or physical feelings. Induction encourages a state of internal focus, while external distractions are reduced or limited. The induction can be carried out in a number of ways (visual, auditory or kinaesthetic, or a combination of these), depending on the patient's responses to questions in the introduction section.

Eye closure is not absolutely essential, although there are studies which demonstrate that when a person has their eyes closed they are more aware of emotional stimuli (for example, from music) (Lerner *et al.*, 2009). Sometimes a patient may be so anxious that they do not feel able to close their eyes because they will feel too vulnerable. If this is the case, the practitioner can tell the patient that they may keep their eyes open, but must focus on a point in the room (for example, a picture on the wall behind and above the practitioner). This way, the patient will have something on which to directly focus their attention, but will also get muscle fatigue in the eyes, as focusing in this way causes strain. With the practitioner still in view, the patient will start to feel reassured that they are going to be safe and, with a gentle suggestion further into the induction, will close their eyes when they feel ready to do so.

The most effective methods of inducing hypnosis involve utilising the modes in which the patient already relaxes. By recalling the memories of these relaxed states, the patient will begin to remember the physical state of relaxation and this will in turn amplify their potential to experience the hypnotic state. Broadly put, the practitioner will take note of which sense the patient involved in past relaxed states, and will use this sense as a guide to ways of taking them into hypnosis. For example, if the patient states that they listen to music to relax, auditory stimulation would be used. Conversely, if the patient swims for relaxation, a technique using physical (kinaesthetic) stimulation would be utilised. The only occasions when these relaxation states would not be used to assist in recalling a certain state would be if the patient used 'false friends', such as alcohol, drugs or smoking, to enable them to relax. All of these are contraindicated for a positive experience of relaxation, and they are often harmful to the patient. It is of interest that, if a patient does use these methods of relaxing, this is an indicator of poor coping strategies in response to stress, and this may also need to be dealt with as part of the therapeutic process.

VISUAL INDUCTIONS

Visual inductions involve suggestions for focusing the eyes on one specific location or paying attention to the muscles of the eyes. An example of this would be when a practitioner asks the patient to focus on a spot on the ceiling, and notices eye fatigue. If the patient has an eye impairment (for example, glaucoma), a visual induction may be contraindicated. If the patient has eye problems as a symptom of the presenting condition (for example, migraine), visual inductions should not be used.

All inductions involve fixation of attention at some level where the patient is then focused upon one specific location, sense or idea. The purpose of a formal induction is eye closure.

AUDITORY INDUCTIONS

Auditory inductions involve suggestions to stimulate the auditory cortex. An example would be when the practitioner asks the patient to listen to the sound of his or her voice. In auditory inductions the patient is also directed to deselect other sounds around them so that they become part of the background. Another way of increasing internal focus in an auditory manner is to ask the patient to focus on internal, rhythmic sounds, such as breathing or a relaxed heartbeat.

KINAESTHETIC INDUCTIONS

Kinaesthetic inductions involve suggestions to stimulate the physical sensations or feelings. An example of a kinaesthetic induction would be to give suggestions of hand levitation, inducing a physical dissociation. Other examples would include asking the patient to focus on experiencing warmth or feeling their muscles become progressively looser and more at ease. In each of these examples the feelings are associated with sleep or relaxation.

AUTHORITARIAN VERSUS PERMISSIVE

In the delivery of suggestions, there are two other main variations in the ways in which induction can be achieved, and these can fit into any of the above categories.

The first approach to be discussed is that of authoritarian presentation, in which suggestions are made in a directive, commanding manner. The advantage of this type of approach lies in its rapidity. The disadvantage is that, if the patient fails to comply with the suggestion, the rapport that was established in the pre-induction section of the session will be eroded. This method is favoured for patients who already have a mindset of accepting suggestions unquestioningly, whether as a result of their career choice, or their temperament, or the severity of their condition. It is worth remembering that those patients who are used to issuing orders and having others comply with them also respond better to this way of presenting suggestions. In extreme cases, such as emergency circumstances, authoritarian suggestions are favoured over permissive suggestions because they are thought to capitalise on the freezing reflex that occurs before the 'fight or flight' response. In the instance of hypnosis being induced at this moment, a rapid dissociation away from the experience of the immediate surroundings occurs. Similarly, use of direct suggestions can be seen from the work of Dr Patterson at the University of Washington Burns Centre, who developed a virtual-reality programme to suggest that the patient is flying around a snow-filled canyon while dressings are being changed.

The second approach involves the use of permissive suggestions. These are requests and invitations, rather than orders. They involve repetition and presentation of ideas in gentler terms. This type of approach is favoured for those patients who are anxious, for younger patients, and for those who are experiencing hypnosis for the first time, as it allows them more apparent control over the process. The advantage of this approach is that it gives the practitioner more time to calibrate the patient response. The possible disadvantage is that the patient may become so relaxed that they sleep before therapeutic suggestions can be made. When permissive suggestions are used it will take longer for the changes to take effect, as repetition and invitation involve allowing the patient to analyse the suggestions before taking them on board, so there will be a longer period of time between suggestion and response.

It is worth noting at this stage that when a patient comes for a second session, they may be more open to a more directive/authoritarian approach, as their mindset will have changed in relation to themselves, their problem, and their capacity to change. They will also be more receptive to the process than they were during the first session, because they will have had an opportunity to note the benefits which have occurred as a result. Making note of this attitudinal change will allow the practitioner to vary their approach so as to maximise the efficient use of time in the session, as more authoritarian approaches can be delivered more quickly.

DEEPENING

This is the section of the script where the patient is taken deeper into this focused state of relaxation, or into a heightened state of internal awareness. The patient is asked to continue to focus on physical changes, such as breathing becoming deeper, or the experience of dissociation from immediate surroundings that occurs. The patient becomes progressively more aware of unconscious processes and functions, theoretically producing a corresponding change in the brain whereby the brain centres that are involved in apparently unconscious thought and activity also become more active. When this takes place, and suggestions for change at this level are made, the patient is more likely to be able to take control over these thoughts and activities which were unconscious, and therefore inaccessible, at a more conscious level.

The practitioner can effectively personalise the deepening part of the script by interspersing the patient's methods of relaxation within the framework of a deepening script. For example:

> counting down . . . ten . . . going deeper relaxed . . . deeper relaxed . . . you can start to feel as relaxed as you would in a wonderful . . . warm . . . bath . . . nine . . . eight . . . going deeper relaxed now . . . a warm . . . relaxing bath where no one can disturb you . . . seven . . . six . . . and you can let go of all your tension as you start to relax . . .

By doing this, the practitioner demonstrates that they have paid thorough attention to the patient. In turn, this is more likely to be reciprocated by the patient paying attention to the post-hypnotic suggestions than if the patient feels that they are being read to, or that the practitioner is merely going through a generic procedure.

The practitioner aims to take the patient into as deep a state of hypnosis as possible. However, the patient will only go as deep as they feel is comfortable and appropriate for them. Calibration of when this has taken place is made by observing changes in the patient's physiology. When the state stabilises, and after suggestions have been made for waking, post-hypnotic suggestions are made to the patient. Also known as 'therapeutic suggestions', these are the suggestions for positive changes which are to take place after termination of the session.

THERAPEUTIC SUGGESTIONS (POST-HYPNOTIC SUGGESTIONS)

These need to be:

➤ phrased positively
➤ restricted to one subject at a time
➤ achievable
➤ realistic.

As mentioned already, suggestions must be of a positive nature. It has been observed that the brain receives suggestions more efficiently when the latter are made in sets of three, so if you are doing self-hypnosis, try to find three different ways of making the same suggestions. For example, when giving your auto-suggestions to feel more calm generally, you could phrase these in the following way: 'I can be more relaxed . . . more able to deal with any situation . . . more in control of my own responses.' In this way the mind can select whichever is most appropriate to gain the outcome of being calm, no matter what the situation.

These post-hypnotic suggestions are made most effectively *after* the patient has been told that they will be woken as they will then go to their optimum depth of hypnotic state.

This is for a number of reasons. The patient may be enjoying the relaxed state and therefore relax a little more, or, in some cases, the patient may experience relief that they have not been given any suggestions to change and can therefore continue to operate within the status quo. Whatever the reason, the patient is more receptive at this point, and suggestions based upon the discussion in the introduction section are made. Only suggestions previously agreed upon are made, and these should be made wherever possible using the patient's own words and language patterns.

EGO-STRENGTHENING SUGGESTIONS

These are suggestions for general physical and emotional health and well-being, and they are interspersed with the therapeutic suggestions for the awakening. These suggestions are based on the patient history (for example, 'You can feel as happy as you did when you passed your driving test . . .') and positive future scenarios (for example, 'You can look forward to enjoying life now that you no longer smoke . . .').

Ego strengthening can be a therapeutic process in itself – for example, in confidence building. Here the post-hypnotic suggestions would involve the patient focusing on feeling confident and relaxed in future scenarios. The additional aim of ego strengthening is to help the patient to think in a positive manner generally, and therefore to be able to apply this mindset to the specific problem that they have been experiencing. Ego strengthening is not suitable for all conditions or patients, as the suggestions it involves may be unrealistic for the patient because of their current mindset (for example, reactive depression).

The primary purpose of ego strengthening is to act as motivational fuel to encourage the patient to carry out the post-hypnotic suggestions, and to encourage them to be more positive and generally better able to cope.

AWAKENING

The purpose of awakening is to bring the patient to full conscious alertness with hypermnesia of any suggestions that need to be carried out post-hypnotically. During this process, any suggestions that have been made explicitly for the purpose of the hypnosis, such as limb heaviness or tiredness, are removed. Suggestions for general health and well-being are also made at this stage. A signal, such as counting, is usually given before the awakening process to prepare the patient to be brought out of the hypnotic state.

POST-HYPNOSIS

At this point the patient is given an opportunity to ask further questions, and this includes the practitioner answering any questions that may have arisen as a result of the patient's experience of the hypnotic state. This reassures the patient that they remained in control throughout the process, and any feedback can be used for future sessions to tailor suggestions more effectively. After the debriefing process, the practitioner can then reinforce any suggestions made during hypnosis and encourage the patient to observe any changes occurring in themselves.

When the session is used to teach self-hypnosis, at this point the patient should be encouraged to practise the technique while with the practitioner. This allows the patient to feel safe, and demonstrates that suggestions made in the hypnotic state were fully understood.

Some practitioners suggest to their patients that they should not discuss the process with anyone else during the following 24 hours. This is to encourage the unconscious processing of the hypnotic event during their sleep. Amnesia of the specifics of the hypnotic state is more likely to occur when these suggestions are adhered to.

HOMEWORK

Once the formal therapeutic element of the session has been concluded, the patient may be instructed to do homework. Homework is the name given to specific tasks, thought processes or behaviours which the patient is directed to action after leaving the session. This may include practising self-hypnosis. If self-hypnosis has been suggested, the practitioner should reinforce the process at this stage, reminding the patient of how to do the self-hypnosis.

For activities relating to the patient's interaction with their condition, the practitioner will repeat the suggestions made as part of the formal hypnosis session, unless amnesia has been used to induce a deliberate 'forgetting' of the suggestions. This might be used, for example, for patients who smoked to say to themselves 'I have no desire to smoke' and to distract themselves deliberately when in a situation where they used to smoke, or for phobic patients to press the tip of the thumb and first finger together to produce relaxation in a specific situation.

The purpose of homework is to reinforce therapeutic suggestions, and also to break the associated patterns of thought, feelings or actions which were associated with the condition.

Use of CDs/MP3s

Some practitioners use CDs or MP3s to reinforce suggestions made in the hypnosis session. If this is to be done, generic CDs which work on motivation, confidence, general health and well-being, reducing anxiety or improving coping strategies are most effective within the context of this hypnotherapeutic model. This is especially true if the practitioner is going to leave three weeks between sessions. I shall discuss this in more depth in Chapter 7, 'Hypnotic diagnostics.'

FUTURE SESSIONS

When the patient is clear about what is expected of them after the session, dates for any future sessions (if necessary) are then set. The timing between sessions is dictated by the condition and the speed at which the patient responds, or a more formulaic approach incorporating the psychocybernetics framework can be taken. The main reason for this variance is that some conditions (and patients) will need reinforcement as soon as possible, whereas others will need time for the changes to be accepted and acted upon before continuing with the therapeutic sessions. As with the use of CDs/MP3s, I shall discuss this in depth in Chapter 7, 'Hypnotic diagnostics.'

CHAPTER 4

Questions patients ask

During a clinical hypnosis session, patients are given an opportunity to ask questions. Questions asked by patients at the start of the session will differ from those asked just before the practitioner takes them into hypnosis. This difference relates to the fact that patients will feel more comfortable and relaxed, and will ask more detailed questions about hypnosis further into the session than at the beginning when they are unsure about exactly what is going to happen. A competent practitioner will recognise that most patients who are new to hypnosis will have similar concerns and questions, but will wait until the patient asks them.

This chapter provides examples of the types of questions that are often asked by patients, and discusses appropriate responses to them. It is valid to bear in mind that the patient will ask questions not only as a way of uncovering the specific answer to a question, but also as a way of measuring the practitioner's knowledge and competency. A poor answer to a question can break rapport. There is also a danger in answering a question too comprehensively. The practitioner must always keep a balance between education and information.

The purpose of answering patients' questions is therefore twofold – first, to reassure the patient and therefore reduce their anxiety, and secondly, to prepare the patient to safely receive suggestions while in hypnosis. An appropriate answer to a patient's question in this context is one that reassures the patient and informs them of what to expect in terms of their future experiences, while still remaining within the framework of a clinical hypnosis session. Above all, any response will need to emphasise that the patient is in control of both the form and the content of their sessions. As a result of this reassurance, rather than a requirement to accurately inform, some of the answers are linguistic models tailored to the patient's concerns about the process, rather than 'correct' or definitive answers.

IS HYPNOSIS AN ALTERED STATE?

There are non-state theorists, such as Dr Graham Wagstaff of the University of Liverpool, who have conducted studies which demonstrate that events experienced during hypnosis can also be replicated outside this state (Wagstaff, 1981). The conclusions drawn are that hypnosis is not a unique altered state, especially as events reported by those supposedly experiencing hypnosis have varied substantially. This debate will be ongoing until in-depth research based on objective rather than subjective or experiential criteria has been undertaken.

Current developments in fMRI and PET scan technology mean that we now have a much clearer picture of the neurological events that occur during different processes, such as waking, sleeping and hypnosis. Research shows that there is a distinct alteration in brain activity during the induction of hypnotic states, and also during the time when suggestions are being processed (Rainville *et al.*, 2002; Woody and Szechtman, 2003), and the current consensus is that hypnosis is an identifiable brain state, similar to that of meditation (Grant and Rainville, 2005).

HOW WILL I KNOW THAT IT HAS WORKED?

Patients will sometimes ask what happens if hypnosis does not work. There are a number of reasons for this question, one being that the hypnosis itself was not adequately explained to the patient. Another reason for this question may be that the patient has general feelings of negativity and their focus of attention remains on their problem rather than on the therapeutic outcome. If this question comes up, the practitioner will repeat some of the suggestions made while the patient was in hypnosis to move their focus of attention to the benefits of change. The patient is also directed to actively look for the differences between how they were before the session, and what has changed after the session. The terms 'change' or 'differences' are used out of preference when attempting to focus the patient's attention on the future, rather than emphasising the benefits, as the patient will be more willing and able to notice these effects in a non-judgemental manner. If the situation arises whereby the patient informs the practitioner that they did not gain the benefit which they expected, a further session will then be given that refines the specific suggestion and enhances the patient's capacity to focus on the benefits by the use of ego-strengthening suggestions.

WHAT CAN HYPNOSIS DO FOR ME THAT I COULD NOT ALREADY DO FOR MYSELF?

This is a key question in motivating patients to experience hypnosis, and also in enabling them to gain maximum benefit from the therapeutic suggestions. Some patients may have had their condition for such a long period of time that they believe there is no other way for them to be. An example of this would be the migraine sufferer who has no recollection of a time when they did not suffer from their condition. There are others who feel that the situation they are trying to change is such a fundamental part of their life that they could not imagine themselves without their behaviour. Smokers often fit into this category. In either case the explanation of the advantages of using hypnosis will incorporate information on the ways in which the brain best receives suggestions, as well as informing the patient of how the hypnoidal state can help. It will be explained to the patient that there is a major difference between the type of auto-suggestions given out of hypnosis, and suggestions given by a practitioner while the patient is in hypnosis.

This difference is what makes the hypnosis more effective. While the individual is focused mentally and relaxed physically they are more able to receive suggestions that in a full waking state they might reject, or talk themselves out of. The other element here relates to brain function, and it can be simply explained to the patient that when they are in hypnosis, the areas of the brain which relate to controlling responses will be activated and accessible to conscious control. Thus the patient will be able to make the changes necessary on an unconscious level, without having to consciously 'try' to change. Hypnosis effectively acts as a mediator or translator between conscious control and unconscious function, allowing the patient to more easily and effectively make the necessary changes.

IS HYPNOSIS DIFFERENT FROM MEDITATION?

Hypnosis and meditation can be very similar in the way in which they are experienced physically and, with some forms of meditation, the way in which they are experienced mentally. The main difference lies in the specific mental processing that takes place in hypnosis as a result of suggestions. There are some forms of meditation that use guided imagery, and this can also be used in hypnosis, although in hypnosis this usually takes the form of a specific therapeutic metaphor. When an individual is meditating, the emphasis is often on achieving a specific internal state while in meditation. In hypnosis, the primary emphasis is on achieving external changes after the hypnosis session is completed. Research has been conducted on the similarities between hypnosis and meditation in terms of the brain state (Grant and Rainville, 2005), which show similar experiential changes and shared brain mechanisms. Further research (Creswell *et al.*, 2007) has shown that meditation, like hypnosis, activates the left pre-frontal lobe, which is linked to positive emotions, self-control and happiness, and also influences the amygdala, which are effectively the alarm centre of the brain, thereby reducing the potentially harmful effects of stress. One can reasonably deduce from this that any positive benefits which are discerned in meditation can also be experienced as a result of hypnosis.

However, in terms of the individual, hypnosis can be experienced as basically similar to or basically different from meditation, depending on the individual's mindset and previous knowledge of either process.

IS CLINICAL HYPNOSIS LIKE STAGE HYPNOSIS?

For some patients, their fears of hypnosis are based on what they may have seen in a stage show. Their fears often relate to the idea of losing control, or being influenced inappropriately. If this question comes up, the practitioner will need to explain that there are many different events going on in a stage show, and be able to differentiate between what goes on in a clinical hypnosis session and what patients believe they have seen on stage.

It can be explained to the patient that there are a number of components to a stage hypnosis show. The first of these is expectation. When people go to a stage show they already know what to expect of the event, and will therefore already be predicting what they are going to experience. The next process is peer pressure. It is very rare for people to go alone to a stage show – they usually go in groups. Within each group there will be one or two individuals who are more exhibitionistic by nature, and the rest of the group will encourage them to get up on stage. Frequently, people will drink alcohol before arriving at the stage show, and this will encourage the potential participants even further as their inhibitions are lowered.

Once the audience arrives at the stage show, there will be a pre-selection process to discover those who will end up on stage. This usually involves suggestibility tests. The purpose of these tests is not to find the most easily hypnotisable subjects, but to find the exhibitionists. One example of this type of test is the 'hand-clasp test', where members of the audience are instructed to hold their arms straight out in front of them at shoulder height, and to interlink their fingers and press their palms together. Suggestions are then made that, at a given cue, they will be unable to pull their hands apart. These are followed by suggestions returning all sensations to normal. Once this has been done, the audience watchers who are placed around the auditorium will pick out the people who drew attention to themselves by indicating that they could open their hands, and therefore were not hypnotised, but were showing that they were exhibitionists and willing to participate in the stage events. These individuals will often raise their hands up in the air to draw more attention to this fact. They are then selected to come up on stage.

Once up on stage, the hypnotist provides encouragement by directing all of the audience applause to the person 'being hypnotised', and by directing them to engage in more and more outrageous behaviour. The final component in the show will be the abrogation of responsibility, whereby a person on stage can do all manner of things while claiming that the stage hypnotist 'made them do it.' Some stage hypnotists encourage their participants to more outrageous behaviour by telling them that the more they do, the more intelligent or amusing they are, working on the ego of their subject. When the person comes off stage they can tell their friends that they do not remember what they have done, or they were under the influence of the stage hypnotist – so there can be no 'blame' attached to their behaviour. Frequently, the participants in a stage show will be given some free tickets to a future performance. In the mean time, those who went to the show will tell those to whom they give the tickets all that happened, and the stories will become progressively more outrageous. By the time the next group goes to the show they will already be heavily primed for the event, and the exhibitionist of the new group will want to outdo the first performance, and so it goes on.

A hypnotised individual would not be a good performer in a stage show. When a person is in hypnosis they hardly move, and any responses that are shown will be slow and small. Patients who ask about stage hypnosis can therefore be assured that during clinical hypnosis they will become relaxed and quite still, they will only do what they feel comfortable doing, and they will remain in control throughout.

There are instances when people who participate in stage hypnosis shows are genuinely in an altered state (other than that induced by alcohol). This could happen if the participant is a somnambulist or is vulnerable to suggestions as a result of a pre-existing condition or sequence of events, or because they want to believe themselves to be hypnotised, and begin to enter a hypnotic-type state as a result of this belief. Following the sudden death of her daughter, Sharron Tabarn, after she had participated in a stage hypnosis show, Margaret Harper formed the Campaign Against Stage Hypnosis (CASH). The aim of this organisation is to get stage hypnosis banned in the UK.

In the context of the clinical hypnosis setting, with any type of questions that patients may ask, the key is to tailor the reply to their concerns, rather than to attempt to give a comprehensive answer. Patients who ask about stage hypnosis usually want reassurance that they will be safe and in control, and that they will not be 'made' to do anything they do not want to do.

ARE PATIENTS IN CONTROL OF THE HYPNOTIC EVENT AND CAN THEY EXERCISE FREE WILL OVER ACCEPTING THE SUGGESTIONS?

Suggestions that are made in hypnosis will reflect the discussion between patient and practitioner during the pre-induction talk. Suggestions for the purpose of creating and maintaining the hypnotic state, or for the purpose of therapeutic benefit, are based on the pre-induction discussion alone. As soon as they enter hypnosis, the patient will then engage their conscious awareness to analyse what has been said to ensure that they feel safe and comfortable with the suggestions that are being made. They will bring themselves out of hypnosis if they are not comfortable with the suggestions, or if new suggestions are introduced. Even at the somnambulistic level of hypnosis, the patient remains in control and would respond to suggestions with an awareness of their personal safety still intact. If the practitioner asked the patient to do anything that they did not feel safe and comfortable with, or made suggestions which were outside the framework already discussed in the pre-induction talk, the patient would bring him- or herself out of hypnosis.

No one can be forced or encouraged to do something that they would not already be inclined to do. The ability to reject suggestions is enhanced by the focused state of attention that is pivotal to the experience of hypnosis. It therefore follows that anyone in hypnosis will be able to reject or accept suggestions in the same way as they would in a normal state. However, the capacity to act upon positive suggestions is enhanced by this state of physical relaxation and focused concentration.

CAN ANYONE GET STUCK IN HYPNOSIS?

This type of question again relates to patients' concerns about how much control they have over the experience. The easiest way to reassure patients in this situation is to inform them that they control the experience throughout. Another aspect of this concern is what would happen to them if something was to distract, disturb or in some way incapacitate the practitioner before they had brought the patient to full conscious alertness. Patients who ask this type of question need to be reassured that they would, in these circumstances, bring themselves out of the hypnotic state. The practitioner will tell the patient that it may take a little longer for full reorientation to occur, as part of the 'waking up' procedure includes the return of all sensations to normal. However, reassurances are made that the patient will be normal and fully alert after a short while, even if some unforeseen event occurs and they have to do this for themselves.

CAN A PATIENT BE MADE TO FORGET WHAT HAS HAPPENED?

Remembering and forgetting events, as well as restructuring them, is all part of memory codification (David *et al.*, 2000). Patients in hypnosis are able to remember everything that is of value for them to remember, and can give themselves permission to 'forget' (a more appropriate term would be 'neglect to remember') anything which is causing them disturbance. As with the issue of control, patients can be reassured that no other person can force them to forget, but that forgetting is sometimes part of a natural process for healing and change, and that if it is appropriate for them to forget about something which concerned them, they may choose to do so. Thus clinical hypnosis is described as working in a similar way to the natural process of memory, by either kick-starting a memory association or re-creating an emotional link.

WHEN A PATIENT EXPERIENCES AN ABREACTION IN HYPNOSIS AND NEEDS AN EXPLANATION OF WHY IT HAPPENED

An 'abreaction' is an emotional response that is triggered by a memory or state. This is experienced while the patient is in hypnosis, and can often disturb or upset the patient – usually because it was unexpected. On awakening it is important to reassure the patient that the experience was an appropriate one, and give them time to discuss it, should they need to do so. Abreactions can be described to the patient as an emotional discharge that, as they were not able to experience the emotion at the time of the original disturbing event, needed to be experienced now – for example, being told as a child not to cry. Now that they have done so, there is no further requirement for the symptom. Occasionally, abreactions occur spontaneously, with no apparent origin. The main emphasis here should be to assure the patient that the abreaction was natural and appropriate, and that they can now move forward. A simple model for the practitioner to use as a way to reassure the patient is to state that the abreaction will only occur when three elements are in place. First, the patient is able to deal with the abreaction, secondly, the abreaction is relevant to the problem, and finally, the abreaction will be cathartic and help the patient to move forward. When the event is described in these terms, the patient is reassured that the abreaction occurred because it is part of the process, and they can therefore understand why it happened.

Management of the patient during an abreaction is discussed fully in Chapter 8, 'Creating the hypnotherapeutic protocol.'

PATIENTS VIEW THEIR CAPACITY TO ENTER HYPNOSIS AS AN ISSUE OF WILLPOWER

Hypnosis is *not* about the practitioner exercising their willpower over that of the patient (Conn, 1980; King and Council, 1998). It is appropriate to inform the patient that they require willpower to experience hypnosis, and that they will only experience the state depending on how much willpower they have. The hypnotic state can then be described as one that gives the patient *increased* levels of willpower over their own thoughts, behaviours and emotions. This runs counter to some of the research available. However, the issue here is one of motivation. Would a patient wish to be hypnotised if they felt that they lost rather than gained control over events? The answer is obvious, so here it is appropriate for the practitioner to utilise a model of behaviour which will help the patient to respond to the hypnosis, rather than hindering this process.

PATIENTS WHO RECALL MEMORIES WHILE IN HYPNOSIS

Patients who approach their condition analytically often benefit from experiencing events in hypnosis that could give them a rationale for their behaviours, thoughts and feelings. If a therapeutic process involving evocation of memories is to be utilised, it is vital to inform the patient of the malleable quality of memory, and to assure them that the event may not be 'real' in the way that they are experiencing it, and that this memory is only their current perception of an event, real or imagined, designed to assist them in making a beneficial change in their life.

Some patients are afraid that they will recall events which they would rather not remember, or of which they have little or no recollection – memories which they have deliberately chosen to forget consciously. If a patient does re-experience a memory spontaneously, the emphasis in the therapy is on the patient permitting the recalled information to allow them to move forward. The practitioner will always emphasise that any memory which is recalled in hypnosis may not be a strict representation of the actual event, and as a result is only their current perception of the event. As a perception it can be understood and worked through. If a patient spontaneously recalls a memory of which they had no previous conscious awareness, the practitioner will explain that this has only happened because they feel safe enough to allow it to happen, and because this memory has some relevance to their current situation.

PATIENTS WHO EXPECT HYPNOSIS TO BE SIMILAR TO A GENERAL ANAESTHETIC

If the patient expects to be completely unaware of their surroundings and the internal experience during hypnosis, on being reawakened they may feel that they were not hypnotised (Matheson *et al.*, 1989; Pekala, 2002). Before inducing hypnosis, the practitioner needs to describe the state in such a way that the patient will understand their experience of the event as it occurs. One possible way to describe the hypnotic state is as being similar to that of sleep at the physical level (so the patient can move around if they want to, but they may experience sensations of limb heaviness and tiredness), while the mental processes are in a state of heightened focus whereby the patient hears and can analyse everything as it is suggested to them. In this situation the explanation must also include the suggestion that it is important for this mental awareness and processing to continue as the patient will need to be aware of the suggestions so that they can decide which of them are most appropriate to take on board. It can also be explained that as the patient enters deeper levels of hypnosis there may be times when their awareness of their surroundings will vary in intensity.

PATIENTS WHO DO NOT BELIEVE THEY CAN BE HYPNOTISED

If a patient has this mindset, it is usually based on preconceptions of hypnosis as a form of mind control. The patient can be assured that they will only be hypnotised if they wish to be hypnotised, and that hypnosis is a naturally occurring state which they have experienced before – for example, when driving along a familiar road or absorbed in a piece of music. After the hypnosis session it can be useful to ask the patient how long they believe they have had their eyes closed. The majority experience the time as being considerably shorter than it actually was. This in turn acts as a convincer that the hypnotic event was different from simple eye closure.

PATIENTS WHO ARE UNSURE ABOUT THEIR POTENTIAL TO EXPERIENCE RESULTS

If the patient questions whether hypnosis will work for them, the practitioner can first explain that hypnosis works with their personality to enhance the positive aspects that are already in place. During the hypnosis session, suggestions are made to direct the patient's attention on to positive changes in the future. The practitioner can reinforce these suggestions in the post-hypnotic section by suggesting that the patient looks for any 'differences' in the way that they are experiencing life events.

PATIENTS WHO BELIEVE THEY ARE ASLEEP DURING HYPNOSIS

If a patient does fall asleep during hypnosis, this can be easily recognised, as there will be more movement, and changes in breathing patterns will occur. A patient in hypnosis is generally quite still, whereas someone who is sleeping will make irregular and jerky movements, change their position, and their breathing can become louder and quite stentorian.

However, some patients go so deeply into hypnosis that there are times when they do not register everything that is being said. This occurs when they are fully comfortable with what is being said and, raising no conscious objections, allow themselves to go deeper into the hypnotic state than they expected. When this situation occurs, the practitioner will explain this to them and reassure them that everything which is of significance for them to remember will be recalled. The key to differentiating between patients who believed they were asleep, and those who actually went to sleep, is whether they responded to the awakening script. The practitioner will then highlight this as an indicator that they were in hypnosis rather than actually sleeping, because if they were truly asleep they would not respond.

PATIENTS WHO BELIEVE HYPNOSIS MAY CONFLICT WITH THEIR RELIGIOUS BELIEFS

Some patients are concerned about suggestions made because of religious considerations. As with many of the questions that patients ask, this is the result of concerns about mind control, or fears that suggestions made by another person might in some way contradict the patient's belief structure. If this is an issue, it is essential that the practitioner finds out the nature of these concerns. Once this has been done, an explanation of how the process of clinical hypnosis helps individuals to take more control of themselves is given. Reassurance is also given that hypnosis is not about another person gaining influence over the patient. This can be amplified if appropriate with the suggestion that the patient's faith will be secure throughout and can even help them to experience the therapeutic effects of the session at a more profound level.

There are some events that occur in charismatic churches whereby an individual enters an altered state on a given cue or trigger from a central figure (Galanter, 1983). The individual may experience an abreaction, such as crying or shaking, and in some instances may gain specific benefit from the experience. If a patient comes along who has seen this event occur and believes that hypnosis is something similar, it is vital to explain the parallels and the differences. The parallels are in the aspects of expectation and trust in the other individual (in this case the preacher or healer), and the differences lie in the fact that in charismatic healing the benefits gained are attributed to the power of their God, whereas in clinical hypnosis they are attributed to the individual him- or herself. For patients with a religious framework, emphasis will be placed on the fact that no one can be forced to do anything outside their moral, social or religious beliefs in any form. To further reassure a patient with this mindset, the practitioner can take useful parts of their belief system to create a motivational scenario. By describing clinical hypnosis in a way that reinforces the positive aspects of the patient's belief system, the practitioner can utilise the patient's beliefs to strengthen the suggestions for change.

PATIENTS WHO EXPECT A 'CURE' FROM HYPNOSIS

Some patients have completely unrealistic expectations of clinical hypnosis. They believe that, once hypnotised, they will be completely 'cured' of their condition. The first point to make here is that the term 'cure' is not used within this therapeutic framework. Cure implies total and permanent remission from all symptoms. Patients who talk of cures will often be those who believe hypnosis is something that is done *to* them, as opposed to their being an active participant in the event. They will often describe their understanding of the process as an expectation that they will hear, feel and remember nothing until they are woken up, and at that point they will be symptom-free – similar to having a tooth out under general anaesthetic. These individuals may have this belief structure as a result of expectations generated by the media or stage hypnosis, or because they do not wish to take any responsibility for maintaining their symptom, because they have a secondary gain to maintain.

In any event, the practitioner will need to emphasise to such patients that the process is a therapeutic partnership, in which they need to take an active role. It should be further emphasised that it is in fact essential for the patient to hear, feel and remember during the process, so that they only take on board suggestions that are safe and comfortable for them. The final element in the explanation creates flexibility in the outcome, with the patient being allowed to notice the changes as they take place, so that they become natural to them, rather than waking up from the hypnosis having had a totally new way of behaving installed in them. This would feel unnatural, and would obviously very soon be rejected. Thus the unrealistic expectations are broken down and reconstructed into a sequence of statements that will allow the patient to experience hypnosis as a relaxed and pleasant state, and therefore experience positive effects from the suggestions.

PATIENTS WHO BELIEVE THEY CANNOT BE HYPNOTISED BECAUSE THEY ARE TOO ANALYTICAL, INTELLECTUAL OR INTELLIGENT

Analytical, intellectual or intelligent individuals often have as part of their characteristic make-up a tendency to believe that no one can hypnotise them, as they often believe hypnosis to be some kind of trick or mind game. This attitude stems from a commonly held but now very outdated belief that only people with a weak will can be hypnotised. In these circumstances, the patient will be told that the more analytical, intellectual or intelligent they are, the deeper into hypnosis they will be able to go. To go further, the practitioner will actively encourage the patient to continue to apply this characteristic all the way through the hypnotic state. The other element here, namely fear of losing control or being tricked, is also overcome by the practitioner actively promoting the patient's analytical, intellectual or intelligent character trait as part of them taking control of their experience of hypnosis, and exercising direct choice over the suggestions that they decide to accept.

PATIENTS WHO BELIEVE HYPNOSIS TO BE POTENTIALLY DANGEROUS

Some patients believe that hypnosis is in some way dangerous, that they could get stuck, or that the practitioner could make suggestions to them which would be harmful or make them reveal personal information which they would not otherwise disclose. Anxious patients may focus on apocryphal stories of hypnosis sessions in which patients were subjected to unpleasant experiences and were subsequently traumatised. To reassure the patient that this is not the case, the practitioner will often point out that any individual for whom hypnosis could potentially be dangerous *cannot* be hypnotised, and that this is a self-defence mechanism. Anyone who is able to experience hypnosis will be able to control the experience throughout, and to hear all of the suggestions that are made, so will therefore be able to filter out any suggestions that are potentially harmful to them. It is also appropriate to mention that if the patient does not have these fears dealt with appropriately, they will remain in an anxiety state and will then be unable to enter hypnosis properly, if at all.

PATIENTS WHO BELIEVE THAT HYPNOSIS WILL HELP THEM TO EXPERIENCE PAST LIVES

The popular press has much to answer for with regard to past-life regression. Whenever there is a newspaper article or television or radio programme about this subject, people will contact hypnosis practitioners with a view to experiencing a past life. There are a number of issues which need to be dealt with here. First, clinical hypnosis is not something to be experienced purely for the purposes of experimentation. Secondly, if an individual wishes to gain some therapeutic benefit from the process, there may be other methods that would be more appropriate. To ensure that those people with genuine need are assisted in the best possible way, the practitioner will ask a series of evaluative questions before the pre-induction talk to clarify the reasons why the patient wants past-life regression rather than any other specific protocol. These evaluation processes are discussed in later chapters. It is worth noting that there are a number of religions which include past lives as part of their structure, and therefore the potential therapeutic value of past-life regression for these individuals is valid (Pyun and Kim, 2009).

PATIENTS WHO COME FOR CLINICAL HYPNOSIS TO PERFECT THEIR NEUROSES

There are some individuals for whom the specific benefits of retaining their symptoms are greater than those to be gained from getting better. These secondary gains will often create behaviours by the patient to maintain the symptoms. These strategies can often include the patient attempting many different ways of gaining remission, from medication to therapeutic approaches, and in some extreme cases, unnecessary surgery. This allows the patient to maintain the symptom while still appearing to attempt to find ways to improve their situation. The mindset of such patients will prevent them from being open to any types of suggestions that could help them to make the appropriate changes to get better. They will then be able to continue to maintain their symptoms on the basis that they are 'trying everything, but nothing is working for them.' With this type of patient there are a number of directions that can be taken. One approach is for the practitioner to undertake ego strengthening rather than approaching the condition per se, with a view to encouraging the patient to find better ways of coping and opening their mind to the benefits of change. Another approach would be to encourage them to visualise the future, and to begin to imagine how life could be for them without their condition. Either way, it is neither appropriate nor conducive to a productive outcome to attempt to deal directly with the symptoms of their condition before the mindset of the patient has been changed to a more positive one.

PATIENTS WHO DO NOT WANT THE THERAPEUTIC OUTCOME

Sometimes patients come along for clinical hypnosis, but do not want to be there. This may be because, as described in the previous section, they have secondary gains that are keeping them in their problem state. It is also possible that the motivation is not theirs. This occurs when, for example, a partner or a GP books a patient in for smoking cessation, but the patient him- or herself has little or no motivation. If this situation occurs, the practitioner could consider using the hypnosis to change the patient's mindset, or could conduct the session anyway, emphasising the positive effects of change. In clinical hypnosis, motivation plays a key role in the recognition and acceptance of change and patient suggestibility. It is a good idea for the practitioner to speak to the patient before they come for the session, so that they can pre-assess whether hypnosis is going to be appropriate for them. Whenever another person telephones to make a session booking on the patient's behalf, this is a fairly good indicator that their focus of attention is not on the session. As a result, a seasoned clinical hypnosis practitioner will insist on speaking to the patient him- or herself before the session, to avoid the possibility of a poorly motivated patient arriving in the consulting room.

CHAPTER 5

Hypnotic events, application and contraindications

Before discussing the patient experiences that can occur as part of the hypnotic state, it is useful to identify the indicators of 'levels' or 'depths' of hypnotic state that can be experienced (Pekala *et al.*, 2006). Although there are no clearly defined delimiters between levels of hypnosis, there are a number of visible and experiential indicators which can be observed. Not all patients will experience all hypnotic events, nor will they necessarily experience different levels. Each patient will experience the event in different ways, depending on the following:

➤ **Personal history:** Patients who have prior experience of hypnosis, or who have experience of meditation states, will often be more comfortable and notice more of the phenomena that are taking place in hypnosis. Patients who are generally stable and who have a strong ego state will have fewer concerns about suggestions being made, and will therefore exercise more free will when responding. This in turn allows them to experience deeper states than patients who are not so comfortable with themselves. If patients are highly motivated to achieve the therapeutic outcome, this will influence their receptivity to suggestions. It is important to note that there are individuals who come for clinical hypnosis as a last resort and want the hypnosis to work for them so much that this counters their ability to enter a hypnoidal state. They are so anxious for success that this anxiety prevents them from focusing and relaxing sufficiently to enter hypnosis.

➤ **The condition:** If the condition includes symptoms of anxiety or the patient has problems relating to control, these can make it more difficult for the patient to experience relaxed states. Most conditions, whether physical or psychological in origin, will be worsened by stress, and the more stressed the individual, the longer it will usually take to induce hypnosis. This is why it is so important to reassure patients that they dictate the level of hypnoidal state which they will experience, and that they remain in control throughout the event. Patients will achieve a level of hypnosis at which they feel most comfortable. At this level they will experience the optimum relaxed state from where they will be able to experience the therapeutic components of the hypnosis. Once they have reached this level they will remain there until they have gained sufficient insight into their condition, or received the unconscious signals which they need to move forward. Suggestions for change are most often made in the hypnosis script immediately after the patient has been told that they will soon be woken up. It is generally believed that this is the most effective level at which to make suggestions, as patients will often hold back from achieving their deepest potential of hypnotic state due to fear of letting go, or anxiety about change.

➤ **The content and method of delivery of suggestions given by the practitioner:** The content and delivery of suggestions are directly influenced by the patient's way of operating in and viewing the world (Feldman, 2009). Suggestions are created from this worldview, and are enhanced by the practitioner feeding back in hypnosis the type and form of language that the patient uses to describe their symptoms and the outcome that they require. If the content of the suggestions is appropriate to the patient's interaction with their condition, they will continue to achieve progressively deeper levels of hypnosis. This happens as they become comfortable and familiar with more of the hypnotic phenomena with each session. As a result, their capacity to enter hypnosis increases with increasing levels of experience until they plateau at their optimum potential depth. If the method used by the practitioner to deliver the suggestions is one with which the patient is comfortable (e.g. the chief executive officer of an organisation being given direct authoritarian suggestions), the levels of hypnotic state that are being experienced can also increase for the patient.

➤ **The level of rapport established with the practitioner:** The practitioner needs to demonstrate three main attributes, namely competence, an understanding of patients and their conditions, and the ability to create clear objectives for the therapy with patients. Competence is demonstrated by a confident and open approach, and the ability to communicate with patients in their own language. Understanding comes from listening and interpretation skills, allowing the patient to *feel* that they are being listened to and that the practitioner demonstrates empathy where appropriate (Mercer *et al.*, 2002). The creation of clear objectives for therapy involves all of the skills described above, whereby the practitioner takes what the patient presents, and in partnership with them creates a clear and specific objective for therapy which will be achievable and acceptable to the patient. Rapport skills can be learned, but as each experience of working with a patient will be unique, it is worth noting that when this process is done well, it is invisible to the patient.

JUXTAPOSITION OF SUGGESTIONS

Throughout the various levels, a skilled practitioner of hypnosis will introduce suggestions that direct the patient's attention to ongoing hypnotic phenomena or events. This is done to enhance the patient's awareness of hypnotic phenomena, or to direct their attention away from external events. One example would be 'Your limbs are starting to feel heavy and tired . . . so you can notice that you are starting to relax . . .' The first part of the suggestion directs the patient's attention to the experience of limb heaviness that is often characteristic of medium-depth hypnosis, while compounding the suggestion with the idea of relaxation. As a result, the patient will begin to associate the events of the hypnotic state with relaxation.

INDIVIDUAL APTITUDE

Positive attitude and expectation, the patient's motivation to achieve change and the rapport that is established between practitioner and patient are all factors that determine whether a practitioner can induce a hypnotic state. Influencing these factors is therefore a part of the pre-induction section of the clinical hypnosis session.

Evaluating the potential of an individual to enter hypnosis or to accept hypnotherapeutic suggestions is problematic, and there are few accurate tests or indicators of susceptibility. The Barber Suggestibility Scale and the Stanford Hypnotic Susceptibility Scale (Ruch *et al.*, 1974), the Harvard Group Scale of Hypnotic Susceptibility (Shor and Orne, 1963) and the Hypnotic Induction Profile (HIP) (Hilgard, 1981) are often referred to in clinical publications. These measures use standardised performance-based psychological tests to check for hypnotic susceptibility. It has been discovered that although susceptibility can be measured, it is not necessarily an accurate indicator of whether therapeutic suggestions will be accepted more readily. It is best to use evaluative processes that are based on the patient's responses in the pre-induction section of the hypnosis session as a method of calibrating unique hypnotic susceptibility, and to base a treatment protocol on these responses rather than using hypnotic suggestibility or hypnotic susceptibility tests, which can damage the rapport between patient and practitioner.

Nor does the ability to experience the hypnotic state change much throughout the patient's lifetime, although studies of different age groups appear to show that responsiveness peaks between the teenage years and the age of 35 years. The ability to be hypnotised appears to follow the normal bell-shaped distribution curve for performance, with the younger and older age groups tending to demonstrate relatively lower responsiveness. Longitudinal studies of college students have shown that the ability to be hypnotised remains as stable as IQ over a 25-year period (Piccione *et al.*, 1989).

Other factors that influence performance relate to patients' ability to experience hypnosis-related phenomena outside formal hypnosis. An example of this is found in studies by De Groot *et al.* (1988) and by Nash *et al.* (1986), which show that patients with active imaginations are more likely to experience hypnotic phenomena, and therefore access deeper levels of hypnosis. Alongside this, Tellegen and Atkinson (1974) developed a scale of absorption to attempt to measure this phenomenon. The ability to become absorbed in a subject is an accurate indicator of the ability of a patient to experience hypnosis.

Restricted environment stimulation therapy (REST) is the only process currently known to demonstrate the ability to enhance the individual's capacity to experience hypnotic states. As it implies, the patient is subjected to a restricted environment, such as a flotation tank. Studies by Barabasz and Barabasz (1989) on patients with chronic pain conditions demonstrated an increased aptitude for hypnosis when the REST technique was used.

NORMAL STATES OF CONSCIOUSNESS

One remark commonly made by those experiencing hypnosis is how similar it is to the waking state. Their expectations and belief structures, which are discussed elsewhere in this volume, are a factor in this. This is why it is important for the practitioner to explain the hypnotic state in terms of commonly occurring focused or altered states. Telling the patient about daydreaming, or how it feels to be absorbed in a piece of music, is often a good way of leading them into an appreciation of how hypnosis can be experienced. It is always useful to describe the hypnotic event in terms of something familiar to the patient, as this ensures that they feel in control, enhances their receptivity to suggestions, and can build on positive mental associations.

PHYSIOLOGICAL AND PERCEPTUAL INDICATORS OF STAGES OF HYPNOTIC STATE

There are no fixed delimiters to levels of hypnosis, nor do these levels have specific significance in terms of which will be most effective for the patient to receive suggestions. Each patient will settle on a level at which they feel comfortable and receptive at that time.

LIGHT HYPNOSIS

This is the first stage that any patient can enter, and in a formal hypnosis induction it commences as soon as eye closure is achieved, or if eye closure is not achieved, when sufficient focused attention is in place to create pupil dilation. With certain conditions and patients, this state is one that is a symptom of their condition – for example, if the patient is dissociated. This can be observed particularly when patients are discussing their condition during the pre-induction talk, and physical indicators of dissociation are already present – for example, a fixed gaze and slow responsiveness to questions.

The following events can be observed:

➤ eye closure
➤ a reduction in movement
➤ a more pronounced swallow reflex
➤ posture and facial features beginning to relax
➤ breathing beginning to deepen
➤ external indicators of tension beginning to decrease.

MEDIUM HYPNOSIS

Medium hypnosis is the next stage of hypnosis, in which the awareness of the patient moves from external events to a more intensive concentration on internal events. The patient may notice their stomach rumbling, or become more aware of other internal processes such as their pulse.

The following events can be observed:

➤ characteristics of light hypnosis become more pronounced
➤ movement of the head from an upright position further backwards or forwards than usual
➤ a slumped posture
➤ the mouth may open
➤ skin pigmentation heightens
➤ a feeling of lethargy
➤ a feeling of tiredness
➤ decreased awareness of the immediate surroundings
➤ retardation in responsiveness
➤ a reduction in sensory awareness
➤ twitching movements in the peripheral nervous system
➤ increased lachrymation
➤ breathing moves to the abdomen
➤ yawning.

DEEP HYPNOSIS

Not all patients are able to access this level, and it is worth noting at this point that when no further trance phenomena can be observed, and the patient appears to 'plateau', they have reached a level of experience with which they are comfortable. In addition to this the response time to suggestions increases as greater depths of hypnosis are achieved, so more time may need to be given for the patient to respond.

When the patient reaches their plateau, attempts to deepen further are usually ineffective, and it can be observed that they will start to shift around if the practitioner attempts to further deepen the trance.

The following events can be observed:

➤ further enhancement of the characteristics of light and medium hypnosis
➤ partial or total amnesia of the hypnotic events
➤ partial or total amnesia of suggestions made during hypnosis
➤ depersonalisation
➤ increased capacity to experience analgesia or anaesthesia
➤ enhanced capacity to experience hallucinatory states
➤ periodic closing down of external awareness
➤ deep abdominal breathing
➤ sighing.

SOMNAMBULISM

When experienced during the hypnotic state, somnambulism allows the patient to experience sensations and events as if they were awake. This is similar to the somnambulistic state that occurs during sleep. It is a rare occurrence, as the potential to experience somnambulism in hypnosis correlates with patients already having experienced these states in their sleep. As a therapeutic state it is not considered to be useful, as the amnesia that occurs as part of this state prevents the patient from recalling suggestions once they are conscious. Even during the somnambulistic hypnotic state, the patient remains aware on some level and will not accept suggestions that fall outside their moral, social or emotional framework. In other words, no one at any stage of experiencing hypnosis or post-hypnosis can be 'made' to do something that they would not otherwise have been inclined to do.

The following events may be observed:

➤ eyes open
➤ tension in body and facial features
➤ walking or talking may occur
➤ amnesia during and after the hypnotic event
➤ failure to respond to suggestions.

ABREACTIONS

An abreaction occurs during hypnosis when the patient gains access to emotional states that have not been experienced appropriately, or when there has been no opportunity for the patient to fully come to terms with an event (Loewald, 1955; Bob, 2007). Abreactions are cathartic in nature, and allow the patient to discharge their emotions in a safe environment. While a patient is experiencing an abreaction, the practitioner needs to ensure that the patient feels safe and is given permission to experience the emotion. An abreaction may take many forms, for example tears or laughter. It is essential that the practitioner does not make any assumptions about the nature of the abreaction while the patient is in hypnosis – for example, to assume that tears necessarily denote sadness. Neutral language at this point is vital, and suggestions such as 'You are safe' and 'It's fine to let it out' can be made.

On waking the patient after an abreaction it is appropriate to give them time to discuss it if they wish to do so, but they should not be questioned about the event. Often patients experience feelings of tiredness after abreactions, and it is appropriate to compound suggestions in the post-hypnotic section of the session by suggesting that they will feel much better after a night's sleep, and therefore reduce any tendency to unpick the therapy as a result.

An abreaction is not a requirement for therapeutic change to take place during hypnosis, but its presence can be used as an indicator that change is occurring. Nor is an abreaction essential for patients to access emotional states or memories, and care should be taken to ensure that no suggestions of this kind are made. If a patient abreacts spontaneously (Yanovski and Bricklin, 1967) – that is, outside the framework of any suggestions being made at that time – it is important to reassure them that they abreacted because they felt safe to do so, and it will be of use for them. This is particularly important when patients express an opinion that they feel worse rather than better after the experience, so the abreaction is then reframed as part of their progress, rather than otherwise. You may wish to use the model of a healing crisis to reframe the abreaction. This model utilises the image of a fever, which worsens before it improves, and suggestions are made that the abreaction is like the peak of the fever – things can now start to improve. The practitioner should not be first to comment on the abreaction on waking the patient, as some individuals will have amnesia of the event.

The following events may be observed:

➤ laughter or tears
➤ shaking
➤ increased movement
➤ tension in facial features
➤ alterations in posture
➤ verbalisation of emotion
➤ alteration in skin pigmentation.

Managing patients during an abreaction

If a patient abreacts, the practitioner will need to acknowledge that they are aware of the event. This is done to reassure the patient that they are being observed, and that the practitioner is not unduly concerned about the abreaction. This will give the patient a comfort zone in which to experience the event in any way that will be cathartic to them. The acknowledgement will be given by the practitioner using phrases such as 'That's fine . . . you are safe here . . . you can let it go . . .'. Care is taken to ensure that the phrases are neutral – in other words, that the practitioner is not assuming anything. Tears may signify joy – for example, at the birth of a child – or laughter may be a way of discharging angry feelings. Neutral, reassuring phrases or even silence from the practitioner will allow the patient to go through the abreaction until they tire of it. If the patient appears to be becoming very distressed by the abreaction, but still does not come out of hypnosis, the practitioner can ask for a signal, such as a head nod, to signify that the patient would like to be brought out of hypnosis.

Another way of getting the patient away from the abreaction is to take them below the hypnotic level at which they are experiencing the event. Direct, authoritarian suggestions, such as 'Deep . . . deep sleep', can be made to take the patient away from the event and further into hypnosis. Deciding when to allow and when to intervene comes with experience. An abreaction often looks worse than it actually is, and as a general rule it is better to allow the patient to experience it in a safe environment, rather than having it continue to have some effect on them. Abreactions occur when patients feel safe with the practitioner, and they do have a cathartic effect, even if they may seem quite unpleasant for the patient at the time. They are *not* a necessary component of the efficacy of the hypnotherapeutic outcome, and for this reason the practitioner does not explain the possibility of such an event occurring before the induction, as this could induce anxiety and act as a self-fulfilling prophecy.

FALLING ASLEEP DURING HYPNOSIS

It is important for the practitioner to continue to observe the patient throughout the process for many reasons, not least of which is to ensure that the patient does not fall asleep during the process. This might occur if the patient is particularly tired, if they have been very stressed, or if they have not relaxed for a while. Older patients are also more inclined to drift off to sleep when relaxation suggestions are made.

It is preferable to prevent sleep from occurring. At the first indicator that the patient is moving from hypnosis into sleep, the practitioner can raise their voice or increase the speed of suggestions to hold the patient in the hypnotic state. However, if the patient is already asleep, they can be brought back from sleep to hypnosis using one of two methods. The first is for the practitioner to gradually increase the rate at which they are breathing. This produces an atavistic response in the patient, during which the brain interprets the raised rate of breathing as heightened alertness – or potential anxiety in the practitioner – and therefore a situation has arisen to which the patient may need to pay more conscious attention. The patient's brain will then send out signals to wake and assess the situation. This is the response that was observed during the Blitz in the Second World War, when mothers of young babies were able to sleep through the noise of bombing, but would wake if their child began to stir. Another way of gradually moving the patient from sleep to hypnosis is to increase the pace and volume of the suggestions, or to vary the pattern of suggestions made. This also needs to be done gradually in order not to jerk the patient out of hypnosis. If the practitioner is observing and calibrating the patient's changing responses, the patient should be able to move from sleep to deep relaxation without coming all the way out of hypnosis.

As has already been mentioned, this change in state from hypnosis to sleep can be observed by changes in breathing patterns and increased movement. If sleep does occur, the practitioner has a choice. If therapeutic suggestions have been made *before* the patient fell asleep, the practitioner may wish to allow the patient to sleep and wake normally when they have gained sufficient benefit from the relaxation. If therapeutic suggestions have yet to be made when the patient falls asleep, it is more appropriate to bring them out of sleep and aim to keep them in hypnosis.

If the patient does fall asleep during hypnosis, and then states on waking that they do not recall any of the therapeutic suggestions, it is appropriate for the practitioner to inform them that they slept *only* because that was a more immediate need, and that getting some rest was more important than hearing the post-hypnotic suggestions. The suggestion is then made that by allowing him- or herself to sleep, the patient will then be able to process the post-hypnotic suggestions fully at a later stage, perhaps in their sleep that night.

CONTRAINDICATIONS TO THE USE OF CLINICAL HYPNOSIS

Not everyone is able to experience hypnosis, or is receptive to the therapeutic suggestions. There are certain individuals and specific conditions which have, as part of their modus operandi, the equivalent of a switch that prevents them from being receptive to the type of altered state which is experienced during hypnosis and, by default, the therapeutic suggestions.

Conditions

Any condition for which the patient is currently undergoing medical intervention and for which they are taking medication requires the clinical hypnosis practitioner to gain permission from the prescribing medical practitioner. There are no absolute rules with regard to what can and cannot be treated using hypnosis. The capacity to treat depends on the setting (for example, in a hospital, and under the supervision of a medical practitioner), and also on the other competencies and skills of the person doing the hypnosis (for example, a midwife using hypnosis for childbirth).

Medications

If the patient is taking medication that is designed to alter the chemistry of the brain, it can alter the patient's susceptibility to suggestions. If this is the situation, it becomes a factor in deciding whether to use hypnosis. Certain medications for depression, for example, fall under this heading. In addition to this, there may be side-effects of medications which are similar to hypnotic phenomena, and which could therefore make the experience of hypnosis a less than positive one for the patient.

Symptoms

Some conditions have symptoms that the patient may experience as phenomena when in the hypnotic state. One example of this would be the sensations of drifting or floating which are sometimes experienced during hypnosis, and which might be associated with the symptomatic dissociation of depression, or sensory hallucinations, which might be disturbing for someone with migraine, and be sufficient to bring on an attack. It is therefore essential that the practitioner takes full note of the ways in which the patient experiences their symptoms when deciding on the appropriateness of clinical hypnosis as a treatment.

Individuals

The normal states of awareness (7±2)

It is important at this point to be aware that although most individuals can be hypnotised, there is a framework that can be used to evaluate whether hypnosis is appropriate, and what type of suggestions would be applicable to this type of individual. For this I use the 7±2 model. Although the theory that 7±2 pieces of information are stored in short-term memory is no longer considered to be accurate, it does provide a useful framework when evaluating the current state of mind of the patient, and where they currently fit on the 'neurotic–normal–lethargic' continuum.

Briefly, the '7±2 model' refers to the number of pieces of information that can be stored in the short-term memory at any one moment in time. Seven is considered to be normal functioning. When eight pieces of information are present, the individual is operating above normal levels, and the term for this is 'neurotic.' Neurotic functioning is still healthy so long as, when the requirement to process the extra piece of information is no longer present (that is, when the individual no longer has the heightened workload or problem to deal with) they return to a normal level of functioning (seven). If a further item is added to the list, and the individual has nine items of information in short-term memory, this processing is described as 'psychotic', and is outside the range of healthy functioning. The psychosis may involve voices giving instructions (suggestions), and the individual will certainly be on medication. Therefore patients at this level of processing are not suitable candidates for hypnosis, as they are unable to rest sufficiently to enter hypnosis.

At the other end of the scale are those individuals who have six items in short-term memory, and are operating at the slower end of the scale. The term used for this scenario is 'lethargic', and, like neurotic functioning, it is still considered to be healthy functioning so long as the individual can shift gear into normal functioning when necessary. The final category is that of 'catatonic' processing, with five pieces of information in the short-term memory at any one moment in time. As with psychotic processing, these individuals are outside the range within which hypnosis can be used. They will be on medication, and will find the focus required to enter hypnosis very difficult, if not impossible.

In summary, the normal (seven items), neurotic (eight items) and lethargic (six items) categories all fall within the range of functioning where clinical hypnosis may be used. For individuals who are experiencing their lives at the neurotic end of the scale (i.e. they are stressed and have a lot to cope with), suggestions can be made to reduce the level of stress or let go of their neurosis. For individuals who feel lacking in energy and who could identify with being at the lethargic end of the scale, suggestions for motivation and focus can be made. Individuals who are processing information normally may wish to break a habit or alter an unwanted thought or behaviour. From this we can see that the way in which individuals function will have a bearing on how they manage their condition, and will therefore influence the selection of the most appropriate strategy with which to treat. Using this 7±2 model can help the practitioner to identify how well the patient is coping and/or behaving generally, over and above their interaction with the problem.

Common-sense considerations

There are also some common-sense indications as to when it is not appropriate to use hypnosis. Examples would include situations where the patient is unwilling to experience it, or when the suggestions are not for the direct benefit of the patient. If the patient is under the influence of alcohol or recreational drugs, or in any form of artificially induced altered state, it is not advisable to attempt to induce hypnosis. Nor will the therapeutic suggestions be received in a controlled or useful manner. In addition, the use of hypnosis for entertainment (which, although a different event, has the same name) is not appropriate for those who practise it in the medical setting, so if someone wants to experience clinical hypnosis purely as an experiment, it is unlikely to work or to be experienced at any profound level.

As a further note, if individuals do ask for hypnosis but they do not have any specific reason for wishing to experience it, this can fall into one of three categories. The first is the prospective patient who does not wish to disclose the nature of their condition, the second is the individual who is simply curious about the experience, and the final category is the individual for whom the process would not be appropriate because they have an undiagnosed pre-existing condition, or an inappropriate objective for the hypnosis session. An example of this is the individual who believes that something has happened to them and if they can only uncover what it might be, then 'everything will be all right.'

It is important for the practitioner to use safeguards to ensure where possible that they can assist genuine cases, and deselect those for whom the process could be harmful or dangerous. If the practitioner suspects that the patient is being less than truthful about the nature of their requirement to be hypnotised, the recommended course of action is for the non-medical practitioner of hypnosis to request that the prospective subject of hypnosis visits their own medical practitioner and has a medical evaluation. The prospective patient is then asked to request written permission allowing the clinical hypnosis practitioner to treat, and this is to be obtained before any hypnotherapeutic session can be booked. The net result of this is that the clinical hypnosis practitioner will then be safe in the knowledge that the patient has been properly evaluated for the symptoms of their condition, and those for whom hypnosis would not be appropriate have been identified. This also means that the safety of the practitioner and the prospective patient is, where possible, ensured. It is generally recognised that individuals who have reasons other than those initially given to the clinical hypnosis practitioner will rarely visit their doctor, and so deselect themselves from the process. There is always the possibility that individuals who could be helped will slip through the net at this point, but the lay practitioner of hypnosis does not have the medical knowledge to diagnose a condition, and referral to a medical practitioner is the appropriate ethical course of action to take in these circumstances.

To summarise, before making a decision to use clinical hypnosis, the individual, the condition and the patient's interaction with the condition (symptoms and effects) will need to be taken into account and evaluated. Here lies one of the reasons why clinical hypnosis research currently fails to meet the research criteria required for its use within mainstream medicine. At present there are numerous protocols for using clinical hypnosis with medical conditions. The failure in research seems to lie in the inability to agree standardised procedures that relate to the pre-evaluation process. Research up to now has mainly consisted of a large number of small-scale research projects, each employing different methodologies, which cannot be compared with each other, and which fail to reflect the wider potential of clinical hypnosis. A common conclusion drawn in many clinical hypnosis trials is that more clinical trials are required to assess appropriately the use of clinical hypnosis as a mainstream medical intervention. The key here is to recognise that the pre-evaluation process, and the way in which decisions are made about the form and content of hypnotherapeutic suggestions, are an essential component of the protocol. This process can be identified and standardised. Some clinical hypnosis practitioners would argue that by doing so, the freedom to utilise instinct when selecting suggestions or building rapport is taken away, and that this would adversely affect the potential results. To some extent they are correct. However, for clinical hypnosis to achieve the status of a recognised medical tool, efficacy might need to be compromised in order to create standardised procedures that can then be modified according to the preferences of the individual. This is one of the reasons I set up the Medical School Hypnosis Association (MSHA), whose *raison d'être* is to coordinate and promote research into clinical hypnosis.

CHAPTER 6

Therapeutic approaches within hypnosis

Before any decisions can be made about the type of approach to be used, the components that will make an individual more receptive to one approach rather than another need to be identified and evaluated against the following criteria:

➤ motivation to experience hypnosis
➤ stress as a component of their condition
➤ the mindset of the individual
➤ the patient having a specific therapeutic objective.

The motivation to experience hypnosis has already been discussed elsewhere in this volume. How to use this information to select the appropriate approach for an individual patient, and set therapeutic objectives, is covered in Chapter 8, 'Creating the hypnotherapeutic protocol.'

STRESS AS A COMPONENT OF PATIENTS' CONDITIONS

Stress will cause patients to further focus attention on themselves in a neurotic or unhealthy manner, which then exacerbates the symptom. Consider, however, that when individuals are given better coping mechanisms for stress, their confidence increases, their ability to function more appropriately increases, and their sense of perspective about their problem will necessarily increase. All of these factors will have an effect on the symptoms and affects of the condition.

THE MINDSET OF THE INDIVIDUAL

Provided that an environment is created that will help the patient to feel able to relax, their mindset can be adapted to one which will be effective in helping them to make changes. The practitioner must therefore evaluate each condition in relation to the mindset that the patient brings to their approach to treatment. The patient's expectations of hypnosis will have a bearing on the efficacy of treatment. Interestingly, patients who expect hypnosis to 'cure' them, or who strongly desire to experience hypnosis, will rarely gain maximum benefit from this intervention. As already mentioned, an extreme desire to experience hypnosis will increase anxiety levels, and result in a failure to enter the relaxed hypnotic state. It may be that the patient's expectations are so high that personal motivation to change remains low. Whichever is the case, it is those patients who present with a creative, open mind who appear to be the most responsive (Gibson and Curran, 1974; Lynn and Rhue, 1986; Glisky and Kihlstrom, 1993).

Once all other factors have been taken into consideration and a specific objective can be identified with the patient, the type of protocol to be used can be decided upon.

The following are a number of different hypnotherapeutic approaches. These have been selected on the basis that the pre-selection criteria already discussed in this book can be applied in mapping the internal structure of a clinical hypnosis session, and then personalising it to the patient. The practitioner is then able to qualify and quantify the decisions made in relation to the approach selected. There are other hypnotherapeutic approaches which are potentially no less effective, but as the decision-making criteria are not so transparent, they have not been included here.

The approaches discussed here vary widely from the strictly clinical to the borderline esoteric. It is essential to remember when selecting the approach that it is the opinions of the patient that are paramount in choosing which is the most appropriate approach. (If the practitioner does not favour that approach because of their own personal beliefs, these beliefs are best put aside while working with that particular patient, unless the practitioner believes that the approach favoured by the patient could be potentially harmful.) In the clinical hypnosis framework, the practitioner operates as a *tabula rasa*, and should not impose their belief structures on the patient, otherwise they will end up selecting a treatment base which is appropriate for their own ways of doing things, but not necessarily for those of the patient. This is a classic example of the therapist treating him- or herself – not the patient!

When first practising clinical hypnosis, there are occasions when practitioners do not choose the most obvious or appropriate approach for their patients because they themselves do not like it, or they are not confident about the technique. As the practitioner gains more knowledge and experience, the approaches that they will use should increase in number – otherwise their range will become increasingly narrow and they will only be effective with a small number of patients with an ever decreasing success rate. Having a wide range of approaches from which to select the most appropriate will allow the clinical hypnosis practitioner to help a greater number of individuals with a wider range of conditions. Furthermore, adopting the same approach and using it with a small group of individuals can eventually reduce the practitioner's motivation and involvement, and even rapport and observation skills, as boredom and over-familiarity set in. The best clinical hypnosis practitioners will have one field of personal expertise, but will continue to practise different approaches and treat patients with other conditions as a way of continuing to refine their skills.

It is an interesting fact that a specialist in one condition or approach rarely sets out to work in that area. It will often be the case that they have a success with a particular condition, and that other individuals with that condition will come to see them as a result of their success, and that they will refine their skills by working with large numbers of individuals with that one condition. By this time, the practitioner's skills will be attuned to the nuances of how these patients interact with their condition, so their expertise will be enhanced. In effective clinical hypnosis tuition the student is encouraged to attempt approaches which are outside their personal experience or comfort zone. In this way, individuals become less judgmental and more open when selecting approaches for the benefit of their patients, rather than because of their own personal reasons or prejudices. It is also a recognised fact that when practitioners use an approach which they would not have selected, and they observe this technique working with a patient, they will incorporate it into their range of experience, become comfortable and proficient with it, and their personal outlook will therefore broaden and benefit both themselves and their patients. That is not to say that an individual will become comfortable with using all approaches, but merely that it is important to continue to learn techniques, and to further develop the range of skills when practising clinical hypnosis on a regular basis. It is equally important for the practitioner to utilise self-hypnosis regularly (the benefits of this are discussed elsewhere in this volume).

SPECIFIC HYPNOTHERAPEUTIC APPROACHES

What follows is an introduction to the many ways in which therapeutic processes can be conducted within the framework of hypnosis. Regardless of the form of clinical hypnosis protocol selected by the practitioner, the primary aim is the alleviation of a symptom or a problem. In no circumstances should an untutored practitioner use these techniques for experimentation. When dealing with the mind of another patient, or even oneself, it is possible to inadvertently trigger emotions or apparent memories, which would then need to be processed in an appropriate manner. Only in an educational setting or some other controlled environment under supervision is it appropriate to experience these techniques without a clearly defined outcome in mind.

As has already been discussed, the practitioner does not need to have a specific belief structure in order to utilise any of the following methods. An open attitude is all that is required. Under the protocol headings below are suggested conditions or types of individuals that would respond well to each. However, the lists are by no means exhaustive.

Ericksonian

This technique is based on the work of Milton H Erickson, who is regarded as the father of modern-day hypnosis. In its purest form, Ericksonian hypnosis involves open-eye hypnosis, where there is no formal induction of a hypnotic state. The practitioner will give indirect or open-ended suggestions based on the personality and environment of the patient, and will focus the patient on the possibilities of change. This technique aims to elicit the solution to their condition from the unconscious of the patient, often using 'confusion as the gateway to learning.' This approach places emphasis on suggesting through open-ended questions and the use of analogies. This encourages the use of different ways for the patient to think about their condition and draw alternative conclusions about the ways to act and respond. Ericksonian hypnosis provides the linguistic structure on which many other hypnotherapeutic approaches are based, including neurolinguistic programming (NLP).

Applications
➤ Analytical individuals.
➤ Confidence building.
➤ Anxiety.
➤ Habitual behaviours.

Traditional
This form of hypnosis includes a formal induction, involving eye closure, and a deepener that is usually based on physical suggestions such as progressive muscle relaxation. The therapeutic suggestions are usually delivered in the form of direct suggestions based on the specific objective for therapy which is uncovered in the pre-induction talk. This type of approach can utilise suggestions that are more authoritarian in nature, and is best used with patients who have a healthy ego state and a clear idea of their objectives. To refer back to the section on 'The mindset of the individual' earlier in this chapter, these would be the people with seven pieces of information in their short-term memory – those individuals who are otherwise 'normal', but who might wish to break a habit or refine a behaviour.

Applications
➤ Habit breaking.
➤ Motivation.
➤ Performance enhancement.

Esoteric
Esoteric techniques include any form of hypnosis that incorporates the patient's belief structure but which may not, initially, appear to be directly related to the problem. An example of this would be rebirthing or past-life regression therapy. With an esoteric approach, the patient would usually have expressed the belief that this particular approach will work for them, and will be able to explain the ways in which they believe it will benefit them. In the clinical setting, esoteric approaches are not necessarily to be considered as the first choice – unless the patient has built the expectation that this approach will be the most effective for them into their mindset about hypnosis. Before choosing an esoteric approach, the practitioner will need to identify clear objectives for the patient, as some esoteric techniques do not readily lend themselves to creating specific and realistic outcomes for therapy.

Applications

➤ Relationships.
➤ Grief.
➤ Indecision.
➤ Individuals with a personal belief structure with regard to the process.

Rebirthing

This process is one of reliving one's own birth process within hypnosis. The objective of rebirthing is to re-experience any associated feelings, and to revivify a component of the birth event in order to release the individual from any perceived traumas which occurred during their birth. The theory of this technique states that once this has taken place and been processed fully by the individual, a remission from the associated symptom can be obtained. An example of this might be a patient who has claustrophobia, and experiencing the rebirthing process 'uncovers' a traumatic birth experience during which they recall having the umbilical cord around their neck at the time of delivery. Once the experience has been processed consciously, the requirement for the symptom is then eliminated. Rebirthing is also used outside the framework of clinical hypnosis and can involve a physical process which is used to simulate the experience of birth.

Applications

➤ Individuals with a personal belief structure with regard to the process.
➤ Analytical individuals.

Direct suggestions

A direct suggestion is one in which the content is explicit. Direct suggestions are goal driven and are therefore based on what the patient requires in terms of change (for example, more energy), rather than what they do not require (for example, not feeling tired). Direct suggestions are effective in habit breaking, in confirming events, and in ego strengthening to direct the patient's attention towards external events which already exist, but to which they have not previously paid attention. When in hypnosis, the patient appreciates the certainty of direct suggestions, as the practitioner will use them to confirm positive states and to affirm new behaviours and thought processes. Direct suggestions are more authoritarian than permissive, as they involve instructing the patient as to what to do. If the patient is anxious or depressed, or their mindset does not lend itself to being told what they should do or what to experience, direct suggestion should be used sparingly, if at all.

Applications

➤ Habit breaking.
➤ Performance enhancement.
➤ Phobias.
➤ Stress management.

Indirect suggestions

This type of suggestion uses terms such as 'may', 'can' and 'if you wish' to direct the patient's attention in a specific way without engaging conscious objections. In clinical hypnosis this approach incorporates a factor known as 'apparent choice.' Apparent choice involves presenting two or more alternatives to the patient and asking them to make an 'either/or' choice. The practitioner will either direct the patient's preference to one of the choices, or regardless of which choice the patient makes the objective is achieved. Therefore, implicit in any indirect suggestion is the objective – for example, 'You may find your eyelids becoming heavy and tired . . . wanting to close . . . they may wish to close now . . . or they may wish to close later.' Either way, the objective of eye closure will be achieved. Indirect suggestions can allow the practitioner to express one suggestion in a number of different ways, and to repeat suggestions until they are accepted by the patient. This type of suggestion is also known as a 'permissive suggestion.'

Applications
➤ Chronic pain.
➤ Anxiety.
➤ Children.
➤ Patients who are experiencing hypnosis for the first time.

Neurolinguistic programming-based techniques

Neurolinguistic programming (NLP) is a framework created by Richard Bandler and John Grinder, and is based on the works of Milton Erickson. NLP is a methodology of communication that identifies the modalities in which individuals communicate. It utilises structured language patterns, and places value on the levels at which we communicate, either at a deep (meaning) level or at a surface (social) level. It is used to evaluate behaviour and thought processes, and to create specific structures to change and improve them. Clinical hypnosis can use NLP techniques within the hypnotic state, and can incorporate these communication patterns into the therapeutic suggestions. This allows the patient to receive suggestions in a structured manner, and to incorporate them into their thoughts and behaviours in a way that will be acceptable to them. However, NLP is most obviously employed in clinical hypnosis in the pre-induction talk and within the context of the specific therapeutic suggestions.

Applications
➤ Low self-esteem.
➤ Confidence building.
➤ Phobic responses.
➤ Performance enhancement.

Hypno-desensitisation

This is a hypnotherapeutic protocol that utilises the well-documented psychological approach of desensitisation. The patient is required to produce a scale of disturbance (known as a Subjective Units of Disturbance Scale or SUDS) itemising the least to the highest anxiety-evoking situation within the framework of their condition. Once the scale has been produced, hypnosis is induced and a signalling device is installed. The practitioner will then describe the events, commencing with the least anxiety-evoking situation, and will make suggestions for relaxation at each point. Where no or minimal anxiety is experienced, the next event on the hierarchy is presented. Where anxiety is experienced, additional relaxation is suggested, until minimal or no anxiety is experienced. This process is continued throughout the hierarchy.

Applications
➤ Phobias.
➤ Pain control.
➤ Performance anxiety.
➤ Stress management.

Quantum therapy

In the context of clinical hypnosis, quantum therapy uses two basic strategies. With the first strategy, the practitioner seeks to assist the patient in moving outside their habitual thought processes or behaviours. The second strategy relates to the concept that the patient maintains the problem by continuing to pay attention to symptoms at an unconscious and conscious level. Guided imagery is used to lead the patient into a state of momentary 'chaos', from which a new version of reality will be created. At that point, appropriate thoughts and behaviours will then become accessible.

Applications
➤ Behavioural changes.
➤ Indecision.
➤ Dermatology.
➤ Neurotic conditions.

Polarity

Polarity-based techniques utilise the concept that if you have experience of one type of state or event, you have a latent knowledge of the opposite state and can potentially experience it to the same degree. In this framework, the mindset that created the condition contains recognition of an equal and opposite mindset. The end result will be a balanced state, in which both ends of the scale are recognised at the same time.

Applications

➤ Creativity.
➤ Decision making.
➤ Repetitive negative thought patterns.
➤ Over-stimulated nervous system (e.g. due to hormones).

Creative visualisation

Creative visualisation can be incorporated into a number of other approaches. The basic principle here is the use of suggested images to create a representational system. Once an image has been created to represent the patient's condition, or the patient's interaction with their condition (symptoms or affects) or even of their objective, this image can then be altered. Once the patient has taken control of the images, they become able to make those changes in reality. An example of the types of changes that can be made would be assisting recovery from cardiovascular problems, where the scarring on the heart is visualised and the image is changed to a strong, healthy heart as recovery takes place. Other creative visualisations are more analytical in intent, where the individual produces a safe environment in which they can come to terms with an aspect of their problem. Metaphors, quantum and mind–body techniques fall into this category.

Applications

➤ Recovery from surgery.
➤ Grief.
➤ Coping with cancer and the side-effects of medical intervention.
➤ Abuse.

Psychoneuroimmunology

Psychoneuroimmunology (PNI) is a mind–body technique that uses imagery primarily to stimulate the immune system (Schubert and Schussler, 2009). PNI is used as an adjunct to conventional approaches, and is best known for its use in oncology and pain management. PNI works with stress, the psyche and the immune system to create distractions, enhance the patient's perception of control over their condition, and enhance the efficacy of medication and other treatment strategies.

Applications

➤ Oncology.
➤ Pain control.
➤ Immune disorders.
➤ Healing after physical injuries.

Time distortion

Time distortion techniques in clinical hypnosis are used to expand time for individuals who need more time, and to contract time for those for whom time drags. As time distortion is a symptom of some common conditions, particularly those that involve anxiety, this approach allows the patient to alter their perception of time so as to increase or decrease the time experience. The phenomena of time distortion in the hypnotic state can be used to help to convince the patient that something different from the normal state of awareness has occurred while they were hypnotised.

Applications
➤ Premature ejaculation.
➤ Memory and learning.
➤ Childbirth.
➤ Recovery and healing.

Dissociative techniques
Dissociative techniques operate on the premise that a condition has a component over which the patient feels that they are not in control when experiencing a symptom. This is often described by the patient as 'a part of me which seems to take over when bingeing (or some other symptom).' Dissociative techniques follow a sequence whereby:

➤ the part in control of the symptom is identified
➤ the needs of that part are identified
➤ these needs are negotiated
➤ the part is reintegrated into the whole individual and the symptom is returned under the direct control of the patient.

The patient may then require a further technique to gain full remission from the symptom. This usually takes the form of deconditioning (hypno-desensitisation or direct suggestions to eliminate the habitual component of the symptom).

Applications
➤ Nail biting.
➤ Binge eating.
➤ Obsessive-compulsive disorders (such as trichotillomania).
➤ Trauma.

Regression
Regression, when utilised in hypnosis, allows the patient to experience a past event (real or imagined), through which they can analyse and gain insight into their current situation or condition. Unlike revivification, regression allows the patient to view the past event while maintaining adult knowledge and experience, so they are effectively dissociated. The retention of adult knowledge allows the patient to review that event and process it differently. When using clinical hypnosis, the purpose of the patient experiencing the past event while in hypnosis and in a safe and controlled environment is purely to assist them to move forward. A more rare use of regression is to allow the patient to experience an event in order to recall a

specific element of that event, perhaps an emotion, or, for example, if an object has been lost and the patient cannot consciously recall where they put it.

Applications
➤ Hay fever.
➤ Memory recall.
➤ Blushing.
➤ Reconnecting with older, more appropriate behaviour patterns.

Esoteric regression
Also known as 'past-life regression', this is a process in which the patient accesses a 'past-life experience' that they perceive to be in some way relevant to their current situation or condition. During the past life the patient undergoes various stages of progression whereby they can gain insight into feelings and events, thereby experiencing catharsis.

Applications
➤ Relationships.
➤ Maladaptive behavioural patterns.
➤ Analysis of current behaviours or responses.

Non-verbal communication
Non-verbal suggestion is a method of supplementing other techniques either in or outside of the hypnotic state. By being congruent in tone, pitch and volume with the verbal suggestions it is possible to amplify them, or by being incongruent it is possible to encourage the patient to question the veracity of the statement. Physical movements or the use of pauses between statements can also be part of this technique.

Applications
➤ Hypnosis for the deaf or hearing-impaired.
➤ Hypnosis with children.
➤ Kinaesthetic patients.
➤ Gaining insight into unconscious knowledge.

Automatic writing and drawing
This approach uses the ideo-motor movements of the hand as a medium for communicating information directly from unconscious to conscious awareness without the need for it to travel via the language centre. It is most useful for uncovering information that has not been spoken of, or an experience that took place during a trauma, such as a traffic accident. An example in this instance would be recollection of a vehicle licence plate that had previously been 'forgotten.' Automatic writing and drawing can also be used with regression, and the patient will write as they would have written at the age to which they have been regressed. Only the

patient can interpret the writing or drawing, which will look sketchy and indistinct, similar to doodles.

Applications
➤ Discovering lost objects.
➤ Gaining insight into events.
➤ Trauma.

Ideo-motor response techniques

These techniques use fine motor movements, primarily finger movements, to allow the patient to communicate otherwise suppressed information. Ideo-motor response (IMR) therapies draw upon the concept that the patient has the answer to their condition within their unconscious. IMR techniques allow the practitioner to operate as a facilitator in the negotiation between the patient's unconscious desires and conscious processing. This negotiation can be carried out in a content-free manner, allowing the patient to release a neurotic symptom without consideration of how this process is going to occur.

Applications
➤ Behaviour modification.
➤ Blushing.
➤ Anxiety.
➤ Decision making.

Hypnodrama

Similar in concept to psychodrama (Julius Moreno), both of these techniques involve the creation of a framework whereby the patient can explore their responses, and those of other participants in an event, in a number of different situations. This in turn helps the patient to 'play out/act out' or direct the scene in various ways. The insight that results from experiencing the viewpoint of others, observing their own behaviour in different ways and manipulating scenes then influences the patient's attitudes with regard to their own behaviour and that of others. The advantages of hypnodrama over psychodrama are twofold. In psychodrama the individuals involved in the events will be physically present, or represented externally. In hypnosis the patient can experience a much wider range of situations and emotions safely, and will be able to stop and start the scenes at will in order to explore variations on a theme. In both hypno- and psychodrama the patient may also play different roles. The objective is to gain insight and perspective. The other advantage of hypnodrama is that it involves a relaxed state, and the patient will therefore be able to process the information more rapidly. Lastly, because hypnosis is a multi-sensory experience, it is a potentially more enriching experience, as the practitioner can make direct suggestions, while the patient is in hypnosis, on more appropriate ways of feeling, thinking and acting in the scenario that they have just experienced.

Applications
➤ Assertiveness training.
➤ Anger management.
➤ Drug or alcohol abuse.
➤ Physical or emotional abuse.

Inner game
This therapeutic application, which is based on a coaching technique, utilises the premise of an inner game and outer game being played out when an individual attempts to make changes. The outer game involves logic and practicality and is concerned with influencing external events, whereas the inner game involves emotions, preconceptions and beliefs about the self. When applied in the context of clinical hypnosis, the inner game uses these structures to create an inner event that is congruent with the outer requirements, so that the individual can achieve peak performance. As with hypnodrama, the use of the hypnotic state enhances the images that are required to produce this state of positive self-belief, and will amplify the benefits by the use of future projection (whereby the patient pre-experiences achieving the required changes) and sensory imagery (whereby the patient can feel what it is like to achieve their goals).

Applications
➤ Motivation.
➤ Self-sabotage.
➤ Goal setting.
➤ Sensory modification.

Lucid dreaming
This technique also exists outside the framework of hypnosis. It is used in hypnosis as an analytical method that aims to direct the patient to use their dream state for processing information which will then help them to gain remission from their symptom. Suggestions are made during hypnosis that the patient can first become aware of when they are dreaming (hence lucid), and they then experience the required outcome with regard to their problem during the dream. This technique is most effective for patients who have a Jungian framework, patients who have previously found that after sleeping well they can find the answer to some of their problems, or patients who have an analytical approach to their condition. Some of the more esoterically minded will also appreciate this technique.

Applications
➤ Nocturnal enuresis.
➤ Nightmares.
➤ Enhancement of creative states.
➤ Sleep disorders.

Glove anaesthesia or analgesia

This technique is taught to patients as a method of pain control. It is a kinaesthetic technique in which suggestions of numbness or coolness are made to produce a dissociative event in the hand, coupled with hallucinations of the suggested change in sensations. It is known as 'glove anaesthesia' because the hallucination of changed sensations in the hand is created with suggestions that the patient is wearing a thick leather glove. It is used to bring about alleviation of physical pain by manipulating the sensations at the site of the pain.

The ability to create anaesthesia in the hand is taught to the patient, and the patient is then taught self-hypnosis to increase the profundity of the anaesthesia or analgesia. The patient is then shown how to relocate the numbness or coolness from the hand to the site of pain. The relaxation induced by the self-hypnosis and the ability to manipulate the pain sensations generally improves the well-being of the patient, even if full anaesthesia is not achieved. This technique is frequently taught to reduce pain during labour, and is also effective in dermatological conditions.

Applications
➤ Pain management.
➤ Phantom limb.
➤ Healing.
➤ Childbirth.

Metaphor

A metaphorical suggestion uses a simple story that contains a covert or secondary meaning. The intention is to keep the conscious processes occupied with the story while the covert meaning is taken on board without engaging the critical processes. It is most effective with analytical patients, as it allows them to analyse part of the process (the story) while accepting the inherent meaning.

Applications
➤ Hypnosis with children.
➤ Pain management.
➤ Healing trauma.
➤ Fertility and pregnancy.

Hypno-analysis

This process involves identifying and analysing the origin or the construction of a problem. This method operates on the basic assumption that once this information has come to the level of consciousness, the impact of the problem can be reduced or removed. This process often involves regression to the time of origin, and is used for patients who have a perceived requirement to understand their behaviour or condition before expressing a willingness to move forward.

Application

➤ Comprehension of thoughts, behaviours and emotions.

Cognitive–behavioural therapy

This technique is based on changing negative self-beliefs. Once these belief patterns have been identified and amended, the associated behaviours can then be eliminated. When used in the framework of clinical hypnosis, this technique can enhance the patient's capacity to make the necessary mental connections, with less conscious objection, and therefore improve their capacity for change more rapidly.

Applications

➤ Maladaptive or repetitive thought processes.
➤ Working with limiting belief structures.
➤ Pattern breaking.
➤ Abuse of drugs or alcohol.

CHAPTER 7

Hypnotic diagnostics

Before looking at the specifics of creating the hypnotherapeutic protocol, I feel it is important to have an overview of the process itself in terms of where it 'fits' into other treatment approaches, and how best to assess whether the individual is suited to the hypnotherapy.

Within this chapter, I shall consider whether there is an optimum time frame between sessions, and how best to ensure that the sessions themselves work towards the objective of the patient, rather than that of the practitioner (as can sometimes happen). The goal of this chapter is to move the individual who wishes to incorporate hypnosis into their current practice towards a clearer appreciation of where clinical hypnosis fits into medical and psychotherapeutic practice, and away from a mindset about therapy which may have been gained within a different discipline, or from other literature about hypnosis. It is also essential for those who come to the subject 'fresh' to gain the insight that will bridge their knowledge from being a subject of hypnosis to a potential practitioner. I wish to emphasise here that the framework and time frame which I shall discuss are based primarily on, and refined by, my own experience in clinical practice (supported by the available research), but do not constitute the *only* way of conducting sessions. I have found that before commencing tried and tested hypnotherapeutic protocols, there often is a requirement for an initial phase of treatment, one designed to motivate the patient, give them confidence in the process, and create rapid benefits.

I shall also touch on my thoughts about other time frames and approaches for hypnotherapeutic protocols, specifically as these may be of relevance to the patient if they have had hypnotherapy before, or if they are having or have had other treatments for their condition, or their expectations differ from the process that they will experience in your sessions.

The simplest way to convey my hypnotic diagnostic concept is to use what I call the 'three-ringed circus of therapeutic change.' Within this, there are three distinct components or 'rings' which interlock to form the patterns shown in Figure 7.1. Within this, any one of the three components – the individual, the condition, or the patient's interaction with their condition and the world outside – can be influenced. Changing any one of these components will change the interlocking

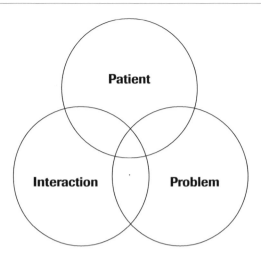

FIGURE 7.1 The three-ringed circus of therapeutic change.

dynamic between all three of them, and will result in the potential for therapeutic change. In classic hypnotic diagnostics, the practitioner focuses their attention on the problem, looking at the case history in terms of the following:

➤ when the symptoms started
➤ how they developed
➤ how the symptoms manifest themselves
➤ the physical, emotional and psychological effects on the patient.

This narrows the range of potential change to that of the problem only, and the outcome in terms of the presence or absence of the symptoms. The absence of the symptoms then becomes the objective for treatment.

To view the application of clinical hypnosis purely from this perspective is, I believe, to diminish its potential for bringing about change, and this is why I created the three-ringed circus as a way of explaining the ways in which clinical hypnosis can influence the life of the patient, and for practitioners as a model for extracting information. Why is this so important? First, and most importantly, there will be situations when the condition (and the associated symptoms) cannot simply be viewed as something which is happening to the patient. There are actions and reactions involved in maintaining symptoms, and there will be exacerbating and ameliorating factors which can be taken into account when treating the patient with hypnosis.

An example of this three-ringed component approach would be the case of a patient who suffers from obsessive-compulsive disorder. In this situation, the patient experiences an intensification of the symptoms when they are stressed. Teaching self-hypnosis will reduce that stress, and will therefore reduce the intensity of the symptoms. This involves changing the *interaction*. Another approach would be to build up the patient's confidence. The practitioner would then be influencing the *patient*. The practitioner could also use hypno-desensitisation to work on the *problem*. So, within this example, there are three ways of commencing treatment to effect immediate change.

TREATING THE PATIENT

Treating the patient involves uncovering in the case history any areas *outside* of the patient's interaction with the problem, or the problem itself, which are of concern to them at this time. This may be an immediate problem, such as a deadline at work, or it may be a chronic problem, such as a sick parent or an underlying illness of the patient him- or herself. Uncovering this information will give the practitioner a good indicator that the patient may not be in their optimum state to make the therapeutic change – in other words, this may not be the best time for them to have therapy. The clinical hypnosis practitioner can teach the patient techniques which will allow them to manage their stressors better, or to dissociate from those stressors sufficiently to be able to make the therapeutic change. Techniques for dissociating or coping can then be utilised by the patient whenever this is necessary in future.

TREATING THE INTERACTION

The interaction in this context consists of the ways in which the patient maintains and identifies with their problem. This may include behaviours, feelings and a belief system. By working on the belief system, breaking down behaviours or helping the patient to come to terms with their feelings, the practitioner is easing the patient into a less involved relationship with the problem. Often the patient will have a belief that there are things that they 'have to do', 'must do' or 'can't imagine not doing', and by breaking down these self-limiting beliefs and allowing the patient to test their new actions, the dynamic of the three rings or components changes.

TREATING THE PROBLEM

This component is more familiar in therapy. Here we treat the symptoms by trying to reduce the intensity, duration or even occurrence of the symptoms. When the practitioner works with this aspect, it is in an attempt to provide the patient with an immediately noticeable change. This change may not persist in the long term, but it is often sufficient to give the patient confidence that the process can effect change and that it is therefore worth adhering to any homework which is given.

The three stages of a problem

When taking the case history, I find it useful and valid to track the progression of the problem as a separate entity from the patient. The following questions need to be asked.

➤ When did the problem begin?
➤ When did it change?
➤ What prompted the decision to come for therapy at this time?

Looking at the relationship between patient, problem and interaction at each of these three stages gives a clear indication about the relevance of other surrounding issues. For example, when looking at the time when the problem began, the patient describes themselves as they were *then*, and their perception of the problem historically. Identifying when it changed will provide the practitioner with the information relevant to the stage at which the condition became a problem (i.e. moved from being manageable to being unmanageable). Identifying the additional factors which came into play at this stage, such as a change in work situation, or the birth of a child, identifies the issues relating to the patient's interaction with their problem, and may therefore require additional stress management techniques. Finally, identifying why the patient is coming for therapy at this time gives clear indications about motivation (for example, the woman who comes for therapy in order to lose weight, because she is getting married and wishes to be slim for her wedding).

I have found over the years that presenting this framework to the patient (time before, time of change, and current time) results in the questions having a less invasive tone. By giving them specific value it also focuses the patient's mind on events which they may not have previously believed were relevant, but which they now understand play a significant part in their problem.

DECIDING WHICH COMPONENT RING TO TREAT

When patients come for treatment, they will often focus on one aspect of the problem as they see it. This may be a way of thinking, an action or a feeling that they wish to change. By making note of how much emphasis the patient puts on this aspect of their condition, the practitioner can make choices about which component ring will be the easiest to influence, and the quickest in which to bring about changes. The decision as to whether to initiate the treatment protocol by treating the patient, the problem, or the patient's interaction with the problem is therefore quite straightforward. The patient has a need to see change, and will often want it quickly. The way to facilitate this is to change the component ring that will maximise immediate benefits (i.e. whichever component ring is the easiest to change). The net effect of this is that the patient will be more motivated, more committed to the process, and more willing to enter hypnosis in subsequent sessions, as they have already experienced a benefit from the process. The less obvious effect of this change is that the dynamics of the component rings will have changed and weakened.

Once the benefits of the process have been experienced by the patient, the practitioner can then identify from the pre-induction talk in the second session with the patient which of the three components is most significant to them (not which one is the easiest to change, which was covered in the first session). With this in mind, the practitioner can then select an approach that will facilitate the change required by the patient.

GIVING THE PATIENT CONTROL OF THE PROCESS

When initiating a hypnotherapeutic partnership with the patient, the more control the practitioner can hand over, the more relaxed the patient will feel. This is particularly important for those patients who are having hypnosis for the first time, and for those for whom anxiety is a component of their problem. This control is usually apparent control, and is used in a similar way to that of Milton Erickson's 'apparent choice'. By this I mean that the practitioner will give the patient suggestions throughout the pre-induction talk that this process is a 'therapeutic partnership' and 'together we will decide on the most appropriate course of action for you.' By explaining the post-hypnotic suggestions that will be used, and discussing them with the patient, the practitioner is effectively gaining the patient's tacit agreement. An example of this would be if the practitioner explains that there are two ways in which the problem could be addressed, and then goes on to explain both approaches. By discussing the merits of each approach with the patient, the practitioner is getting the patient to decide which of the two options they find most acceptable to them, and is gauging how they will respond. It is a choice, but not an open one. Some practitioners would have a problem with this approach, as they feel that it is a requirement of hypnotherapy to maintain silence about the mechanisms behind it. I think this has more to do with the ego of the practitioner, and that by withholding information the practitioner may be unwittingly creating more anxiety about the process than is helpful.

With regard to the hypnosis itself, the process can be described as one which is being taught to the patient, so they have a choice as to how much they respond, and when. By adopting this approach I have found that patients go much deeper into hypnosis because they know that at any point in time they can bring themselves to a lighter level of experience. I often use the metaphor of swimming. When a person learns how to swim, they make sure that they only go as far as they feel safe into the water, and as they become more confident in their ability to swim, they can go much deeper. Patients respond well to this metaphor, and to the fact that I explain why I spend so long in discussion before I do the hypnosis itself. I will explain to patients that if I made any suggestion which was not pre-agreed in the pre-induction talk (hence the time spent), they would immediately pull themselves out of hypnosis and be fully alert. This reassures the patient that they are in control, and they will therefore often allow themselves to go so deep into the hypnosis that they feel as if they 'blanked out' the suggestions that were made during the hypnosis. This is usually a positive indicator that they are relaxed about the suggestions and therefore do not need to consciously register them in the hypnosis itself.

IDENTIFYING THE 'GOOD' AND 'BAD' CANDIDATES FOR HYPNOTHERAPY

There is a large body of research and tests available on selecting the best candidates for hypnosis, but whether these 'highly responsive' individuals are also good candidates for hypnotherapeutic change is another matter. I am not alone in recognising that there are patients who go very deep into hypnosis, thoroughly enjoy the process as they are experiencing it, but do not necessarily go on to benefit from the post-hypnotic suggestions. I believe that a number of factors are potentially at work here, including the following:

➤ motivation for change

➤ timing of the session (for example, too soon after a tragedy)
➤ secondary gains in maintaining the problem
➤ inappropriate protocol selection
➤ fear of change
➤ inability to conceive of life without the problem (for example, 'I can't imagine life without smoking').

Over the years, I have also observed that those who, in the context of the hypno-therapeutic session, become very deeply relaxed, and even feel that they have fallen asleep, are often those individuals who, at the time of the session, are very stressed or have poor sleeping patterns. As a result, I have come to the conclusion that the failure of the hypnotherapeutic process in this context is due to the fact that the patient has unconsciously identified their need for rest as more immediate and important than their need for therapeutic change. Remember that an immediate need will always override an ongoing one. For this reason (in the context of the three-ring components), I treat the *patient* first, and teach self-hypnosis and relaxa-tion techniques *before* attempting to move on to the therapeutic change. Once the patient is rested, and sleeping better, the protocol can be attempted again, and this time it is much more likely to be effective.

TIMING AND NUMBER OF SESSIONS

Single-session protocols

With habits, such as smoking and nail biting, there should not be a requirement for more than one session. Such habits can be treated simply with direct suggestions and homework. However, it is still valid to give the patient the opportunity to feed back their progress to the practitioner via a phone call or email after a three-week period. At this point, the practitioner can give further ego-strengthening sugges-tions or recommendations. If there has been any problem in terms of the success of the protocol, the patient has an opportunity to discuss this with the practitioner and, if necessary, to have a further session.

Multiple-session protocols

With conditions that are more involved (i.e. which have an impact over and above a set of symptoms, and/or have an origin that must be dealt with), multiple ses-sions are recommended. The number of potential sessions should be discussed with the patient before commencing therapy, so that they have an understanding of the maximum number of sessions to expect. This framework is also valid if the process is an educative one, as for example in the case of pain control where glove anesthesia is being taught.

THE USE OF CDs/MP3s

I would emphasise that the use of CDs/MP3s is a personal decision taken after years in practice, and a recognition that some of the work required, such as stress management, habit breaking and ego strengthening, can be done via a generic recording. I would still recommend the use of self-hypnosis, as it gives the patient control, but with a recorded hypnosis track I know that the patient is getting support and benefit *between* sessions. This again is based on my knowledge from clinical practice, as I have found that a significant number of patients, if they did not have something which was designed to support them and to supplement the suggestions from the sessions, would improve initially, but then slip back into old patterns of behaviour and thought.

The track selected is designed to be listened to daily for three weeks, starting the day after the hypnosis session. I suggest that the patient listens to it in bed, just before sleep. This way there is no excuse that they cannot find time to do it, and also because they are generally relaxed at this stage, they will often drift off to sleep while still listening.

CONTACT BETWEEN SESSIONS

As with the use of CDs/MP3s, I emphasise that this is my way of conducting practice, and it is based on a refinement of many different methods attempted over the years. I have found that requesting the patient to contact me via phone or email *three weeks* after their session to give feedback on their progress, and to book another session if necessary, ensures that:

➤ the patient feels a level of control over the process itself
➤ by making the call they have to evaluate their progress since the session
➤ by setting the contact time to three weeks after the session, the patient optimises the value of the post-hypnotic suggestions and has substantial change to discuss
➤ the patient is in control of whether they wish to come for another session.

I feel that this is critical to the motivation and focus of the patient with regard to getting better. Once the patient is able to look back on the three-week period since their first session, and to identify benefits, they are then better able to communicate to the practitioner what, specifically, they need to work on next. To ensure that the patient is able to do this, during the first session, when I bring up the subject of their contacting me three weeks after the session, I tell them that one of four things will have happened during the intervening period. The first alternative is that they will have achieved their objective and there will be no need for them to return for another session. This allows the practitioner to further encourage and motivate the patient with ego strengthening as to how well they have done after only one session. The second alternative is for the patient to notice changes, but not enough. In this case, the practitioner can suggest a second session in which the treatment involves 'more of the same', as this has obviously worked, as indicated by the changes noticed by the patient, but it needs supplementing. The third alternative is for the patient to become aware of an issue which they felt was unrelated, but that has come to the fore. In this instance the practitioner can suggest that this issue has arisen because it is relevant, and that is what they will work on during the next session. The final alternative is for the patient to have noticed no changes at all. Although this is rare, it does happen, and if this is the case, the patient can walk away from the process if they wish to do so, or the practitioner can discuss an alternative approach.

SETTING LIMITS ON THE NUMBER OF SESSIONS

The maximum number of sessions I have set in which to treat a condition using clinical hypnosis is three. This number is a refinement of the research that I have conducted within my own practice, and I have found it to be an optimum for the way in which I work. If there has been no discernible benefit to the patient with three sessions of hypnotherapy, a CD/MP3 track to supplement their therapy between sessions, homework, and the benefit of the nine weeks (minimum) since commencing therapy, then I genuinely believe that the patient is not a suitable candidate for this treatment. Setting a limit on the number of sessions focuses the mind of the patient in a way that an open-ended approach to sessions does not. Also, I could cite the law of diminishing returns here. In the first session, when the patient has low expectations of the hypnotic event and of therapeutic change, any benefit, no matter how small, is noted. As the patient experiences more hypnosis and their expectations are altered, they start to expect change, and if they do not achieve what they feel to be significant improvements on subsequent sessions, they may become demoralised. In addition, if the number of sessions is kept open, there is a risk that the nature of those sessions will change as the patient forms a closer bond with the practitioner, and the sessions can gradually slip from therapy to counselling. This undermines the efficacy of both approaches, and should be avoided at all costs. Speaking of costs, letting the patient know the maximum number of sessions they may be expected to have will reduce any anxiety about the potential financial cost to the patient. Finally, the patient who only needs one or two sessions when they were told to expect a maximum of three will also experience an ego boost, as they 'didn't need to have all the sessions – they got better faster than expected.'

OPTIMUM TIMING BETWEEN SESSIONS

As I work within the psycho-cybernetics framework within my practice (see below for more on this), I generally leave three weeks between sessions. As I have already mentioned, this gives the patient time to do any homework, to appreciate the changes that have occurred, and to identify any other issues that have arisen since the first session and which may need to be addressed. Exceptions do occur, such as pain management as this is more of an educative process than a therapeutic one.

ADAPTING TECHNIQUE WITHIN A PROTOCOL

I have introduced this to highlight the fact that, just as the timing and number of sessions vary between practitioners (and between schools of thought), it is important to be aware that the practitioner is free to respond to the changes that take place in the patient between sessions, and to adapt the protocol accordingly. The most obvious example of this is the change from permissive to authoritarian approaches between sessions one and two, where the patient has demonstrated an increase in their confidence since the first session. The practitioner will *always* take a case history during a session, even after the first session. Subsequent case histories will track the changes since that session, allowing the practitioner to adapt their technique if it is no longer appropriate, or to change it altogether if something of more significance has occurred to the patient during the intervening weeks.

PSYCHO-CYBERNETICS WITHIN THE HYPNOTHERAPEUTIC PROTOCOL

Psycho-cybernetics is a huge topic. For those who wish to read more about it, I would recommend *Psycho-cybernetics* by Maxwell Maltz. Within the context of hypnotherapeutic treatment, I shall only discuss the aspects that are relevant to the process. In psycho-cybernetics there is a model of targeting a neurological 'node', which in this context equates to the seat of the problem, and letting three weeks elapse for the brain connections to re-form and consolidate, thus creating a solution to the problem. Within this context, allowing three weeks to elapse between sessions equates to optimising the time frame of neurological healing, and of the patient being able to consciously register positive change. There is considerably more to this process, and I would recommend those practitioners who wish to use the same framework as I do to read up on the subject. It is also a wonderful way of fleshing out the models that a practitioner may utilise to describe the workings of the process they are about to use. This is particularly important for those who have tried (and failed) with others.

HYPNO-ANALYSIS: A NEW ANGLE

Hypno-analysis has had something of a bad press, especially with concerns about regressions and the possible suggestion of false memories (Berger, 2002). Although I would discourage practitioners from attempting to utilise hypnosis to uncover memories and then attempting to directly analyse the content and/or validity of those memories, I do recognise a use for this process when the practitioner puts the implication of the uncovered memory to a specific use. To clarify, if a memory comes up in therapy, the practitioner can assure the patient that this particular memory has only arisen at this time because the emotional discharge associated with its recall will have a cathartic and therefore therapeutic value in the context of the change that they are attempting to achieve at this time.

NOTES FOR THE PRACTITIONER
The importance of continuing professional development

Continuing professional development (CPD) is vital to good clinical practice. The practitioner who completes their initial certificated training and then makes no further attempt to continue to learn skills and benefit from new research will find that their skills, their motivation and their stamina for practice will diminish. Having taught thousands of practitioners over the years, I am aware that the drop-out rate in practice is high, with around 80% leaving the profession after two years. Having been able to monitor these numbers from within a professional organisation, I am aware that those who undertake CPD continue in practice, while generally those who do not undertake it will leave.

Apart from this consideration, there is the fact that maintaining an awareness of research and development, continuing to read about the subject, and taking the opportunity to attend conferences and workshops all contribute to the sharing of ideas, as well as support.

Clinical supervision

Talking about the importance of support leads naturally on to the concept of clinical supervision. It is a given that working with the public, particularly those who are stressed or troubled, can have an impact on the professional. Clinical supervision provides a safe framework in which to share experiences in practice, and to offload in a controlled and appropriate manner. Those who do not experience clinical supervision or peer support will find that their clinical practice can take its toll, and there is an unfortunate tendency for the problems of their patients to find their way into conversations in the practitioner's private life – which is neither appropriate nor professional. I would encourage anyone who is going to use clinical hypnosis in practice to at least make him- or herself aware of clinical supervision groups (information about virtual support can be found at www.msha.org.uk).

Self-hypnosis for the practitioner

Clinical supervision or peer support may not always be accessible or available. This is where self-hypnosis comes into its own for the practitioner. Having a 'safe space' where the practitioner can talk to their own personal therapist (or higher self, depending on how the practitioner wishes to frame this) within hypnosis is a wonderful self-help tool. The practitioner can use the self-hypnosis to change state from practitioner to private individual, in the same way that many people have certain clothes for work, and others for home life, thus allowing them to mark a distinction between the two roles.

Self-hypnosis for the practitioner will also help them in clinical practice. Rapport is easier to achieve when the practitioner him- or herself is relaxed, and this will naturally lead the patient into a more relaxed state. Mirror neurons have a part to play in this. By using self-hypnosis, the practitioner is also able to manage their own stress, and to set goals not only for therapy, but also for professional practice or personal development.

Patients want to see fit, healthy, motivated and successful practitioners, irrespective of their field of endeavour. This is particularly true for therapists, as the process should above all be aspirational and inspiring. It almost goes without saying that no one would want to go to a therapist who can't 'fix' him- or herself.

CHAPTER 8

Creating the hypnotherapeutic protocol

THE USE OF QUESTIONS TO CREATE THE HYPNOTHERAPEUTIC PROTOCOL

This is a large topic, and this chapter can only give an overview of how to create the therapeutic protocol. The skills of observation, active listening and interpretation come with experience, but they can also be learned. These skills will become part of the decision-making process as the practitioner gathers examples of ways in which the protocols can be best put together from their own practice. This chapter contains examples of the types of questions that are necessary to devise an appropriate protocol, and it also includes a simplistic model of how to put this information together.

There are two types of questions that are relevant when creating the hypnotherapeutic protocol, namely questions designed to uncover factual information and those designed for evaluative purposes. How these questions are delivered is not important, provided that they are put in such a way that the patient feels comfortable enough to disclose the relevant information. Later in this chapter the structure follows the headings from Chapter 3, 'The structure of a clinical hypnosis session', and gives examples of the types of questions that can be used to elicit the information required for each component of the session. A session cannot be completely scripted, as the practitioner will respond to the patient when eliciting information. The questions are to be used as prompts where the patient does not otherwise offer the relevant information when relaxed and a good rapport has been established. Once patients feel comfortable talking about themselves, they will often furnish the relevant information unprompted.

The questions are asked during the pre-induction discussion, except where otherwise stated.

Areas to be covered in the questions include the following:

➤ the condition
➤ the most appropriate protocol
➤ the optimum time frame for a remission from the symptoms or affects

> the patient's language patterns
> the patient's success states
> specific symptoms or affects
> the duration and history of the condition
> the expectations of hypnosis and hypnotherapy
> selecting the modality for delivery of therapeutic suggestions.

To recapitulate, there are six stages to a clinical hypnosis session, namely introduction, induction, deepening, post-hypnotic suggestions (therapeutic suggestions), the awakening stage and the final stage (post-hypnosis). The final stage consists of debriefing the patient. The questions are asked mainly during the pre-induction talk, except where otherwise stated. Questions will be shown in this chapter under the most relevant heading, so that it can be clearly seen to what the questioning refers.

To create the hypnotherapeutic protocol, four areas need to be addressed, evaluated and taken into consideration. The rationale behind this is to personalise the treatment, and to ensure that where possible the patient takes control of the process as part of the therapeutic partnership described elsewhere. A failing in some hypnotherapeutic processes is that the focus for the patient remains on the condition, and the practitioner then attempts to treat the problem only. An example would be the assumption that, for a patient with a phobia of flying, the patient wished to be able to fly in an aeroplane, when in fact their specific objective may be to be able to look at one in the sky without experiencing anxiety. It is for this reason that clear and specific objectives are required from the patient before the hypnotherapeutic process can commence.

The four areas for consideration and evaluation are:

> the patient
> the condition
> the interaction between patient and condition (the symptoms and effects)
> the objective.

The practitioner will need to first isolate each of these components and evaluate them individually, and then take an overview of their interaction with one another. This takes place during the first contact (which may be a telephone call or email enquiry) and in the pre-induction talk. It will also continue as part of the post-hypnosis feedback session.

FIRST-CONTACT ASSESSMENT

The first contact may be a telephone call, an email or the first session itself. The purpose of the first contact is to reject any prospective candidates for hypnotherapy who may not be suitable because of individual characteristics, or because the condition with which they are presenting is contraindicated for the use of hypnosis. This process may seem an obvious one, and is for the protection of patients and practitioners, and any patient who is not deemed suitable for hypnotherapy can be assured of this. Once this process has occurred (*see* Chapter 5, for the evaluation criteria), the patient's objective in general terms must then be identified.

The following are key phrases that can be used to elicit this initial information. Such phrases can be used as guidelines on how most appropriately to construct questions:

> 'How can I help you?'

This phrase is used as a way of identifying the presenting condition, and will give the practitioner an indication of the patient's preconceptions and level of motivation, all of this taking place without the patient needing to focus on the problem. This negative focus of attention would be the case if the practitioner asked 'What is the problem?'

Implicit in the 'How can I help you?' question is the statement 'How do *you* think hypnotherapy can help you?', which will encourage the patient to focus on the role of hypnotherapy in creating the change that they require.

The patient's response to the question when phrased in this way will be to present their condition, and often to identify their conception of the role of hypnosis in helping them. An example would be 'I want to stop smoking, and a friend of mine told me that hypnosis is a good way of doing this.' From this the practitioner can start to evaluate the mindset of the patient. Conversely, if the patient says 'I don't *really* want to stop smoking, but my doctor told me to come here', the practitioner is also gaining information that the patient's motivation will be an aspect that they need to incorporate into the script if they choose to go ahead with the session.

With most conditions, it is appropriate to ask whether the patient is seeing a medical practitioner or taking medication for their condition. If this is the case, it is appropriate for the practitioner to say:

> 'You will need to visit your GP and let them know that you are intending to have hypnotherapy. I will need to have their consent in writing.'

This has the effect of including the prescribing physician in the information loop, so when writing up the case the clinical hypnosis practitioner can send them a copy for the patient's medical records. In addition, if the patient has not seen their medical practitioner, they can do so and have the condition diagnosed appropriately. There will be some people who, when asked to do this, will choose not to, and therefore do not come back to make the appointment. There may be any number of reasons for this. For example, some individuals will decide that they have a phobia, this decision being based on nothing more than a magazine article they have read. It is important to be aware that this process of ensuring that the medical practitioner has seen the patient first is put in place as a safeguard for non-medical practitioners to ensure that they are working with properly diagnosed conditions.

If the presenting condition falls within the category of habit breaking, or any other condition that could affect anyone within the 'normal' range of experience, it is still appropriate to ask:

> 'Are you seeing a medical practitioner for any other condition?' or 'Are you currently taking any medication?'

By asking this question, any other considerations which might be contraindicated can be identified. If the patient is taking medication which has side-effects similar to the phenomena of hypnosis, or which is a mood mediator, this can compromise the efficacy or even the appropriateness of hypnosis.

INTRODUCTION

This is the pre-induction talk in which most of the information gathering and evaluation will be covered.

INFORMATION GATHERING

Pinpoint the condition and review the information gathered from the first contact. This is kept to a minimum:

> 'You have told me on the phone that you would like to [pinpoint condition – for example, *stop smoking*].'

The framework of the session is then introduced to the patient. This will enable the patient to know what to expect of the session, and begin to reduce their anxiety levels induced by fear of the unknown:

> 'What will happen in the hypnosis is you will have your eyes closed and I will make some suggestions to relax your body (or focus your attention). Then you will hear me make suggestions based on what we will discuss in this part of the session. I will only suggest what we have discussed. In fact, if I make any suggestions which you have not already agreed, you will, of course, wake yourself up and reject them. When this part of the hypnosis is over, I will wake you up, and you will become alert, feeling refreshed and relaxed. You will remember everything that is important for you to remember.'

Information about the patient as an individual is then requested. This is done in order to relax the patient, to develop rapport, to begin to learn about how they process information, and to gain insight into the individual's personality and how resource states can be elicited. By starting with general, non-threatening questions, the patient will feel more comfortable and begin to speak freely. The information obtained at this stage mainly relates to individuals and how they operate outside the framework of their condition:

> 'Tell me a little about yourself. What do you do for a living?/Where do you live?/ Are you in a relationship?' etc.

These types of questions are designed to allow patients to talk about themselves in general terms, and will give indicators as to whether they are potentially stressed (for example, in a work situation), or if there are possible difficulties to be faced when they have achieved their therapeutic objective. An example would be if a patient had a problem with confidence and was in an unsupportive relationship.

Current anxieties or potential stressors can now be identified from the feedback given by the patient to the last question:

'You mentioned [pinpoint the stressor]. Can you tell me a little more about this?'

These types of questions are used to prompt the patient to identify potential triggers for their condition or specific symptoms. It is worth noting that often a patient may have had a condition for some time and will be able to identify when it gets worse, but will not always recognise times when it gets better. Patients do not go for help when they are coping well, so it is legitimate to assume that there will be some additional trigger or stressor which has induced them to take therapeutic action. Suggestions for reducing stress or improving coping strategies may need to be included in the hypnosis script. Other questions that are useful at this point, and which will often pinpoint this stressor or trigger, include the following:

'Why have you come for hypnosis now?'

'Is there any particular reason why it has become important for you to deal with this problem now?'

Any future anxieties of the patient with regard to potential change can then be identified. If the patient identifies that there is no particular reason or stressor, this may be a factor in motivation, and an additional impetus may need to be identified:

'What do you want to get out of this process?'

This question can focus the patient's attention on the positive benefits of change.

When taking note of the responses to these questions, the practitioner will also need to be aware of the ways in which the patient is delivering this information. If the patient talks about how they feel, or will feel, the suggestions can be delivered using this kinaesthetic emphasis. An example would be a patient who responds to the above question by saying 'I want to feel in control.' The post-hypnotic suggestions should then include suggestions that incorporate positive states and feelings as a way of linking in with this desire for control – not just in relation to the condition, but generally. Patients who describe their future states once they have achieved their objective in visual terms will have the suggestions delivered in pictorial form – to 'see' themselves achieving their objective. Lastly, those patients who talk about the future state in auditory terms can have it described back to them in hypnosis in terms of what they may hear when they have achieved their goal – for example, hearing positive feedback from people around them who notice the changes in the patient.

More time and emphasis are focused on the patient at this point in the session. The benefits of change are emphasised, rather than the condition, as a way of initiating the required perceptual changes. It is said that a good physician will first tell a patient what is right, and then tell them what is wrong – the emphasis is therefore on the positive:

'Tell me a little about yourself.'

'Is there anything specific happening in your life at the moment?'

A clear and realistic outcome for treatment will then need to be established. This can be done by applying SMART principles to the objective (SMART stands for **S**pecific, **M**easurable, **A**chievable, **R**ealistic and within a given **T**ime frame). The patient's objective is then evaluated against these criteria. Many patients will have a clear idea of what they do *not* want, and this part of the session often requires care, as it may be the first time that the patient has considered their problem from the viewpoint of a possible solution. The following are examples of questions that can be used to initiate the idea of looking at the problem from a different angle:

'Tell me specifically what you want out of the process.'

'Describe how things will be different for you.'

The patient will then be able to build up a multi-sensory image of the way things will be for them when they have achieved their outcome. An example of this would be a person with insomnia, who initially tells the practitioner that they 'want to be able to sleep normally.'

Questions can be used to make the outcome:

➤ specific ('Tell me specifically what you mean by a good night's sleep')
➤ measurable ('How many hours' sleep would you need to wake refreshed?')
➤ achievable ('What are you going to change to make sure this will happen?')
➤ realistic ('How do you expect to be able to do this?')
➤ time frame ('How soon do you want to do this?').

The end result will be an objective that fulfils all of these criteria, which will lend itself to the creation of practical and therefore more readily acceptable suggestions.

CASE HISTORY

Now that the patient is more comfortable, the specifics of the condition can be discussed. The patient will be more relaxed and more willing to provide the information necessary for the practitioner to be able to create unique suggestions. The questions used in this section will be direct, and wherever possible will be phrased using positive language.

Questions that direct the patient to recognise what they are already capable of doing are most useful at this point. These are asked in order to assess motivation and gain an understanding of the current ego state of the patient:

'What are you good at?'

'Tell me about some of the things you are proud of.'

'What are your achievements?'

The patient's responses can be linked with positive suggestions for change in relation to the presenting condition.

The next stage is to introduce questions about how the patient developed this condition:

'Do you remember when this started?'

'Was there a time before the condition developed?'

Questions to analyse how the patient currently manages their condition can be introduced at this point:

'Has there been a time when the impact of this problem was less than it is now?'

'Do you remember when you were able to cope better?'

The next question:

'Is there anything which you currently do that helps?'

is used to create positive memory associations when making suggestions. An example would be the patient with tension headaches, who finds that if she lies down in a dark room with her eyes closed the tension begins to ease. Suggestions can then be constructed using the idea that while in hypnosis she can imagine herself lying down in a darkened room and noticing her tension starting to disappear.

Next, questions to gain an understanding of the interaction between the patient and their environment as a result of this condition can be asked:

'How does this condition affect you?'

'What are the symptoms?'

'Does it prevent you from doing anything specific?'

'How do you feel when you [for example, have a panic attack]?'

These types of questions will allow the practitioner to gain a deeper understanding of the unique relationship between the patient, their condition and their interaction with that condition. How the patient feels about him- or herself and the condition, and how or whether the symptoms create associated behaviours, can all be identified at this point.

RAPPORT

As well as collecting information for use in the creation of the script and selection of the appropriate protocol, the practitioner will also need to demonstrate that they are interested in the patient, and understand their requirements. Rapport in this context denotes the interaction between patient and practitioner that makes the patient feel relaxed and able to speak freely about their condition. Rapport is constantly monitored throughout the session. Part of this process will utilise mirroring, pacing and leading the patient until they are in a sufficiently relaxed state to enter hypnosis. Mirroring involves the practitioner noting the physical positioning of the patient – for example, with folded arms and legs – and then adopting a similar posture and mirroring the way in which the patient speaks. This is not mimicry, but rather a modulation of the practitioner's normal way of speaking to make the patient feel that they are dealing with someone similar to them. Leading and pacing involve adopting similar but more relaxed postures and behaviours in order to lead the patient to a more compliant state. If done well, this process will not be noticed by the patient and will continue throughout the introduction session to a point at which the physical transition to hypnosis is barely discerned by the patient, as they will be very relaxed by this time.

DISCUSS THE HYPNOTIC STATE

Identify any previous experience:

'Do you know anything about hypnosis?'

'Have you ever been hypnotised before?'

This question is asked in order to allay any fears and misconceptions based on that experience. At this point the practitioner should take the patient's previous knowledge or experience of hypnosis (or lack of this) and create a model based on what they previously understood, which will reassure them. It is also important that, if the patient has had a previous experience of hypnosis which was not entirely positive, the practitioner has this information in order to ensure that they do not accidentally replicate the experience.

What to expect of the experience

At this point the practitioner will create an appropriate model for the patient to describe the events of hypnosis. This model is designed to fit into the patient's worldview and create a framework for positive changes (*see* Chapter 4, 'Questions patients ask').

Ways in which clinical hypnosis can potentially help

The final part of the preliminary section includes 'selling the benefits of the therapy.' In this section the practitioner will create a further model, including the effects of the therapeutic suggestions, and specifying what input the patient him- or herself will need to add to the process – for example, suggestions to *notice* the differences in their skin condition. With this model, the patient has explained to them, starting with their worldview, how specifically the clinical hypnosis process will work for them. A good example is the patient who identifies him- or herself as being quite analytical. This characteristic can be built in at this point:

> 'Only the really analytical person will make sure they only take on board suggestions after they have fully analysed them and made sure that they are right for them.'

The aim of this section is to assure the patient that this process will not change them as an individual, and that in fact it can enhance characteristics which will be useful for them.

PSYCHO-CYBERNETICS

The final explanation involves describing to the patient a model of the time frame for change. For this, the model of psycho-cybernetics is modified. It is described to the patient in simple terms that it will take around three weeks for the changes which they have initiated in the session to be fully taken on board by their unconscious processes. In other words, it will take about three weeks before they stop being aware of the change. It can be suggested that this occurs during the REM phases of sleep, where the individual reviews new knowledge and learning from the previous day, and plans the next. In the context of therapeutic change it can be linked to the Émile Coué concept that 'every day in every way you are getting better and better.' Patients will then feel comfortable about self-monitoring the changes for a while, and then let go of them as they become accommodated into what the patient considers to be normal.

LAST OPPORTUNITY FOR QUESTIONS FROM THE PATIENT

> 'Any questions before we start the clinical hypnosis?'

Even at this stage some patients may have further questions. This gives them a final opportunity to ask them. Patients who are still asking 'What if?' questions at this point (for example, 'What if it doesn't work?') may have some secondary gain to holding on to the condition, or may still have some anxieties.

RECAPITULATE ON THE OBJECTIVE

At this point the practitioner will run through the SMART goal, and check with the patient that they are absolutely clear that this is what they are setting out to achieve. The patient may wish to refine some part of the objective at this point.

A PRACTICAL POINT

'Do you need to go to the bathroom before we start?'

'Are you wearing contact lenses?'

'Are you comfortable closing your eyes with your lenses in, or would you prefer to take them out?'

'Is there anything else you need to tell me? For example, do you have any hearing problems?'

Statements are then introduced to guide the patient into hypnosis:

'When you are ready to let go of this problem, you can . . . start to relax . . .'

or:

'You can start by making yourself comfortable. Let your arms rest on your lap and place your feet flat on the floor.'

MODULATION OF VOICE QUALITY AND PATTERNS

The practitioner selects the way in which they will modulate their voice while conducting the hypnosis itself, based on the way in which the patient talks. If the patient is softly spoken, the practitioner will moderate their voice accordingly during the pre-induction talk. If the patient speaks more loudly and more rapidly, the practitioner will replicate this, but in this instance they will begin to lead the patient by example to speak more slowly and gently.

INDUCTION

The simplest way of selecting an induction is to base the decision on the modality in which the patient currently relaxes. If the patient does this by reading a book or watching television – that is, anything which engages the visual field – a visual induction is appropriate. For patients who listen to music or enjoy social interaction as a way of relaxing, auditory inductions are appropriate. For those who prefer more active forms of relaxation, and engage in physical activities, kinaesthetic inductions are more appropriate.

The following types of questions are used to elicit this information:

'What do you do to relax?'

or, for patients who say that they do not relax, or do not know how to relax, or who relax by using a 'false friend' (for example, cigarettes or alcohol), the question can be phrased differently:

'How would you choose to spend a day if you had nothing to do?'

SAFETY NET: INTRODUCING THE HYPNOTIC AND POST-HYPNOTIC EVENTS TO THE PATIENT

This section is optional, and involves walking the patient through the process and explaining how they will experience each event. This is designed to reassure the patient, and for those who do fall asleep or feel that they have failed to consciously register the post-hypnotic suggestions at the appropriate section of the script, it will mean that they have *already* heard the post-hypnotic suggestions while in hypnosis. This is particularly useful for anxious patients, and also when amnesia is required for some suggestions. If, for example, Parts Therapy is used (in which a behaviour that is no longer required is 'put to sleep' or 'put into the past'), this concept can be introduced to the patient at this early stage. An example of a way to script it is as follows:

'You will become very relaxed in this session . . . and . . . when I have made all the suggestions for you to carry out . . . (*such as having no desire to smoke, or having strong, healthy nails*) . . . at the very end of this session . . . you will hear me count up from one to ten. . . . And as I do . . . all normal and healthy parts of you will wake . . . except the part that used to (*smoke/bite your nails*) . . . that part of you can remain deeply asleep . . .in the past . . .'

By 'prescripting' this concept, the patient will often forget that it has been said, as it is so early in the hypnosis. The practitioner then does not need to repeat the part over which they wish the patient to have amnesia (i.e. the dissociation and therefore removal of the maladaptive part by leaving it asleep or in the past).

DEEPENING

Deepening processes can be devised using the modality within which the patient has identified their relaxation state. Those patients who have kinaesthetic ways of relaxing will respond well to suggestions that involve warmth and changing sensations in the limbs (such as heaviness or lightness), and those for whom social interaction is one way of relaxing often respond well to suggestions that include positive emotions or memories. Those whose modality of relaxation is visual can be asked to imagine themselves relaxing, or see their body as it starts to become more limp and relaxed. Auditory patients can be asked to focus on the sound of their breathing as it becomes deeper, or on internal sounds such as their heartbeat. The practitioner may also shift the emphasis to the sound of their voice as a sound which will relax them. Interspersing the personal relaxation modes with the deepener scripts such as the Elman 100–1 countdown makes the deepener much more profound, as well as personal.

If the patient has experienced hypnosis before, the practitioner can offer them an additional way of making the hypnosis deeper, as well as encouraging them to take control of the process. One way of doing this is to suggest that the patient mentally counts down themselves, silently, using their out breath to time the numbers. This will give them something with which to occupy their conscious awareness, moving attention away from the outside world and the words of the practitioner, but it also emphasises that they are taking control. The implication is that by taking control of the process they are leading themselves to take control of the events of the post-hypnotic suggestions, and ultimately the therapeutic change itself.

THERAPEUTIC SUGGESTIONS

Therapeutic suggestions need to be:

➤ phrased positively
➤ related to one subject at a time
➤ SMART.

When therapeutic suggestions are made, rapid eye movement can often be observed as the patient processes the information. These suggestions will consist purely of the patient's objective as discussed in the pre-induction talk and verified before the hypnosis commenced.

AUTHORITARIAN VERSUS PERMISSIVE

The decision as to whether to use a permissive or authoritarian form of suggestion for therapy can be made simply on the basis of the ego state of the patient (the weaker the ego, the more permissive the suggestions), and also on how the patient describes the way in which they believe clinical hypnosis can help them. An example of patients' different ways of describing their belief structure can be seen in statements such as 'I just want to be told that I will sleep through the night' or 'I think that it might be quite nice if I could get some rest for a change.' The first statement is direct, while the second is more passive. The delivery of suggestions needs to be congruent with the patient's approach to the process of hypnosis itself.

Generally, during the first session the practitioner tends towards a more permissive approach, which can then be modified to a more authoritarian one as the patient responds to the process, gaining confidence in themselves, in the practitioner, and in their own ability to change. This comes not only from the experience of the hypnosis and post-hypnotic suggestions, but also from the ego-strengthening suggestions which are such an important part of the session, both within and outside the hypnosis.

EGO-STRENGTHENING SUGGESTIONS

The modality on which to base the ego-strengthening suggestions can be taken from the section when the practitioner asked about success states. The rationale behind this is to reawaken in the patient an awareness that they have succeeded in the past. By using the modality in which they described their successes (whether auditory, visual or kinaesthetic), the patient will be stimulated to think in a similar manner. To bring together past success and future achievement, the two events can be linked together using a linking statement – for example, '*You can feel* as in control during your driving test [the objective] *as you did* when you sang solo in the choir [the past success event].' As the purpose of ego strengthening is to reinforce the therapeutic suggestions and generally to make patients feel more positive about themselves, the delivery of suggestions can be more upbeat and motivating, in order to reflect this.

If the patient cannot remember a time when they were successful or positive (and they are not suffering from depression), the practitioner can suggest that they think of someone who has the same attitudes and approach to life as they themselves want to have, and then make the post-hypnotic suggestions on an 'as if' footing. Alternatively, these suggestions can be made from the viewpoint of an observer from the future, who now has these characteristics, and is a representation of the patient when they are better. This future self can be introduced into the ego strengthening as a coach who will come to them during their dreams, and help to create the feelings and behaviours that the patient needs in order to change.

AWAKENING

Any suggestions that were solely for the purpose of the hypnotic event are to be removed at this stage (for example, heavy and tired limbs). In the awakening, suggestions for amnesia may be made. This is appropriate if the patient has recurrent patterns of thought, feeling or behaviour which appear to hold them back from making the change. There are many amnesia scripts available. One example of the type of suggestion that could be made is as follows:

> 'When you remember that there are many things which you have already forgotten, then you may forget those things that it is no longer appropriate for you to remember.'

There will often be an element of confusion in amnesia scripts, allowing analytical patients to analyse the amnesia suggestions, whereas the post-hypnotic suggestions that the practitioner wishes the patient to 'forget' consciously will bypass the critical faculty. When the patient then carries out the post-hypnotic suggestions they will feel that they are making these changes for themselves, rather than having had them imposed upon them.

POST-HYPNOSIS

From this point, the following suggestions and statements are made in the post-hypnosis session once the patient has been fully awakened.

The first post-hypnosis task is to ensure that the patient is fully re-oriented. This can be detected in the patient's posture and speech, and by the practitioner being able to obtain appropriate eye contact. If the patient is not fully alert, the practitioner will tell them to once again close their eyes, at which point the awakening script will be repeated, this time more emphatically. Once the patient is fully re-oriented, an optional question is to ask:

'How long did that seem since you closed your eyes?'

By asking a question about the form rather than the content of the hypnotherapy, the practitioner is asking the patient to move their attention to a different part of the event, namely their awareness of time. The patient will often state a much shorter time than has actually passed. This acts as a convincer that something unusual has taken place, as well as increasing the likelihood of amnesia of the specific post-hypnotic suggestions that were given while the patient was in hypnosis. The practitioner then asks:

'Do you have any questions?'

'Is there anything you would like to discuss at this point?'

This gives patients an opportunity to reassure themselves about any event in the hypnosis of which they were not sure, or that they did not expect. The practitioner will *not* remind them of any of the events that occurred during the hypnosis, as this will only serve to bring the patient's critical faculty to the event. It may even make the patient anxious if they did not remember the event as recounted to them by the practitioner. They may start to wonder what else they have 'forgotten', and begin to reject the post-hypnotic suggestions.

HOMEWORK

In some of the hypnotherapeutic protocols there will be specific homework for the patient to do, such as deliberately blushing, or paradoxical advertising in which they draw attention to the aspect of their condition that most concerns them (for example, their anxiety when giving a speech).

In addition, there are more global statements that are used to encourage change:

'Do not discuss the process with anyone – not today, and preferably not at all.'

This will allow the suggestions to be taken on board by the patient during their sleep processing phases. In addition, if language in the form of speech is not added to the experience, the cortex will not be fully engaged, allowing suggestions to be taken on board at a deeper, limbic level. This statement has the added effect of ensuring that if the patient does know someone who may wish to talk them out of making that change, they can say that they are not allowed to discuss it, and that this is part of the process.

'What is your next goal?'

'Now you have . . . [insert therapeutic objective – for example, stopped biting your nails], what are you going to do next?'

The following questions are designed to enhance the future focus of the patient, thereby putting the condition into the past, and also focusing the patient's attention on their *next* objective, either in the context of the therapy or beyond.

FUTURE SESSIONS
The questions and statements relating to this section will all focus the patient's attention on noticing developments between sessions.

'How do you see yourself differently/think things will be different/want to feel in the future?'

'What do you want to be able to achieve before we have our next session?'

PUTTING THE PROTOCOL TOGETHER
Putting all of this information together is like doing a jigsaw puzzle – the picture gradually emerges as it is being done. At one end of the scale there are patients who are analytical in their interaction with their condition, and an analytical approach can be favoured. At the other end of the scale there are process-based patients, who are only interested in gaining remission from their symptoms, and straightforward direct suggestions to this effect can be chosen. In between is a sliding scale of decisions, balancing the needs of the individual, the condition itself and the way in which the patient approaches that condition.

The practitioner will need to take note of which aspect the patient places most emphasis upon when talking, and this is the obvious keystone. Once this is changed, the patient's whole relationship with the condition will shift, and can therefore be controlled and then eliminated. If the patient spends most of their time talking about themselves, this is the aspect that the practitioner can most obviously choose to change, and he or she will select a protocol that influences the self, such as inner-child work, ego strengthening or a dissociation. If the patient's focus of attention is on the condition and its symptoms, a protocol that emphasises changing this area is appropriate – for example, cognitive–behavioural approaches. For a patient whose focus of attention is on achieving the objective, a goal-focused approach is favoured, such as the inner game, or solution-focused hypnotherapy.

It is the unique interaction of the patient with their condition and the symptoms and effects which will determine which protocol is required. There is no single neat formula. However, if the practitioner listens, observes and prompts where appropriate, the patient will identify the most appropriate approach for them.

The next five chapters take this information and relate it to specific conditions in order to better recognise where the information fits together when individualising the hypnotherapeutic protocol.

CHAPTER 9

Smoking cessation

The following framework is a one-session treatment which operates on the basis that smoking is primarily a habit to be broken. The types of general suggestions to be included are highlighted. However, the efficacy of the framework depends on personalising this protocol for the patient. In addition, emphasis is placed on ensuring not only that the patient breaks the habit, but also that they remain a non-smoker. There are thus two distinct objectives.

The first element of this process that the practitioner needs to be clear about is that it is rare to meet a smoker who 'really wants to stop.' Those who really want to stop do just that, without help. It is not useful to ask a smoker 'Why do you want to stop smoking?', as they will often explain, in well thought out and logical terms, precisely why now is not a good time for them to stop. Smokers are very good at justifying their habit. There is also little value in attempting to scare smokers from their habit, as they are fully aware of the dangers and still continue to smoke. Aversive techniques on their own are of little long-term benefit in this situation, as smokers already know that cigarettes taste and smell bad, and they are aware of the long-term health problems associated with being a smoker. They can and will frequently find excuses for continuing their habit. This particular protocol emphasises stopping smoking as well as making sure that the patient does not start smoking again.

USEFUL MODELS FOR EXPLAINING WHY HYPNOSIS WILL HELP TO BREAK THE HABIT

Models for explaining the hypnotic event will be used with all patients. It may also be necessary to put forward a model of how clinical hypnosis will affect the therapeutic changes, specifically in relation to the presenting condition. When patients have failed to make the necessary changes for themselves, it is useful to put clinical hypnosis into the context of being a mental amplifier or booster. The hypnosis can be described as a process that enhances the patient's willpower, uses their personal characteristics and puts the information where it needs to be. The process is described as a treatment with two components – stopping smoking, and ensuring that the patient does not start smoking again in future. With all this in place, the patient will be able to effectively break their smoking habit *and* remain a non-smoker.

'Can you remember when you first smoked?'

This question establishes whether the patient has a clear memory of when they first smoked, and their body responded by rejecting that smoke. If they can remember, and most smokers will be able to do so, this is also used to make the patient aware that they are only moments away from being someone who never smoked – that is, moments before they inhaled their first cigarette – and as there was a time *before* they ever smoked, there can be a time *after* they smoked, as this treatment protocol emphasises connecting with the 'part of you that knows how to enjoy life without smoking . . . the part of you that was active before you ever smoked . . .'

River or canal: brain pathways

Some patients state that they do not think they can stop smoking. Using this model, it can be explained to the patient that the clinical hypnosis session will not stop them smoking, but will reconnect the neural pathways that were in place *before they ever smoked, when their body knew how to enjoy life without smoking.* So the smoker is not going to learn something new, but merely revert to the behaviour that was in place before they ever smoked. It can be easily described by using the following metaphor: 'A canal is man-made (*smoking habit*) . . . but when it is no longer in use . . . the water flows back along its natural course (*life as a non-smoker*).'

Conscious logic and unconscious behaviour

The practitioner can explain that one of the main reasons why the patient has not been able to stop smoking before is that they have tried to use their conscious, logical thought processes. This part of their mind already knows how bad it is for them to smoke, but it is not the part of their mind that controls their habit. It is the unconscious part of their mind – the part of their mind that contains memories of being a smoker, and controls unconscious processes such as breathing and heart rate and, more significantly, their habits – which needs to get the picture that this person is now a non-smoker. The unconscious part of their mind knows all the triggers for smoking, and it is in this part of their mind that patients need to be able to imagine themselves involved in all of those activities, but without a cigarette, and being in control. Hypnosis is described as a process that allows the conscious part of the mind to relax – while the unconscious part of the mind can take on board the suggestions. Patients will often respond better to the word 'memory' than to the term 'unconscious mind', as the latter's undertones of analysis can put some people off.

Nicotine withdrawal

Nicotine takes around 48 hours to leave the system, during which time some individuals feel tired, sluggish and irritable. Because their immune system is working hard to eject the nicotine, some people can be more susceptible to infection, and may feel quite ill. This will often give recidivists an excuse to revert to smoking, by convincing themselves that 'they felt better when they smoked.' Obviously this is not actually the case, so a model can be used which will explain their situation. A post-hypnosis suggestion that the feelings will only last for a couple of days can be utilised to overcome this. However, this model will only be introduced to the patient if they describe having stopped before and having experienced these effects, or if they express a particular concern about this.

In the post-hypnotic suggestions, and included in the homework given to the patient, is the suggestion to sip fresh fruit juice during the 48 hours after the session. The reasons for doing so are to clear the palette of any taste of nicotine, to give the patient something to do to occupy themselves during the times when they used to smoke, and to top up their vitamin C levels. The latter is valid because smoking depletes the levels of this vitamin, and some patients may start to feel ill when they stop smoking. By sipping fruit juice the patient is encouraged to focus their mind on wellness rather than ill health, and the emphasis is on prevention of negative symptoms. This is a very effective strategy.

POINTS FOR INCLUSION IN THE SMOKING CESSATION SCRIPT

The script incorporates the following:

➤ physical relaxation
➤ permissive hypnosis
➤ direct post-hypnotic suggestions
➤ stress management and ego strengthening
➤ distraction
➤ dissociation.

In addition, there will be post-hypnosis suggestions for homework.

HYPNOTIC SCRIPT: PHYSICAL RELAXATION

Smokers will often identify that smoking is a form of relaxation for them. They will report that they smoke as a treat, or as a punctuation point between activities, or even as a means of getting away from their desk for a break at work. If this is the case, they will benefit from the physical relaxation of the hypnosis itself. Even if this is not the case, the deepening techniques, which use suggestions of warm, relaxed muscles, are well received and will also go some way towards setting up a counterbalance to any expectation of tension or anxiety associated with withdrawal from nicotine. The process should therefore be as relaxing as possible, taking into consideration the ways in which the patient currently relaxes (apart from by smoking). As discussed in previous chapters, the modality chosen for the induction can reflect the patient's preferred method of relaxation, with the proviso that this does not involve smoking!

HYPNOTIC SCRIPT: PERMISSIVE HYPNOSIS

Each smoker will have a different pattern of behaviour, but the reasons for starting smoking are often common. An individual who smokes may associate smoking with rebellion, being more interesting or exciting, or being adult. This goes back to the time when they started smoking, when those feelings may have been in place, but are now no longer relevant to their habit. Smokers are also aware of the prohibited nature of their habit, and will be used to being told not to smoke, either by people or by circumstances. The net result of this attitude is that no smoker likes being *told* what to do in relation to their habit. Therefore the suggestions that are made as part of the induction and deepener will be invitations rather than instructions. The individual is encouraged to relax, and it can be suggested to them that they can simply enjoy the relaxation part of the hypnosis – for example, 'The more you relax, the more easily you will be able to take the suggestions on board.'

For the patient who is experiencing the hypnosis, relaxing will then be associated with the suggestions of being a non-smoker. It also helps if the practitioner gives the patient something to do as part of the deepening process, as smoking can be a control issue, so the more control the patient feels over the process, the more involved they are in the therapeutic change. Having them count down from 100 to zero, using their out-breath to time the numbers, and interspersing these numbers with a red stop light and the words *free from smoking*, or something similar, will not only give them apparent control over the deepening process, but will also distract their attention away from the specifics of the practitioner's suggestions. It doesn't matter whether the patient completes the count, as it is the involvement in the process that is important. I often ask smokers what phrase they would like to have come into their mind in the situations that they have associated with smoking. I will then feed that phrase into the deepener for them to say to themselves.

Suggestions made as part of the induction and deepener can also include phrases which imply that the patient does not need to do anything in order to become a non-smoker, thus utilising the individual's inertia. For example:

> 'there is no need for you to pay close attention to the words that I say . . . simply the sound of my voice can help you to relax . . . all of the suggestions which will be useful to you will be remembered . . . there is no need for you to do anything at all . . . just relax.'

HYPNOTIC SCRIPT: DIRECT POST-HYPNOTIC SUGGESTIONS

The post-hypnotic suggestions will need to be clear and directive, tailored specifically to the times, moods, places and situations in which the patient used to smoke. The practitioner will need to go through the patient's smoking habits one by one and suggest that they will have 'no desire to smoke . . . [in the specific situation].' Smoking is one of the few conditions where the SMART criteria are not required. The objective for the patient is to stop smoking, and to remain a non-smoker. Anything else will fail. There can be no such thing as a social smoker, or an occasional smoker – patients either smoke or they do not smoke. The practitioner will be very directive in suggesting that patients will not be able to trick themselves into smoking:

> 'Now that you are relaxed and can pay all of your attention to breaking the smoking habit . . . and remaining a non-smoker . . . you can find that you will never trick or fool yourself into smoking ever again . . . no matter where you are . . . who you are with . . . or what you are doing . . .'

This is followed by the suggestions created by the patient which were already introduced into the deepener:

> 'and . . . whenever you are in a mood . . . or a place . . . or a situation . . . where in the past you used to smoke . . . instantly and immediately the phrase (for example, *free from smoking*) will come into your mind . . . and you will forget about smoking . . . distracting yourself with this thought . . . so you can forget about smoking . . . forget about smoking . . .'

General suggestions will also need to be made to direct the patient's attention away from themselves at these times. These are also necessary to ensure that patients do not persuade themselves to smoke:

> 'Whenever you are in a mood . . . or a place . . . or a situation where you used to smoke . . . you will instantly direct your attention away from yourself . . . and become involved in a conversation . . . or find your attention drawn away by another thought . . .'

In the context of the post-hypnotic suggestions, the practitioner can be more authoritarian and directive than at any other point during the script, as although smokers do not like being told what to do, they do like being told what they *are capable of doing*, such as being in control, or making sure that they do not trick themselves into smoking.

The principal suggestion, and one that the practitioner can mention in the pre-induction talk, amplify in the post-hypnotic suggestions and reinforce during the post-hypnosis feedback, is as follows:

> 'The only cigarette you are not going to have is the first one . . . only one cigarette . . . and you will be fine with this . . .'

This suggestion is effective for all smokers, regardless of their patterns or habits, as when smokers try to think of being non-smokers, they will imagine themselves in future situations where they used to smoke. This itself creates anxiety as they start to feel deprived of all the many cigarettes which they will not be able to smoke in future. This concept of the first cigarette being the only one that they will refrain from smoking breaks this anxiety down, and makes the whole idea of being a non-smoker a much smaller and more manageable concept.

IDENTIFYING THE PROBLEM

As with other conditions, however, the practitioner needs to focus on which particular aspect of this is most relevant for the patient. There are some individuals for whom stopping is not a problem, and they will talk about having stopped before, often for years – but the problem for them is remaining a non-smoker. Others cannot imagine themselves without a cigarette in their hand, and any previous attempts to stop have been short-lived. For these patients, the emphasis of the suggestions is on breaking the patterns of thought and behaviour associated with smoking, and imagining themselves in all of the situations where they used to smoke, but without a cigarette, feeling calm and relaxed.

Patients whose focus is on remaining a non-smoker

> 'You will be in control . . . in every situation and mood . . . and . . . you may find . . . as a result of being so relaxed now . . . you will be more relaxed about other situations too . . . situations where in the past you might have smoked . . . but now you are in control . . . you will be more in control over other situations too . . .'

With these suggestions the emphasis is on control, relaxation and being aware of their triggers for smoking. Patients can then remind themselves that they are only 'not having this cigarette, the first one', and they will be able to distract themselves away from the trigger.

Patients whose focus is on breaking the habit

> 'You will be able to see yourself in the future . . . calm and relaxed . . . in the situation where in the past you used to smoke . . . and you have no desire to smoke . . . in fact . . . you are so involved in what you are doing . . . in what is going on around you . . . that you forget about smoking . . .'

Symptoms of smoking

It is appropriate, as with all conditions, for the practitioner to ask whether the patient is experiencing any ill effects from their habit. Some patients will say that they are not aware of any such effects. For those who do identify symptoms, such as tiredness or shortness of breath, these symptoms can be incorporated into the post-hypnotic suggestions. For example:

> 'As a result of the fact that you now no longer smoke . . . you will feel more energised . . . able to breathe deeply and easily . . . just as you are breathing deeply right now . . .'

For patients who do not perceive any ill effects, suggestions for general health and physical well-being should be incorporated. Even if the patient is not aware of any symptoms, they need to be directed to notice improvements in their physical health:

> 'You will begin to notice . . . that generally you feel more healthy . . . more able to do things . . . than you did when you used to smoke . . .'

What does the patient smoke?

In order to personalise the framework thoroughly, the practitioner will need to know what the patient smokes (cigarettes, roll-ups, cigars or a pipe), and whether they smoke anything other than pure tobacco. If the latter is the case, the patient will need to be informed that the aim of this treatment is to stop them smoking tobacco in any form whatsoever. They will not be able to smoke marijuana with tobacco any more, as this could lead them back to smoking tobacco in the form of cigarettes. There is no demarcation line, and for smokers who say 'I would just like to have the occasional cigar/joint', the practitioner needs to re-emphasise that there is no middle way with this process – the patient has to make the commitment to stop completely. To get a more honest and comprehensive answer from the patient, this question is better asked close to the end of the pre-induction section when a good rapport has been established.

What are the specific details of the habit?

In the case history, the practitioner will need to find out the specific details of the habit. The practitioner can ask the patient to describe a typical day of smoking, starting with the first cigarette, roll-up, etc. This will give the information a structure so that it can be fed back logically during the hypnosis in the same order as it was delivered by the patient. It is also worth noting times when the patient does not smoke, or does not think about smoking, and this can be added to the suggestions to reinforce the fact that they already have the capacity to control their habit.

The following suggestion is then given:

> 'No desire to smoke when [insert situation].'

As well as the patterns of smoking, any other specific triggers will need to be identified, as these can be the reasons why patients might be inclined to talk themselves into smoking.

WHAT TO EXPECT IN THE NEXT FEW WEEKS

In order to ensure that the patient has a realistic expectation of events, it is necessary for the practitioner to pre-empt any relapses by telling the patient what will happen.

Physical effects

There are physical cravings associated by some patients with stopping smoking. When an individual makes any change, they are more aware of what is going on within, and this self-monitoring, associated with the symptoms of nicotine withdrawal, can cause the patient to exaggerate, and in some cases to misinterpret, the internal events. Dehydration is often misinterpreted as hunger, and causes the patient to reach for food. When patients are dehydrated they might also feel unwell, and again this can cause them to become more anxious and further associate these feelings with breaking the smoking habit. Suggestions in the hypnosis, such as 'You can drink a glass of water in the situations where you used to smoke', prevent the dehydration and also give the patient something to do with their hands.

Emotional effects

Some patients identify that they are more likely to smoke when they are in certain moods than in others. If these moods are positive, patients can be encouraged to imagine themselves in that mood, without a cigarette, and feeling really good about the fact that they are not smoking. If the mood is a negative one, the practitioner can make ego-strengthening suggestions to alleviate that mood, or give the patient better ways of managing it than reaching for a cigarette.

Mental effects

For patients who believe that smoking helps them to think better, suggestions that include the concept 'Now you no longer smoke . . . you will be able to think more clearly' can be made. It can also be pointed out that once the patient no longer smokes, they will find that their memory will also improve as their short-term memory processes are not taken up with processing their smoking habit.

Tragedy cigarettes

Patients who have stopped smoking before will often be able to identify an unexpected trigger – something happened to them that made them feel out of control, and the result was that they lit a cigarette without even thinking about it. In this instance the practitioner will emphasise that this will not happen in future as they will be 'More in control . . . whatever the situation' and 'Smoking would only prevent you from coping well with whatever happens in your life . . .'

Special occasions

Some patients associate smoking with special events, drinking and socialising, or holidays. In this situation, the post-hypnotic suggestions will include patients being able to perceive themselves in these situations, and having *more* control, being *more* aware so that they can ensure that they do not trick themselves into smoking on these occasions. Patients can be encouraged to advertise the fact that they no longer smoke when in these situations, as a way of reinforcing their decision.

HYPNOTIC SCRIPT: STRESS MANAGEMENT

Occasionally, patients will perceive positive or useful effects of their habit. Patients will often state that smoking helps them to relax. Apart from explaining in the pre-induction talk that smoking stresses the system rather than the reverse, installing suggestions to enable the patient to manage stress more effectively will always be part of the session, and will be tailored to situations that the patient identifies as stressors.

Patients will also often state that so long as they are smoking they feel unable to do other things, such as getting fit, as the smoking invalidates any positive effects which they might gain from the physical exercise. With regard to this, suggestions can be offered about making getting fit their next goal:

> 'Now that you have broken the smoking habit you will be able to go to the gym . . . and feel fitter and healthier than you have felt in a long . . . long time.'

Concerns about being a non-smoker usually relate to stress levels, possible mood swings or putting on weight. If the patient tries to stop and finds any of these situations occurring, this can then become an excuse for reverting to the habit. However, it does not prevent these situations from occurring once the patient has gone back to smoking. For example, the smoker who puts on weight once they break the habit does not automatically lose that weight once they start smoking again. For smokers for whom this is a concern, the additional suggestions that they will have more control in these specific situations can be made.

The ego-strengthening suggestions will emphasise the concept of the patient being in control regardless of the situation in which they may find themselves, and these suggestions can be linked back to situations in which the patient is already in control, which they have mentioned during the case history.

HYPNOTIC SCRIPT: DISSOCIATION

Not always a smoker

Smokers will often associate so strongly with their habit that they cannot imagine life without it, and it becomes a way of defining who they are, rather than a behaviour. It can be suggested in hypnosis that for most of the time they are a non-smoker, and it is only when a trigger occurs that the smoking part of them is activated. Suggestions of this kind are particularly effective for patients who describe the act of smoking as one that they engage in without even being aware that they are doing it (that is, purely unconscious), and that often they do not actually want, or enjoy, that cigarette. This concept of the smoker as only 'a part of you' is further followed through into the awakening script, with suggestions being made for all parts of the individual to wake up, 'except the part of you that used to smoke.' This expression puts the behaviour clearly into the past.

Post-hypnosis: behaviour modification

A number of additional behaviours, referred to as homework, can be suggested to the smoker once they have been awakened from the hypnosis part of the session. One suggestion can be that for the first few days the patient can sip orange juice, especially at times when they would have smoked. This can be linked back to the suggestion that they need to replenish the vitamin C levels in their body. Another suggestion can be that each time they think about smoking, 'the only thing which will come to your lips is a smile as you can be pleased that you no longer smoke.' Finally, the suggestion can be made that it is better to pick up the phone to speak to the practitioner during the first three weeks than to pick up a cigarette. This links with the psycho-cybernetics framework, and acts as an interruption of the thought-to-action process of smoking.

SUMMARY

An appropriate model is presented to the patient, depending on their mindset, with regard to breaking the habit. The hypnosis part of the protocol includes relaxation suggestions, incorporates the patient's modality of relaxation to deepen the state, and has direct suggestions relating to the triggers for the habit. In hypnosis, these triggers are fed back in the same order in which they were presented by the patient in the case history. Any excuses for maintaining the habit are addressed, and suggestions for behaviour modification as well as more appropriate stress management mechanisms are installed. The patient is then woken with full ego-strengthening suggestions which link in with their success states by the use of the same modality. Finally, dissociative suggestions are made for the patient to leave their smoking habit in the past. Distraction and ego strengthening are reinforced in the post-hypnosis part of the session, and the patient is dismissed with the suggestion that they have been very successful and can now look forward to achieving their next objective.

CHAPTER 10

Phobias

Patients with phobias frequently present for clinical hypnosis without a formal diagnosis. Before a session is to take place, the non-medical practitioner must know that a visit to a medical practitioner has occurred, to ensure that the patient is treated appropriately. This protocol describes one form of hypno-desensitisation protocol, which can take place either in a single session or over a number of sessions, depending on the severity of the symptoms.

Hypno-desensitisation utilises the well-documented psychological approach of desensitisation (West, 1967), with the additional benefit of the rapid relaxation and heightened awareness of the hypnotic state. The patient is required to produce a hierarchy of anxiety-evoking events, and to indicate the relative magnitude of the effect of these events by placing them in a logical order (on a Subjective Units of Disturbance Scale, or SUDS), from the least to the highest anxiety-evoking situation within the framework of their condition. Once the scale has been produced, hypnosis is induced, and a signalling device (ideo-motor response in the finger) is installed. The practitioner will then describe the events, commencing with the least anxiety-evoking one, and will make suggestions for relaxation at each point. If no or minimal anxiety is experienced, the next event on the hierarchy is presented. If significant anxiety is experienced, additional relaxation is suggested, until minimal or no anxiety is experienced. This process is continued throughout the hierarchy.

IDENTIFYING THE SPECIFIC OBJECTIVE

Even thinking about their trigger situation can stimulate anxiety in patients with phobias. As a result, they may never have thought about how they wish to be when they have achieved their objective. The result of this is a patient who consistently tells the practitioner what they do *not* want (for example, 'I don't want to be afraid of flying'), as opposed to what they *do* want to achieve. It is essential to create a clear image of what the patient is working towards as the objective, so that they will know when they have conquered their phobia. Creating this image in specific, concrete and clearly defined terms will also give the patient a positive association with the phobic situation, which is their objective.

CASE HISTORY QUESTIONS

The history of the phobic response

When treating a patient with a phobia, it is appropriate for the practitioner to ask the patient to describe the history of their phobic responses. The key questions are itemised below, as well as the rationale behind them.

Asking when the problem first occurred will allow the patient to identify whether they are aware of any initiating event. If this is the case, suggestions can be incorporated into the ego strengthening that takes place after the formal hypno-desensitisation protocol to recall the patient's appropriate response, which was in place *before* this event:

> 'You may start to find . . . as a result of this process . . . you will begin to feel as you did before . . . and will be able to enjoy all the things you did before . . .'

For patients who have no recall of an initiating event, the focus of these post-hypno-desensitisation ego-strengthening suggestions will be on using all their senses to imagine themselves experiencing the SMART objective. For these individuals, it may also be useful to educate them as to why they may be unable to uncover an origin. It can be pointed out that some phobias are inherited behaviours (as, for example, in the case of the child who becomes dog phobic as a result of the parent who becomes scared when near to dogs, and pulls their child away, thereby teaching the child their own fear response), or their phobia may have developed from a number of small and, in themselves, trivial events that occurred sequentially. It is important for the practitioner to reassure the phobic patient at each stage of the therapeutic process, as anxiety is a major component of their problem, and the inability to find an origin may be interpreted by some patients as their personal failure to respond to the treatment process. The patient needs to be assured that the process will still work, even if they are unable to identify the origin. The use of education and reframing will always have a place in good hypnotherapeutic treatment.

Uncovering when this situation changed from being manageable to becoming a problem will identify whether there were any external stressors that exacerbated the phobic response. If this is the case, appropriate suggestions for stress management will be necessary. In addition, if any secondary gains are present, they will often be identified at this point.

The last area to identify in this section is what is going on in the patient's life at present. Patients will rarely present with phobias unless there is an existing situation or a planned future event that requires them to take action with regard to their phobia (for example, the patient who is spider-phobic and has a trip planned to a tropical country, or the patient who is about to lose a partner because they can never go out together, due to the patient's claustrophobia). These events can be built into motivation and ego-strengthening suggestions, allowing the patient to experience in the hypnosis the positive feelings associated with achievement.

All of the information elicited from these questions will give a better overview of the patient's interaction with their condition.

SPECIFIC EVENTS OF A PHOBIC ATTACK
Specific symptoms

The specific ways in which the phobia affects the patient will then need to be pin-pointed. This is done most effectively by breaking the symptoms down into groups. This will allow the patient to discuss each symptom individually and, as a result, to break the symptoms down into smaller and therefore potentially more manageable events. The responses identified by the patient will be those of the fight or flight response. The important factor is to identify them in the order in which they are experienced by the patient – that is, asking what is noticed first, and then tracing the stages of experience, so the practitioner will interject only to keep the chronology of the symptoms intact. If good rapport is maintained, the patient will remain relaxed. This then becomes a precursor to the hypno-desensitisation as experienced during the hypnotic state. Below are described some of the types of information that patients will give at this point.

Physical symptoms

All responses associated with the activation of the sympathetic nervous system – for example, sweaty palms, shortness of breath, 'butterflies in the stomach', or an increased desire to urinate – can be described.

Emotional symptoms

Feelings of panic, fear, anxiety or tearfulness can be described. Anger and frustration can also be symptomatic of the phobic response.

Mental symptoms

Patients may describe thoughts of wanting to run away or escape from the phobic experience. These thoughts are often accompanied by mental images of losing control.

Variations in response since the condition first developed

Since the patient first developed the phobic response, there will have been times when the response was lessened, or became even worse than it is at present. The practitioner can ask the patient to describe these variations. They can then use the variations when creating suggestions of ways in which the patient will be able to cope better with the events that worsened the phobia, and use the times when the phobia was less problematic to create positive associations. These suggestions will form part of the ego-strengthening and motivation suggestions, which come after the formal hypno-desensitisation, and are either made before or included in the awakening script.

Eliciting the information about the specific symptoms will allow the patient to break down the phobic responses into smaller and therefore potentially more manageable events.

USEFUL MODELS FOR EXPLAINING WHY HYPNOSIS WILL HELP TO ALLEVIATE THE PHOBIC RESPONSE

Learned response

The practitioner can explain that the phobic response is a learned response that has become maladaptive. As it is learned, it can also be unlearned. If the patient can remember how they responded before this, that information can be used when creating their objective for therapy. If the patient has no recollection, the practitioner can explain that some phobic responses can be learned from peers or parents, so it is not surprising that they do not remember when it started – in fact, it is not even their problem. This instance of two possible ways of the practitioner responding, depending on how the patient reacts to the initial question, is a prime example of adapting the protocol to the patient. With each of the responses – that of the patient who remembers being able to use this memory, and that of the patient who does not remember – a model can be created by the practitioner to empower the patient. The explanation of the practitioner will need to be logical and factual. In this way, the patient will become more relaxed during the pre-induction talk as the practitioner reassures them that their phobic response can be managed.

Conscious logic and unconscious behaviour

This explanation is similar to that used with smoking cessation, and can be adapted for other conditions. In the case of phobias, the practitioner can explain that one of the main reasons why the patient has not been able to rid themselves of the phobia before is that they have tried to use their conscious, logical thought processes. This part of their mind already knows the appropriate response, but it is not the part of their mind that controls the response. It is the unconscious part of their mind, the part of their mind which contains memories of responding in the inappropriate way, and controls unconscious processes such as breathing and heart rate – and habits – which needs to get the message that this person is now in control and will respond appropriately to the phobic stimulus. The unconscious part of the patient's mind knows all the triggers for the phobia, and it is in this part of their mind that they need to be able to imagine themselves involved in all of those activities, with a relaxed response and being in control. Hypnosis is then described as a process that allows the conscious part of the mind to relax, while the unconscious part can take on board the suggestions.

The role of the conditioned response in a phobia

When discussing their condition, patients will sometimes react with the phobic responses (for example, sweaty palms, shortness of breath). If this occurs, the practitioner will use a model that reframes this response. The reframe consists of pointing out to the patient that it is good that they are able to experience these responses in the *absence* of the stimulus, as the fact that they are able to do this demonstrates that they are also capable of doing the reverse, which would be to experience the stimulus without the negative response – that is, to show a healthy and appropriate response to the situation.

EXPLAINING HOW THE HYPNO-DESENSITISATION WILL WORK

Once the general information has been obtained from the patient, it is appropriate to collect specific data that will be used to create the hypno-desensitisation protocol. Before this happens, a full explanation of how the sequence of events will occur during hypnosis is appropriate, so that the patient understands why this information is necessary. One of the major components of phobias is a fear of losing control. Hypnosis will therefore be explained to the patient as a process that specifically creates *more* control, and the deeper into hypnosis they go, the more control of the process, and of the phobia, they will achieve.

As part of the hypnosis, the patient will be asked to experience the anxiety-inducing situations (stimuli), starting with the least anxiety-evoking one. The practitioner will then explain to the patient that no person can be in two states simultaneously, and the hypnosis will keep them relaxed and safe while they experience the stimulus. It can be further explained that when the relaxation is experienced in hypnosis, it progressively weakens the link between the stimulus and the patient's inappropriate response, also breaking down the habitual connection. The practitioner emphasises to the patient that they will control the pace of the hypno-desensitisation, and will be given ways of signalling to the practitioner if they wish to stop, or to continue. Once this explanation has been provided, and the patient has been given an opportunity to ask any questions, the hypnosis part of the session can commence.

CONSTRUCTING THE HIERARCHY

The patient will then be asked to describe the sequence of events, or individual stimuli, that provoke their phobic response. The framework of a scale of 0 to 100 is then described to the patient, and this becomes their Subjective Units of Disturbance Scale (SUDS). Zero is described as 'no disturbance' and 100 is described as 'the most disturbance they have ever experienced/could imagine experiencing.' Some practitioners will make a graphic representation to use when working with the patient, by drawing a line and placing 0 at one end of the line, and 100 at the other. They will then place evenly spaced marks along the line, with the numbers 10 to 90 on them, as follows:

0	10	20	30	40	50	60	70	80	90	100

The patient is then asked to describe the phobic stimuli and place them on the scale depending on how much disturbance they experience when thinking about that event. The practitioner will take note of the modality in which the patient experiences each event in order to feed back within the appropriate modality when presenting the scene in hypnosis. This ensures that the patient will obtain a clear and rapid image of the event, as they have experience of the modality being active in relation to their condition (for example, seeing themselves in a specific situation, or being aware of a sound trigger). It is best to start on the hierarchy with zero rather than 100, and for the patient to be guided through the hierarchy by increasing the intensity, proximity or any other variables which can be identified in the images presented by the patient. This then becomes a precursor to the experience that they will have in hypnosis. As always, the practitioner will need to be guided by the needs of the patient. It is essential for the practitioner to refrain from enhancing the images or potential disturbance by adding elements that the patient has not already discussed. An example would be the patient who identifies a picture of one spider as rating zero disturbance, and dozens of spiders in a dark enclosed space with her as 100. To create the hierarchy involves manipulating the number of spiders, taking the spider out of the picture, even making that picture into a moving image, or making the space less enclosed or giving it more light. By doing this, the patient can evolve a progression which stays within the confines of the hierarchy. If the practitioner asks 'Have you thought about what unit of disturbance you would be at if these spiders were crawling all over you?', this adds another, as yet previously unconsidered, component, inducing more, as yet unconsidered, anxiety. The result of this will be a hierarchy that says more about the fears of the practitioner than it does about those of the patient. The final hierarchy should consist of a sequence of events, evenly spaced throughout the scale – for example, an event which caused zero disturbance, 10, 20, 30, and so on, up to 100. If the spaces are not even, there will be a sticking point when conducting the hypno-desensitisation protocol, as the increase in anxiety at this point may be too large for the patient to deal with.

POINTS FOR INCLUSION IN THE PHOBIA HYPNO-DESENSITISATION SCRIPT

The script incorporates the following:

➤ physical relaxation
➤ permissive hypnosis
➤ installation of a signalling device (ideo-motor response)
➤ installation of a cue word or phrase for relaxation
➤ scene presentation
➤ stress management
➤ ego strengthening.

In addition, there will be post-hypnosis suggestions for homework.

HYPNOTIC SCRIPT: PHYSICAL RELAXATION

For an induction, the modality in which the patient relaxes can be chosen. The practitioner should try to avoid induction techniques that incorporate imagery, as in the context of this protocol the images will be those relating to the phobic situations. As two opposing states cannot be experienced simultaneously, a deepening technique that incorporates suggestions of physical relaxation is the most productive option. A deep physical state of relaxation is required before the therapeutic process can be effectively commenced.

HYPNOTIC SCRIPT: INSTALLATION OF SIGNALLING DEVICES

Signals are installed in the hypnosis script, and will form a continuation of the deepening process. It is important for the patient to be able to signal to the practitioner non-verbally. A verbal response would engage the conscious processes, and often brings the patient out of the hypnotic state, or at least into a less deep experience. The first signal is used for the patient to indicate when they have the stimulus image clear in their mind, and the second signal is used to indicate how the patient is feeling when these scenes are presented. A head-nod is usually requested to indicate when the image is clear, and the patient is then asked to confirm this by nodding their head to show they have understood the instruction. The other signals installed are finger ideo-motor-responses (IMRs), which are used to indicate 'yes' or 'no' when the patient is asked whether they are feeling calm and relaxed once the stimulus scenes are presented to them. The patient is then instructed to confirm that these IMRs are in place by the practitioner asking test questions. As the patient will be in a very deep state of relaxation, there may be a long response time, as the more deeply relaxed the patient is, the longer it takes for a response to occur.

HYPNOTIC SCRIPT: INSTALLATION OF CUE WORD OR PHRASE FOR RELAXATION

The next suggestion to be installed is a cue or trigger word which, when spoken by the practitioner, will recall the deepest relaxation that the patient has experienced as part of the hypnosis script. This word, spoken on the out-breath for the patient, becomes associated with relaxation. An expression such as 'now', 'relax' or 'calm' can be used, spoken slowly and calmly, as in the following example:

> 'In a few moments' time you will hear me say the word . . . *relax* . . . and whenever you hear me say the word . . . *relax* . . . you will go so deeply relaxed . . . so comfortable and safely relaxed . . . that you will be able to go as deeply relaxed . . . as you are right now.'

This cue word will then be used to relax the patient whenever they give a negative IMR response. This would occur when asked in the script if they feel calm and in control when the phobic stimuli are presented to them and they do not feel in control. The cue word is introduced at this point by the practitioner to take the patient away from their negative response. When the patient shows signs of relaxing (i.e. breathing slowing down and becoming more regular, and skin pigmentation becoming more heightened), the same stimulus can then be re-presented.

HYPNOTIC SCRIPT: SCENE PRESENTATION

This part of the script involves first reminding the patient what is about to happen, namely that each of the stimuli scenes will be described to them, starting with the least anxiety-provoking scene, and that they will be asked to nod their head to indicate that they understand. The practitioner will then begin to describe, using the patient's descriptive modality and terms, the lowest stimulus in the hierarchy. The patient will then be asked to indicate using the finger IMRs whether they feel relaxed and comfortable (in which case they indicate 'yes') or not (in which case they indicate 'no'). The practitioner will note by observing changes to the patient's breathing patterns whether they are demonstrating signs of anxiety. If the patient indicates 'yes', the practitioner will do simple ego strengthening to reinforce the progress that has been made, and will then describe to the patient the next anxiety-evoking stimulus or scene. Again, the patient is asked to indicate by a head-nod when this scene is clear in their mind (rapid eye movement will often be observed at this point), and the IMR indicator of feelings is requested. If the response is positive, and the patient is calm and relaxed, this process will continue all the way up the hierarchy. However, if the patient gives a negative IMR, the practitioner will repeat the cue word, along with suggestions designed to reassure the patient:

> '*Relax* . . . go deeply relaxed . . . calm and relaxed . . . you are in control . . . and I want you to know that you are doing really well . . . really well . . . you can relax now . . .'

The silence of the practitioner can also be used along with occasional suggestions to indicate to the patient that they are fine and safe. This is done until the patient no longer shows signs of distress. Once the patient has relaxed and calmed down, the same scene that caused the negative response is re-presented. This time, with the benefit of additional relaxation suggestions, the patient should be better able to tolerate the stimulus. If they give a positive IMR, indicating that they are relaxed with this scene, the next highest anxiety-evoking scene on the hierarchy will be presented, and so on, until the hierarchy is complete.

HYPNOTIC SCRIPT: STRESS MANAGEMENT

When an individual suffers from the effects of a phobia, an associated symptom may be general anxiety, and this requires suggestions to be 'More able to manage stress . . . so that no matter what is going on around you . . . you will feel in control.' This is particularly relevant to patients who identify a clear link between times when they are under pressure or suffering from stress, and a worsening of their phobic responses. It is therefore relevant to incorporate these within the ego-strengthening suggestions that are delivered after hypno-desensitisation, thus reducing potential occurrences of the negative response in future.

HYPNOTIC SCRIPT: EGO STRENGTHENING

When patients feel that they cannot trust themselves to respond in the appropriate manner with regard to the phobic stimulus, even though on a conscious level they know how they would like to respond, self-doubt can set in. This can affect other areas of the patient's life, and they may start to suffer from a form of mental paralysis when it comes to making decisions. General ego strengthening, that links positive states from the past to potential states for the future, is important. For example:

> 'and . . . now that you have dealt with your spider phobia . . . you can feel as proud of yourself as you did when you passed your driving test . . . you are in control now . . . you are in control . . .'

Finally, suggestions which relate to the ability to change other aspects of the patient's life and to make decisions is important, as suffering from phobias can induce an associated mental paralysis that exists not only in the context of the problem, but also weakens the individual's ability to trust their judgement in other areas of life.

WHEN TO TERMINATE THE HYPNOSIS PART OF THE SESSION BEFORE COMPLETING THE HYPNO-DESENSITISATION

If the patient continues to show signs of distress in response to a particular scene on three or four consecutive occasions, and the relaxation has failed to elicit a 'yes' response that they are prepared to move on to the next stage of the hierarchy, the practitioner can then ask the patient for a head-nod to confirm that they would like to terminate the session:

> 'You can let me know . . . by nodding your head . . . if you would like to end the session at this point . . .'

The practitioner will then reassure the patient that they have made excellent progress in getting to the stage that they have reached, and will inform them that in the next session 'Not only will you be more *relaxed* [or whatever the cue word was] . . . but you will be able to move further than this time . . .'

Further suggestions can be made at this point that the benefit of the relaxation from the hypnosis part of the session will continue, and the patient will sleep well as a result of the session, and continue to process the appropriate response in their sleep.

When the patient is fully awakened, the practitioner will describe how far they have progressed up the hierarchy, and will continue the ego strengthening by congratulating them on reaching this stage. At this point, the practitioner will describe what is going to happen in the future sessions, explaining that they will start with the last stimulus that the patient found manageable, not the last one that they were unable to cope with.

IF THE PATIENT FAILS TO RESPOND

In a small number of cases, regardless of what the practitioner does to suggest creating a SMART goal, or how much relaxation is given or time spent on the case history, the patient remains negative about their potential to gain a remission from the symptom. This could be for one of a number of reasons:

➤ poor rapport between patient and practitioner
➤ failure to identify the appropriate strategy
➤ low patient self-esteem and poor coping strategies
➤ secondary gains from maintaining the problem
➤ lack of patient motivation to achieve the outcome.

The first two reasons have been discussed elsewhere, but the last component, namely motivation, is interesting in relation to phobias. The phobic response can be identified as being one that the patient does not want, but there may be secondary gains to maintaining the symptoms. Using a phobia of flying as an example, it might be that the patient can control the actions of their partner and family by being unable to get on a plane. If this is the case, it often relates back to the third point raised above, namely low patient self-esteem and poor coping strategies. If the patient fails to respond to suggestions when the practitioner is confident that a good rapport has been established, and an appropriate strategy has been identified, comprehensive ego-strengthening suggestions as a full session should be given before attempting to effect a remission from the symptoms. The patient is then taught self-hypnosis as a stress management tool, and informed that they should return to have another try with the hypnotherapy when they 'feel ready to take control.'

The phraseology is significant, as it emphasises that the patient is in control of the change. In relation to this point, maintaining the problem may have secondary gains for the patient. An example of this from my own practice is a woman who could not travel. She had developed a phobia about travelling on trains, buses, cars and planes. This had started 10 years previously, and had become progressively worse. This problem also prevented her husband from travelling – a situation which was an obvious strain on the marriage. Standard hypno-desensitisation did not work, and the patient displayed obvious signs of anxiety when in hypnosis. On discussing the situation with her, and her obvious desire to let go of the phobia, I decided to take a more analytical approach, as she wished to explore the origin of the problem. On doing so, it transpired that the phobia first appeared when she discovered that her husband was having an affair with another woman. From that point, the anxiety developed into a full-blown phobic response to travel – something which she knew that her husband enjoyed. By restricting her ability to travel, she was able to punish her husband for his affair. In hypnosis she abreacted, and in the post-hypnotic session I suggested that she needed to discuss the matter with her husband, which she did. On returning for a second session she was able (and willing) to enter hypnosis, and the hypno-desensitisation process effectively eliminated the phobic response. This was only possible because her need to maintain the problem had disappeared.

BEHAVIOUR MODIFICATION

Suggestions that are made after the hypnosis will relate to testing the patient's new responses. Patients often come for assistance when they have a specific reason for wanting to take control of the phobia. The practitioner can capitalise on this by asking the patient to focus on how they will feel once they have flown to Spain, or visited the cinema, or whatever specific event as described by the patient will tell them that when they do this thing they will know that they are better. If there is no specific future event that can be used to test out the responses, the practitioner can suggest that the patient deliberately puts him- or herself in the phobic situation. When the patient does this, they have made a conscious choice to be there, and will already feel more in control. It is important not to wait too long before testing new responses – usually within a three-week period, while the patient still has the new responses fresh in their mind – as they may start to doubt the effects of the hypnosis, and the benefits of the motivation and ego-strengthening section may start to fade. The patient would then begin to avoid the stimulus as before, so it is advisable to set a date to test out their new responses. The practitioner can suggest that the patient contacts them to let them know 'just how well they did.' This further builds on the ego-strengthening suggestions in hypnosis, compounding the post-hypnotic suggestions and adding further praise and support to focus the patient's attention on their ability to take control of change.

SUMMARY

The key element in this protocol is the breaking down of the phobia into its constituent parts – the stimuli and the responses. This is done first in the case history by having the patient deconstruct their responses. This adds language and therefore cortical activity (or left brain functionality) to the response as a way of redressing the balance, while the practitioner reframes these responses into ones which, as they have been learned, can be unlearned. The hypno-desensitisation part of this protocol includes relaxation suggestions to counter the physical responsiveness to stress, and presents the stimuli in a safe framework in which the patient retains control by the use of signals. Cue or trigger words are installed to relax the patient if they show signs of the phobic response when presented with the stimulus scene, and the scene presentation recommences when the patient signals a positive IMR to each stimulus. The hypnosis part of the session is terminated with stress management and ego-strengthening suggestions. This continues until the hierarchy has been completed, or until the patient fails to respond with a positive IMR when a scene is presented three or four times, in which case the session is terminated with ego-strengthening suggestions relating to the progress that has been made, and the next session will recommence with the presentation of the last stimulus scene that the patient found acceptable. The protocol is complete when the patient is able to respond to the scene that represented 100 on their SUDS scale with a positive IMR. Post-hypnosis suggestions will direct the patient to deliberately put themselves in the way of the phobic trigger, and monitor their new responses.

CHAPTER 11

Performance anxiety

The term 'performance anxiety' is used here to describe an inappropriate response to a future event, which in turn prevents the individual from being able to function effectively. The severity of performance anxiety varies dramatically, from a mild experience of the symptoms of fight or flight, to a complete avoidance and terror of a yet-to-be experienced event, alongside a total inability to function in that event. Any performance requires a certain amount of stimulation of the autonomic nervous system as well as a process of individual preparation (McMorris *et al.*, 2006). If an individual is too relaxed, they may fail to put in the effort necessary to be fully prepared for the event, and this can be a precursor to performance anxiety. Conversely, individuals who worry excessively can feel overwhelmed and produce inertia to act, which in turn prevents appropriate preparation. Either way, the net result is identical – an inability to function appropriately in the event.

The necessity for appropriate stimulation and preparation is a primary consideration when selecting a clinical hypnosis protocol that will stimulate the patient sufficiently, while reducing any inappropriate anxiety and still producing a sufficiently deep hypnotic state to decondition any inappropriate responses.

There are specific areas to be identified and considered when treating performance anxiety. These areas are presented in no particular order, as this information can be elicited at the appropriate time in the pre-induction talk. The patient may introduce the relevant information during the case history, or they may need to be prompted. In the latter case, the practitioner will only ask the questions that are relevant to creating the performance anxiety script. The rationale behind this is that performance anxiety is treated here as a stand-alone event which can occur in individuals who consider themselves to be mentally healthy and 'normal.' These types of individuals will come along for hypnotherapeutic assistance for strategic and practical purposes – rather than for 'therapy.' Asking questions that the patient may consider to be outside the framework of the specific objective will often irritate them, and can break the rapport between practitioner and patient, and confirm the patient's worst fears about clinical hypnosis – as something within which they will lose rather than gain control.

This chapter pinpoints the specific requirements of the protocol, as well as providing an overview of the areas that may need to be considered. If the performance anxiety is a symptom of another condition, the practitioner may need to work with the patient to evaluate the specific requirements of the principal condition by applying the SMART principles, and work towards that objective, rather than treating the associated symptom of performance anxiety. Failure to recognise this as a possibility can result in the patient maintaining the performance anxiety symptoms.

AN IMAGINED RESPONSE OR A REACTION TO A PAST EVENT

When giving the case history, the patient will be able to identify:

➤ whether their current response is one that relates to a specific past event or series of events, or
➤ whether their anxiety relates to the fear of the unknown.

When this has been identified, the practitioner can use this information to ensure that, in the former case, suggestions can be incorporated into the script for the patient to be suitably prepared this time, and in the latter case (fear of the unknown) the patient will have a more appropriate image of what will occur and will be able to pre-empt the fear with a more appropriate response. These suggestions are made in the post-therapeutic suggestion stage of the hypnosis session as part of the ego strengthening, rather than as a specific component of the protocol.

SYMPTOM MANIPULATION

As a certain amount of stimulation is necessary in any performance, there may be a requirement for the practitioner to make suggestions while leaving in place some of the reactions that the patient currently perceives as being symptoms of their condition. An example of this is the heart-pounding sensation, which some individuals perceive as an unpleasant symptom and a forerunner to full performance anxiety. The practitioner can make suggestions which remind the patient that the physical events of anxiety and excitement are identical, and that they are to start looking forward to experiencing the pounding of their heart as it now means that something pleasurable and exciting is about to occur. Another way of manipulating the symptom, other than through cognition, is for the physical awareness of the symptom to be reduced by asking the patient to start to monitor what is going on around them, rather than within them. In both instances, symptoms will be reframed as positive and welcome, rather than as negative and dreaded.

Symptom manipulation is a component of this hypnotherapeutic protocol, and suggestions that alter the individual's physical and psychological perception of the symptoms in a positive way will serve to reduce anxiety, and encourage the patient to experience a positive reaction to the anxiety-evoking event when they experience it in hypnosis. This in turn will act as a template for their response when they experience the event later *in vivo*.

PERFORMANCE ANXIETY AS A STRESS-RELATED CONDITION

Performance anxiety can often be a reaction to stress. If the patient has poor coping strategies, the condition may remain impervious to the therapeutic process. The practitioner can ask questions which relate to what is happening in the patient's life at present in order to ascertain whether there are any additional stressors that are exacerbating the performance anxiety, and can then decide whether there would be a benefit in teaching the patient self-hypnosis as a better way of managing their stress.

Additional methods of assisting patients who have difficulty coping with stress may involve reducing the response to stress by direct suggestion or behaviour modification suggestions, or by including some form of reframing of their stress response. An appropriate reframe is for the practitioner to talk of the patient's responses to stress in terms of hypersensitivity rather than a maladaptive mechanism. When the patient's responses are presented to them in this way, they can begin to consider the use of clinical hypnosis as a way of 'retraining' their system to respond appropriately, rather than viewing themselves as having a 'problem' or requiring 'therapy.'

ACTIVE IMAGINATION

An active imagination is also a component. The highly imaginative individual will play out the future scenario, creating the scene in great detail. If their mindset is a negative one, the outcome will be predicted as negative, and that is the template which the patient will work towards. This ability to visualise makes them an excellent candidate for a successful hypnotherapeutic outcome (Wilson and Barber, 1978). A hypnotic technique that allows the patient to visualise their objective with a positive outcome utilises a skill which the patient already has, but puts it to productive use. The practitioner would do well to emphasise that a good performer needs a good imagination, and that the hypnotherapeutic process will serve to sharpen the patient's abilities. Introducing self-hypnosis techniques, and anchoring for performance, also work well in this context, amplifying the positive states in self-hypnosis and reinforcing them with the use of anchors.

IDENTIFYING THE PROBLEM

When an individual presents with performance anxiety they will have a unique view of the problem in relation to their performance. For some people the performance anxiety becomes an avoidance technique created by low self-esteem, while at the other end of the scale there are individuals for whom the desire for a 'perfect' performance creates constant disappointment and therefore a self-fulfilling prophecy with regard to the anxiety-evoking event or events. If the patient considers these aspects of the condition to be relevant, the practitioner may ask what, specifically, the patient requires of the protocol – that is, whether they feel that it is necessary to deal with these aspects of their cognition in order to gain remission from the condition. If the patient wishes to explore these aspects and a SMART objective can be obtained, the practitioner will work with this. Often the performance anxiety will lessen as a result. The associated behaviour may still need to be addressed as a separate issue, as it may have become a habitual response.

In summary, identifying the problem involves identifying which aspect of the performance the patient perceives to be the problem, and recognising the significance of this aspect in relation to the whole performance. An example would be the athlete who can consistently run at a specific rate when in training, but fails to do so when placed under race conditions.

IDENTIFYING THE SYMPTOMS

When taking the case history, the practitioner will need to discover the specific symptoms and the order in which the patient experiences them – from the first identifiable reaction, through each additional response. These symptoms may be physical, mental or emotional, in varying combinations at different times during the performance. The patient will often find this initially quite difficult. As they start to do this, they are breaking down what had been a global reaction into a sequence of smaller and therefore potentially manageable responses, and it will become easier for them to describe their reactions. This sequence of events will be fed back in the order in which they have been presented while the patient is in hypnosis, with the additional overlay of the previously identified symptom reframe. It is also relevant to identify whether there is a point in the escalation when the patient feels that the symptoms become unmanageable. An additional suggested trigger for being in control can then be suggested to the patient. This control trigger can be linked to a past experience which the patient has identified as having been within their control.

An example of this process would be as follows:

> 'When you notice your heart starting to accelerate [first symptom] . . . so you can begin to feel excited [symptom reframe] . . . as excited as you were when you first experienced driving your car on the motorway [control trigger].'

This collection of suggestions should be made for the first trigger and for any subsequent triggers where the patient notices an escalation of the responses. There may also be a point at which the patient felt that they moved from feeling in control to feeling that they no longer had any control over their response. This stage is particularly significant, and suggestions should be concentrated in this area using the framework outlined above, as well as additional ego-strengthening suggestions which are designed to help the patient to maintain perspective. When observing the patient's body language while these suggestions are being made, the practitioner will be able to identify whether the suggestions are sufficient, or whether additional relaxation suggestions will also need to be made. This can be evaluated by observing any signs of discomfort or anxiety that are displayed by the patient.

IDENTIFYING THE EFFECTS OF THE CONDITION

As already mentioned, the performance anxiety may, in some instances, be a symptom of a broader condition – either stress, or the patient feeling out of control in another area of their life – and this has translated into performance anxiety. It is valid for the practitioner to ask whether the patient wishes to participate in this performance. If their motivation is low, for whatever reason, the objective of reducing the performance anxiety will also be a low priority. Motivation is a key factor in creating and perpetuating new patterns of thought, behaviour and emotions in clinical hypnosis. In addition, the patient may have specific secondary gains which they will identify in the case history. This happens when patients describe the reasons why, specifically, they have not already let go of this problem, or indeed, why they will find it difficult to change at this time. If this occurs, it is worth considering that the symptoms have some value for the patient which they are not prepared to discard, or for which they have not found a more appropriate replacement. For the patient to be appropriately motivated there will have to be an identifiable benefit to them to counterbalance any benefit which resulted from maintaining the symptoms. If this is the situation, the practitioner will need to incorporate further suggestions. The latter can take the form of a thought, feeling or behaviour which brings equivalent, or additional, benefit compared with any benefits that are to be discarded by the patient.

IDENTIFYING THE SPECIFIC TRIGGERS

When the patient discusses the problem they may identify specific external triggers, which will be in addition to the triggers created by the heightened awareness of their internal responses. These triggers may be sounds, or visual or physical triggers (for example, the sound of an audience, or the expression on another person's face, or the touch of their hand on the door handle as they prepare to enter a room). These triggers can then be incorporated into the script as cues for setting off a different response or sequence of responses:

> 'As soon as your hand grasps the door handle [external trigger] . . . you can notice your heart beating more quickly [internal response previously feared] . . . you will begin to feel excitement [reframe of internal response] . . .'

As you can see from the above example, it is more appropriate to retain the internal response and reframe it. This acknowledges the requirement for a certain amount of adrenal response in the performance, while moving the awareness from fear to pleasant anticipation of its occurrence.

IDENTIFYING THE OBJECTIVE

With performance anxiety, the objective can be made subject to SMART goals. The objective will also incorporate how the patient is going to feel once the objective has been achieved, and those feelings are incorporated into the ego-strengthening section:

'When you have passed your driving test [SMART goal] . . . you will feel so proud [feelings of achievement previously identified].'

USEFUL MODELS FOR EXPLAINING WHY HYPNOSIS IS EFFECTIVE WITH PERFORMANCE ANXIETY

As with all other conditions, it is key to the patient's motivation and compliance with therapeutic suggestions that the hypnotic procedure and the therapeutic suggestions are explained in a way that will encourage them to experience both fully. When explaining why and how the clinical hypnosis will influence performance, it is often valid to describe the natural responses to performance itself. This will enable the individual to understand how their reaction has developed. This is particularly useful for the analytical individual who requires some form of rationale to comprehend their responses. As with all of these types of descriptions for hypnosis and clinical hypnosis, they are designed specifically to fit into the mindset of the patient, enhance the positive expectations of the therapeutic process, or reduce or eliminate the patient's negative response to specific triggers.

Explaining the fight or flight response

A simple explanation of the fight or flight response (*see* Chapter 2 and Appendix II, 'Glossary of terms' for further information) is valid in the context of performance enhancement. Once it has been explained to the patient that their response is a natural one that has simply failed to complete, the emphasis on the problem shifts from being one that is out of their control, to one that needs to be completed rather than changed.

Conscious logic and unconscious behaviour

This is another adaptation of the model seen in smoking cessation and phobias. In the case of performance anxiety, the variation centres on the model of the system being appropriately prepared for the performance. In this context, the practitioner can explain that one of the main reasons why the patient has not been able to rid themselves of the performance anxiety before is that they have tried to use their conscious, logical thought processes. This part of the patient's mind already knows the appropriate response, but it is not the part of their mind that controls the response. It is the unconscious part of their mind – the part of their mind which contains memories of responding in the inappropriate way, and controls unconscious processes, such as breathing and heart rate, and habits – that needs to reconnect with the appropriate response. Hypnosis is described here as a process that allows the conscious mind to recognise the responses as appropriate (such as increased heart rate, etc.), whereas the unconscious part of the mind can take on board the suggestions, allowing the individual to be part of the event rather than predicting how they will respond.

Can you remember when you first had this inappropriate response?

If the patient can identify when they first had the inappropriate response, this information can be incorporated into the suggestions in two ways. First, suggestions can be used to revivify in hypnosis how the patient responded moments before they first experienced the negative response. Alternatively, suggestions can be made that in hypnosis the patient can regress to their natural response, and bring this into the present. The aim of this question is to establish that the patient is going to learn how to respond in a way which they already have in place, but have forgotten – rather than learn a new response. Patients whose performance anxiety is based on a real past event can usually recall the time of origin, whereas those for whom the performance anxiety is more of a fear of the unknown will often fail to do so.

POINTS FOR INCLUSION IN THE PERFORMANCE ANXIETY SCRIPT

The script incorporates the following:

➤ patient modality of relaxation
➤ cue or trigger words
➤ performance anchor
➤ de-sensitisation
➤ learning self-hypnosis
➤ ego strengthening.

In addition, there will be post-hypnosis suggestions for homework.

MODALITY OF RELAXATION

As performance anxiety is one of the conditions that is influenced by stress, individuals will often state that they are not doing anything to relax at the moment, or that they feel unable to relax. Identifying what they used to do, or would like the time to do, or even asking them to imagine how, if they had a day off from all this worry, they would choose to spend their time, will help to identify an appropriate modality for the induction. When a modality is selected that the patient already associates with a relaxation state, it will enhance their capacity to enter hypnosis.

It is often the case that with performance anxiety, people do not *want* to relax, as the concept may be incongruent with their therapeutic requirements (i.e. their performance state). If this is the case, the practitioner will agree on a word, such as 'focus', and this can be used in the induction and incorporated into any performance anchors.

CUE OR TRIGGER WORDS

As part of the deepening process, cue or trigger words need to be installed. These words are suggested as cues for the patient to experience deep, rapid relaxation, as well as positive states. Once installed, these words can be repeated during the post-hypnotic suggestions at times when the patient has identified increased awareness of their anxiety. These words are simple instructions, such as 'relax', 'calm' or 'now', and they can also be used by the patient in their self-hypnosis as reinforcement. The phrase 'as soon as' is also useful as a cue for the practitioner to be able to install appropriate responses within the context of the performance. For example:

> 'As soon as you walk into the room where you are to give the talk [external cue] . . . calm and relaxed [cue for positive state] . . .'

PERFORMANCE ANCHOR

When creating a positive future template for the performance, it is useful to use cues. In this instance, the cues need to be actions that the individual must undertake as part of the preparation phase of the performance. This could include turning the key in the ignition in a driving-test scenario, or putting on a specific item of clothing in the case of an actor who is about to go on stage. When this action is linked to a positive state, it will become a performance anchor. Suggestions are made that the patient will:

> '. . . feel . . . [required state – for example, confident] . . . as soon as you . . . [action – for example, first walk out on to the stage].'

Once these positive feelings are linked to the action, the patient can reinforce this in their mental rehearsal, or as part of any self-hypnosis that is undertaken.

DE-SENSITISATION

Individuals with performance anxiety can become overly sensitised to their environment and to any self-monitoring that occurs. As a result of this, they predict what they believe other people are thinking, and become increasingly self-critical. The de-sensitisation suggestions relate to creating a much more realistic perception of the event. De-sensitisation can be undertaken as part of the therapeutic suggestions:

> 'You will become so involved in what you are doing that you forget about yourself . . . and become fully involved in what you are doing.'

In this way the patient is encouraged to refrain from focusing on their environment, or on other people's thoughts and actions, or on the excessive self-monitoring that previously caused additional anxiety. This aspect of the performance enhancement protocol is particularly important to include for those individuals who can perform when there is no audience, or who feel that their performance is not being critically judged. In these situations, the de-sensitisation process can include suggestions that the patient will be able to have a positive experience of the event:

> 'You will be so focused on what you are doing . . . that you become unaware of your surroundings.'

LEARNING SELF-HYPNOSIS

For patients with performance anxiety, learning self-hypnosis fulfils a number of requirements. First, it allows them to mentally prepare for the event while in a relaxed and focused state. Secondly, it can be used as a stress management technique, and as a behavioural prescription whereby the patient can reinforce suggestions made during the clinical hypnosis session, and further supplement them with positive suggestions of their own.

Mental preparation or mental rehearsal

As part of this process, the patient will be asked to discuss the practical preparation that they have undertaken for the performance. If this includes actual or mental rehearsal of the event, the practitioner can ask whether the outcome of the event, when rehearsed, is a positive one. If this is the case, the patient will be encouraged to supplement this rehearsal while in hypnosis, where they can experience as many positive variations of the event as they wish. If the patient is aware that their rehearsal includes a negative outcome, the practitioner will, when teaching the patient self-hypnosis, make suggestions containing the SMART goal that has already been set, which will be reinforced at this point.

Stress management

General responses to stress, or coping mechanisms, can also be addressed as part of this process, particularly if the performance anxiety is symptomatic of a wider inability to manage stress appropriately. The self-hypnosis then becomes a method of relaxation, rather than one of auto-suggestions for change. The benefits of this will be experienced by the patient as improved sleep patterns and an increased perception of control as they start to create a habit of using the self-hypnosis as a method of relaxation.

EGO STRENGTHENING

Ego strengthening is an essential component of this protocol. Individuals who suffer from performance anxiety will often experience periods of generalised self-doubt. By reminding them of those things that they have already achieved, by the use of suggestions which recall past positive experiences, and by future orientating them to the time when they have experienced the success associated with a positive performance, the patient will be placed in a positive state. This then allows them to remain involved in what they are doing, rather than observing it, or predicting their possible performance. Non-specific ego strengthening is also appropriate, with suggestions that the patient can feel more confident and motivated generally.

OTHER ASPECTS FOR CONSIDERATION

As well as the specific requirements of the protocol, there are other areas of which note can be taken and suggestions incorporated as appropriate.

Has anything worked for the patient before?

If this is the case, suggestions that remind the patient of the effect can be included in the script.

Why is it important to deal with it now?

A significant current or future event often motivates individuals to seek help. It is rare for a person to present with performance anxiety where there is not a requirement for them to experience the trigger. An example would be in the case of public speaking, where the patient has been told that they have to give a speech at a wedding, or the patient with premature ejaculation who has embarked on a new relationship which is about to progress to a level of physical intimacy. Obviously, the fact that there is a future event on which to base additional anxiety creates its own stress, with the individual becoming increasingly disturbed. The result of this can be an escalation of the anxiety into other areas of the individual's life. When the practitioner asks questions in order to establish whether there is a specific future event imminent at which the patient feels they are going to be subject to performance anxiety, this can be included as part of the ego strengthening. Individuals can be future-oriented into an image in which they can experience the event in a positive manner. Feelings of achievement from beyond the successful completion can be incorporated into this image and used to further motivate the patient.

Dissociated states

Sometimes patients will discuss the event in a dissociated manner. They may talk of 'a part of them that feels anxious' or, when describing the event, speak of themselves in the third person, or as an observer rather than a participant. If this is the case, it may be appropriate to include a dissociation protocol before deconditioning the performance anxiety using the protocol described in this chapter. The objective of this would be to get the part of the individual that experiences the anxiety back under conscious control, before dealing with the symptoms of performance anxiety.

Alternatively, a simple dissociation/reintegration can be utilised as part of the awakening script, where the part of the individual that is experiencing the performance anxiety can be put to rest, and a positive, confident part brought into play:

> 'In a few moments' time . . . I will wake you . . . you will hear me count from one to ten . . . and by the count of eight your eyes will open . . . and by the count of ten you will be fully wide awake . . . all normal sensations will return to your limbs . . . every part of you will be back in the present . . . except the part of you that used to be anxious when you were in [performance situation] . . . that part of you can rest . . . remain in the past . . . and in the place of this part of you . . . a confident . . . relaxed part of you can wake . . . and . . . whenever you are in . . . [performance situation] . . . you will be confident and relaxed . . . so ready . . . one . . . two . . .'

POST-HYPNOSIS

After the hypnosis has been concluded, the patient will be encouraged to demonstrate their ability to do self-hypnosis. This will allow them to ask any questions and check that they are doing it correctly. Instructions are given by the practitioner as to how often the patient should do their self-hypnosis. Once during the day and again just before they go to sleep at night will be sufficient, but they should also be informed that it will be fine if they wish to do it more frequently.

The patient will be reminded by the practitioner of the instructions suggested in the hypnosis. This is done to reinforce the suggestions, and to remind the patient of any suggestions that they may not have heard. The concept of 'acting as if' can be introduced in the post-hypnosis session. This is where the patient is encouraged to try out their new behaviour as if they can already do it.

PARADOXICAL ADVERTISING

One of the simplest and most effective ways of reducing anxiety associated with a future event is to advertise that anxiety. If the patient has a fear that people might notice that they are anxious, suggestions can be made which give the patient the confidence to advertise that fear to those people whom they fear might notice. In doing so, the patient is taking control of one element of the performance. The more control that the patient can take in that event, the less stress they will experience, thereby directly reducing the effects of the anxiety.

SUMMARY

Using clinical hypnosis to reduce performance anxiety includes initially creating an appropriate model for understanding the patient's condition and the way in which this process can assist in making changes. Once this has been established, a hypnotic process that allows the patient to relax as part of the induction and deepening process is utilised to reduce stress and create a physical state which is in opposition to the anxiety state that was previously experienced as part of the performance. Then the emphasis in the hypnosis moves towards creating a focused, motivated and confident state in which cues direct suggestions for more appropriate thoughts and behaviour within the context of the performance itself. The patient will then have a template for the performance in which they experience a positive outcome of the event. This is reinforced by the use of self-hypnosis and, if appropriate, paradoxical advertising.

CHAPTER 12

Weight control

When creating a treatment plan for weight control, regardless of whether the protocol will focus primarily on the psychological issues or on behavioural patterns, the emphasis is placed on the matter of *control* for the patient. This is because, regardless of the origin of the weight problem (or indeed how it is now maintained), the patient will be aware that when they feel less in control generally, their tendency to over-eat will be exacerbated by the stress experienced. This is why I find it productive to adopt an 'outside-in' approach to taking the case history, where I will take time to discover the character of the individual outside of their relationship with the problem with which they present. This way the practitioner will more effectively establish rapport with the patient, rather than immediately focusing on their problem. By asking simple questions such as 'Tell me a little about yourself. Do you have a family? Any hobbies?' the practitioner will quickly gain a lifestyle picture that will uncover information about how sedentary or active the patient is currently, and can take note of how much emphasis is placed on food within this conversation. By eliciting information in this way, rather than asking direct questions along the lines of 'How much exercise do you take?' or 'What sort/amount of food do you eat?', the practitioner will be able to utilise that information to pinpoint more specific details later in the pre-induction session, when more direct questions can be asked in response to statements made by the patient. An example would be 'You mentioned that you work in an office. How do you get to work?' From this example, the practitioner can then create suggestions for increasing the amount of exercise within this context (for example, if the patient goes to work by public transport, they can get off one stop earlier and walk the rest of the way), or supplementary questions can be asked (for example, whether there is anywhere that they could take a walk during their lunch hour). By discovering the patient's current habits, suggestions can be incorporated into the hypnotherapeutic script that supplement them, rather than creating the necessity for dramatic change. Wherever possible, the changes to eating and exercise habits should be small and manageable, otherwise there will be a tendency for the patient to reject the changes if and when additional stress is experienced.

Finally, it is worth highlighting to you, the practitioner – and for you yourself to point out during the pre-induction talk – that you will not be telling the patient anything that they do not already know. Diet and exercise are the only ways to lose and maintain weight. However, you can emphasise that the essential points about using clinical hypnosis to make the necessary changes are as follows:

➤ Clinical hypnosis helps people to create an image of themselves as they wish to be, and helps them to work towards that image.
➤ By using clinical hypnosis, the suggestions will be taken on board at an unconscious level, so the patient will not be tempted (or able) to trick themselves into old habits.
➤ Using hypnosis for stress management will help to reduce the number of triggers for overeating.
➤ The suggestions will sink to a level at which the new behaviours will become unconscious, and therefore the patient will be able to maintain the changes.

ESSENTIAL ELEMENTS OF THE FIRST SESSION

It is very important to deliver an overview of the protocol to the patient during the first session, and even to include it in the post-hypnotic suggestions so that they can understand the whole concept of past, present and future within the treatment. Furthermore, some patients will only come for one or two sessions, so to ensure that the whole programme is initiated you can *pre-install* the process as part of the deepener. An example of how to script this is given below:

> 'You will become aware of your past, and any relevance that it has to your current state . . . you will begin to pay attention to your habits . . . and notice your behaviour as it changes . . . and you will begin to form an image in your unconscious mind . . . an image of how you will be when you have lost the weight . . . healthy and happy . . . completely in control . . . feeling positive and motivated . . .'

DEFINING THE PROBLEM

Simply put, the question is as follows. Does the inability to lose weight and maintain that weight loss stem from the patient's reaction to unresolved issues from the past, or is it a straightforward matter of behavioural change? In this context, it is not for the practitioner to decide what is or is not relevant to the patient's attitude towards their problem, but it is for them to elicit a framework of belief from the patient which they can then utilise to deconstruct the problem. I shall give two examples of patient statements and practitioner responses, one for each approach, from which you will be able to identify the mechanism underlying the construction of the protocol for each. I will then discuss dissociations in a similar context.

UNRESOLVED ISSUES

> *Patient*: 'My weight started to become a problem after my mother died 12 years ago. Since then I have not been able to get it under control. I have yo-yoed ever since.'

Practitioner: 'In this situation, it is appropriate to look at what was going on at that time, as it may be of relevance to your weight. Would you be happy to take this approach?'

Notice that in the practitioner's response to the patient's statement, the phrase 'may be of relevance' is used. In this way the practitioner is guiding the patient to an understanding that there may be something unresolved which needs to be addressed before the patient can make long-term changes, but does not lead the patient into a preconception that there is necessarily something to uncover.

It is critical when using any type of approach that looks at the past and, more importantly, the patient's relationship with the past, that the practitioner places emphasis on the *relevance* of the past to the problem that the patient is currently experiencing. The patient is encouraged by the practitioner to understand that regression is only used in this context in order to ensure that there is nothing from their past which is preventing them from moving forward, and that they will experience one of three events, any one of which will be constructive in moving them forward.

1 They may recall a specific event.
2 They may experience an emotion associated with a specific event, but not necessarily re-experience the event itself.
3 They may not be consciously aware of any event.

The use of a free-floating regression is the simplest way of achieving this. Here the key phrase within the script is as follows:

'You will go back in time to a time, real or imagined, which has relevance to the changes that you wish to make in the here and now . . .'

Use of this phrase ensures that the patient will select the destination themselves, and allows this to be more of an unconscious process. I emphasise this because often the patient will have a belief that their problem stems from a particular incident, and this may be an erroneous belief. There is an excellent story by Milton Erickson which illustrates this. It concerns a man who came for therapy because he had a recurrent problem in his personal relationships – the women who *said* they loved him would leave him. When this had happened three times, the patient decided that it was not just bad luck, and that his own behaviour must be playing a part. Being of an analytical nature, he had already decided that he must be re-running the same script that he ran with his first partner, and because he did not understand why she had left him, he was replicating the situation over and over again as a way of trying to understand. When Erickson discussed this analysis with him, he asked the patient 'Why, if you understand the origin, do you continue to replicate the pattern?' The patient did not have an answer to this. Erickson went on to suggest 'Perhaps your unconscious is aware of a different origin', and he then used a hypnotic regression which allowed the patient to seek and find a different origin. He described a memory of being a small baby, being left in pain in a hospital room by his mother (the woman who *said* that she loved him). When the patient was awakened, he told Erickson about the memory. He recalled this as the time when he was taken into hospital to have his tonsils removed. He was too young to understand what was happening to him, and his only impression of the event was 'Why is this woman who says she loves me leaving me alone and in pain?' Once the patient had given himself a rationalisation for his current problem, he was then open to making change.

I use this story to illustrate an important point. I will sometimes tell it (or a variation) to patients as a way of opening their minds to the idea that they may have the knowledge that they need to move forward, but it is stored unconsciously, and the hypnosis will help them to understand it. In this context it does not matter whether the event was 'true', in real terms. What is significant is how the patient feels about that event and how a greater understanding of it allows their feelings in relation to their current problems and their perception of them to change in the light of this insight. This runs counter to many hypno-analytic theories of the ways in which a person's history affects the present, and cannot be discussed at length here. I personally feel that the best and most effective way to use the patient's history is only to bring it into the therapeutic process if the patient feels that it has relevance to current events, and only if that knowledge will allow them to change their perception in a positive way. Otherwise it becomes simply another form of psychoanalysis, stretching out the therapeutic process and sometimes leaving the patient less resolved and able to cope with the present than they were before.

In summary, regression in the context of weight control should only be utilised if the patient feels that their past has a direct bearing on the condition and their current ability to make changes in their lives. If a regression is going to be used, this should be done in the first session. The patient can then focus their attention on their current behavioural patterns, and the future template.

THE PRESENT

> *Patient*: 'I have found that, since I started a new job, I have been eating more as there is nearly always a birthday or some other celebration and people bring in cake and biscuits. Also, since I broke my leg a couple of years ago I haven't really been doing as much exercise as I used to . . .'

> *Practitioner*: 'OK, you have given me the specifics about what you need to change – less cakes and biscuits, and more exercise. I shall concentrate on suggestions for these two, as you will be able to notice the changes more quickly, and it will then give you confidence to gradually do more.'

If patients have no interest in their past, and their discussion about themselves in the pre-induction talk focuses on the here and now, the emphasis for the practitioner is to gather as much information as possible about what things have changed since the patient first noticed that their weight was becoming a problem. These are the straightforward 'eat less, exercise more' patients, and with this group it is important to emphasise the specific way in which hypnotherapeutic suggestions will work for them when they have not been able to make these changes for themselves previously.

Patients who come for weight control will often say 'I know what I should be doing – it's just *doing* it that is the hard part.' The practitioner can then utilise this information and build on it to create the hypnotherapeutic model that will be most appropriate for that patient. In this instance, the practitioner suggests that it is precisely *because* the patient knows what to do that the hypnosis will be very effective for them, as it will take that knowledge from the conscious (aware) part of their mind where it is currently, and move it to the back of their mind (their unconscious), where it can become a habit, and therefore something that the patient no longer needs to think about – it becomes something that they just get on with. By building on the belief system of the patient, the practitioner then creates a role for the hypnosis which will allow the patient to feel that the only reason they could not do it for themselves before is that they didn't have the appropriate tool – and that tool is the state of hypnosis. Patients value statements by the practitioner which emphasise that the patient has not failed before, but they simply did not have the capacity to translate what they already knew consciously into unconscious behaviour for change. This is not a trick on the practitioner's part, but forms an essential part of the ego strengthening within the context of the pre-induction talk, which can then be fed back within the hypnosis session itself.

DISSOCIATION

Patient: 'There is a part of me that seems to just reach into the fridge and eat. It's as if something takes over and I have no control . . .'

Practitioner: 'What you have described is called a dissociation, and it is when some of your thoughts and feelings take over. That is why it feels as if you have no control, as you are actually feeding your emotions, not true hunger. What we need to do is to use the hypnosis to get this part of you back under conscious control, so you will never have a situation again where you are out of control in relation to your eating.'

I have found over the years that the more explanation you can offer to the patient for their current thoughts, feelings and behaviours, the more comfortable they will become about the process of change. When dealing with a dissociated part, the practitioner needs to be very aware of what form the dissociation takes, and what behaviour is carried out by the dissociated part. This is relevant when creating the treatment protocol.

As dissociation can be symptomatic of more serious eating problems, such as binge eating disorder or bulimia, the practitioner will need to go into much greater detail. The rationale for this is that if the practitioner goes ahead and treats the patient for straightforward weight control, that treatment will not be effective in the long term until the dissociated part is fully reintegrated. If a decision is made to treat the patient as presenting with an eating disorder, this must be fully discussed with the patient. There are occasions in therapeutic practice when the practitioner may have a different opinion to the patient about what is causing the problem, and how to treat it. It is essential within hypnotherapeutic practice that, if this is the case, the prescribing medical practitioner is involved in the decision-making process. If a patient has a binge eating disorder, or bulimia, it is rare for them not to have sought medical help before coming for hypnotherapy. I emphasise to those clinical hypnosis practitioners who are not medically trained, the importance of ensuring that the patient is appropriately diagnosed. I am aware that some non-medically trained therapy practitioners appear to have no qualms about treating eating disorders without the permission (if the patient is medicated) or the agreement of the general practitioner that there is no more appropriate course of treatment available for them within mainstream practice. I am also fully aware of the number of patients who self-refer for sessions precisely because they do not have faith in general medicine. However, there is a fine line which the non-medically trained clinical hypnosis practitioner must tread, and in order to maintain appropriate ethical practice, I feel that they must err on the side of caution and involve the patient's general practitioner if they are unsure whether their patient is a suitable candidate for treatment using hypnosis.

On the other hand, when the patient describes the 'part of me . . .' situation only within a specific context, they have undergone therapy before, and all the indications are that the patient has resolved the cause of the dissociation, but simply maintains the behaviour on a habitual level, the hypnotherapist can put the part to rest, or into the past, or to sleep. This is on the premise that the dissociated part is now operating habitually, rather than as an active signalling device denoting an underlying unresolved issue. The language of resolution is taken from the patient, by the practitioner asking 'What would you like to do with this part?' In effect, this stage of weight control treatment involves concluding a process (i.e. eliminating the unwanted behaviour), while allowing the therapeutic component (identification, negotiation, resolution, reintegration) to occur on an unconscious level in the three weeks after the session. By working in this manner, the practitioner is initiating a natural process that should have occurred once the therapeutic work previously undertaken by the patient was concluded. If this does *not* happen, the practitioner and the patient have a clear indication that the dissociation is a greater problem than that with which the patient initially presented, and the patient should visit their medical practitioner and obtain permission for the hypnotherapist to treat them, or recommend counselling or cognitive–behavioural therapy to work through the problem.

I believe that clinical hypnosis is an excellent and effective way of treating dissociations. I have made a distinction about how to proceed when treating a dissociated part only in the context of the patient who presents for weight control, but then discloses binge eating disorder, bulimia, or even anorexic tendencies. The emphasis here is to ensure the safety of the patient, and to avoid a situation in which a non-medically trained practitioner attempts to diagnose the condition itself. If the patient presents with an eating disorder that has been properly diagnosed, the practitioner immediately has a different relationship with the patient and can therefore work in a more dynamic manner. A discussion of eating disorders is beyond the scope of this chapter. In fact this is such a large subject that I could not do it justice in a single chapter – it would require a whole book!

THE PATIENT

The patient who presents for weight control will have a history of varying methods which they have tried before in an attempt to resolve the problem. Uncovering what they have used, both unsuccessfully and with success, will help to clarify the most effective suggestions to incorporate into the hypnotic scripts. Also, assessing the varying levels of motivation and expectation experienced by the patient in their previous attempts to lose weight is essential for helping to create suggestions to which the patient will relate. There is absolutely no point in creating suggestions that encourage the patient to go the gym regularly if this is something they have tried before and failed to keep up. Therefore the practitioner who makes note of the small changes that the patient was able to maintain will have a better chance of helping them to change their long-term behaviours and relationship with food and their body. An example would be the person who was unable to keep up their regular exercise classes, but enjoys walking the dog. By making suggestions that they increase the intensity and duration of their walks, something which the patient is more likely to keep up, added to other apparently small behavioural changes, the patient will see results. In addition, their confidence both in the treatment and in their capacity to make changes will increase. The suggestions for change will include having the patient focus on the things which are working, rather than on the things which are *not* working.

When utilising the patient's history of weight control within the suggestions, focus, motivation and confidence are of paramount importance. Finding areas of minor behavioural changes which can accumulate together to make a profound difference, and emphasising memories of confidence within this context, can often lead to a significant mental shift. Add to this a shift in focus towards what is actually producing weight loss, and motivation to continue to follow (and supplement) the suggestions will automatically follow.

ALCOHOL: EMPTY CALORIES

When taking the case history, it is valid to ask whether the patient drinks alcohol, and if so how much and when. The purpose of these questions is twofold – to uncover habitual consumption of empty calories, and to identify whether the patient is using alcohol to reduce stress. In either case, if the patient does drink alcohol frequently, a reduction in consumption or abstinence for a short period will both influence their metabolism and reduce the number of calories consumed. If I find that one of my patients is a habitual drinker – not necessarily of large amounts but, for example, they always have one or two glasses of wine with their evening meal (and nearer to a whole bottle at weekends), I will recommend a three-week fast from alcohol. This suggestion produces interesting responses. By informing the patient that this is the only change they need to make initially, many of them will value the opportunity, recalling the fact that when they have abstained from alcohol in the past they have felt more positive and motivated, and slept better. Others will find excuses for not abstaining, such as an upcoming celebration, or will identify the present time as being particularly stressful, so they do not feel that they could fast from alcohol for the required period. The polarisation of responses between people will give the practitioner a clear indication of the ways in which the patient is using alcohol. If their use is purely habitual, the patient will be willing to make the change and will identify the benefit. However, if the patient finds excuses for not doing this, the practitioner can point this out to them, having identified the need for a more appropriate stress management technique, rather than drinking (known as one of the 'false friends' of stress, along with drugs and cigarettes – the solutions which can be more harmful than the problem). It is appropriate to teach self-hypnosis to the latter group as a more appropriate tool for stress management. In this situation the practitioner will find that the patients who dispute the necessity for or value of stopping drinking for a short period (or indeed their capability of doing so) may be using it to mask an underlying problem that needs to be addressed before their weight can be brought back under control, or they may have a drinking problem. As I can only recommend the changes that the patient can make, I will however point out to them that if they find themselves incapable of stopping drinking for three weeks, they may wish to return to their medical practitioner for them to assess whether there is an alcohol dependency problem. Using this approach, I find that the patients who are able to stop become considerably more motivated, probably to prove to themselves that they do *not* have a drink problem, and that those who cannot do this will either fail to book a further session, or, if they do, will have recognised that there is an underlying problem masked by drinking which they would prefer to work on. This is a win-win scenario that protects both the patient and the practitioner, and allows those patients for whom future weight control sessions at this stage would be less than productive to deselect themselves from the therapeutic process at this time. I can recall scenarios where patients returned to me after one or two years having recognised that the treatment which they had with me became a catalyst for life changes, as they might not have been prepared to acknowledge an underlying problem or alcohol dependency at the time of the sessions, but the awareness registered with them sufficiently for changes to begin to occur.

INCREASING THE OUTPUT FOR THE FIRST THREE WEEKS AFTER THE SESSION

Post-hypnotic suggestions to increase the amount of exercise for *three weeks only* are very effective for patients who want to achieve weight control. Putting the changes into the context of increasing the metabolic rate, too, so that future calories will be consumed more effectively, together with the finite nature (three weeks) of the increased effort, always works well. Conversely, if the practitioner was to talk about increasing the output but did not give the patient a rationale for doing so, or they failed to put a time limit on it, the patient would rapidly revert to their old ways of thinking and behaving. Furthermore, when the patient returns for future sessions, and is enthusiastic about the benefits that they have observed, they are much more inclined to keep it up for a further three weeks. By this time, the new behaviours will have started to become habitual, and the patient is far more likely to continue with them.

HABITS AND CONDITIONED RESPONSES

For patients who identify situations in which they eat or drink habitually (i.e. without thinking), post-hypnotic suggestions to be more aware of what they are doing, or even introducing a pattern-breaking device linked to the situation, are very effective. For example:

> 'Whenever you are at your desk and you notice it is 11 o'clock [the time at which, in the past, they would have had a cup of coffee and a muffin], instantly and imme-diately a red stop-light will come into your mind, and the only thing that will come to your lips is a smile as you realise that *you are in control* . . .'

EMOTIONS AND MOODS

Post-hypnotic suggestions for patients who eat in response to false hunger will centre around controlling the mood or the emotion in a more general manner, rather than focusing on the situation in which they have previously experienced the inappropriate eating triggers. Suggestions such as the following can be produced:

> 'You will notice, as you listen to the CD each day, that you feel much more calm, confident and in control generally. You will start to notice how much more positive you are, and that things from the past no longer bother you in the same way.'

OBJECTIVES AND MOTIVATION LEVELS

In the case history, the patient's objective is assessed against SMART criteria, to ensure that it is appropriate. This will allow a more clearly defined template for future success, which will ensure that the patient knows when they have been successful in the change (i.e. when they have achieved their specific objective).

Motivation to achieve this may need to be installed as a post-hypnotic suggestion or, if the patient is already highly motivated, suggestions that they focus on the benefits of change as they are occurring will be of value. For example:

> 'You will start to notice as you lose weight just how much more confident and motivated you feel as a result.'

NOT JUST ABOUT LOSING WEIGHT, BUT MAINTAINING CONTROL

In my self-help book *You Can Think Yourself Thin* (Century: 2008), I emphasise that there are two distinct components of weight control – losing the initial weight, and then maintaining that weight loss. Just like the smoker who stops and then starts again, the yo-yo dieter will have different needs to those of someone who has never been in this situation before. In such cases, the practitioner needs to emphasise to the patient that successful maintenance of weight loss may require a separate session. This can take place up to three months after the completion of the hypnotherapeutic protocol for weight loss. If this approach is used, the patient is secure in the knowledge that if they do start to revert to inappropriate patterns or habits, they can come back for hypnotherapy treatment *without fear of failure*. This is important, as some patients will not return to complete the process properly if they feel that they have failed in some way, and as a result their confidence in the treatment will be lessened. By emphasising that weight loss and weight maintenance may need to be treated as different problems, this situation is avoided.

FUTURE TEMPLATE

From the case history, the practitioner will uncover a future template, based preferably on a time in the past when the patient was fit and healthy (although not necessarily at their most slim). This is then projected into the future as a template for the patient to work towards. This is introduced into the pre-installation in the first session, and fully installed in the final session.

THE OPTIMUM NUMBER OF SESSIONS

In this chapter I have mentioned allowing at least three weeks between sessions. This is in recognition of the psycho-cybernetics theory discussed in Chapter 8. With time to see the benefits of each session in the intervening weeks, weight-control patients become more focused, motivated and confident in their capacity to maintain long-term changes. I would therefore recommend an optimum of three weeks between sessions to achieve this.

The optimum number of sessions that are required for the patient to achieve sufficient focus, motivation and confidence to lose weight is between one and three, the precise number being dictated by the patient. As the issue of *control* is relevant to weight control, I allow the patient to dictate the number of sessions that they can have, giving an upper limit of three sessions for dealing with a specific issue. This means that patients who have undergone therapeutic processes before, or who are particularly self-aware in terms of what and how they need to change in order to lose weight and maintain that weight loss, can book the first session without the attendant concerns of having to undergo further treatments. Some patients will therefore only require one session of hypnotherapy to get them on track for losing weight. After the first session, a standard weight-control CD should be given to the patient to listen to daily (preferably just before they go to sleep), containing direct suggestions to eat more moderately and healthily, and to include exercise in their daily habits. Additional suggestions for dealing with stress more effectively can also be included. As the suggestions in any recording will be generic, it is valuable to include a section that explains to the patient how to select those suggestions which are appropriate for them. For example:

> 'You will hear and remember everything that is of importance to you . . . and you will only take on board the suggestions that will work for you . . . and . . . as you listen to the track again and again . . . your unconscious mind will start to tailor the suggestions to you . . . you will personalise them . . . so you will feel more comfortable carrying them out . . . as the suggestions are starting to come from you . . .'

During the feedback element at the end of the first session, the patient is instructed to make a note to contact the practitioner (by telephone or email) after three weeks (i.e. when they have listened to the CD for 21 nights consecutively). This will ensure that the patient has had sufficient time to identify all of the benefits of the sessions, and to notice areas where more work is required. The practitioner then books them in for the second session. Working in this way allows the patient to drive the sessions – remember that this is weight *control*, where the emphasis is on the patient taking and maintaining control of the process. Again, three weeks are allowed to elapse while the patient listens to the CD, and they will then contact the practitioner again to book the final session. Some patients will only need one or two sessions, while others will need three or even four if they require a weight maintenance session.

If the first session consisted of a regression, the second session can focus on the present, and on the behavioural, cognitive and emotional changes that are required. The final session then consists of installing the future template and focusing on long-term changes. If any component is not used (for example, if a regression is not required), the order of progress remains the same. Any further sessions that are required by the patient for weight maintenance can take place at any point from three months in the future. This allows the patient to consolidate all of the changes that took place in the weight loss sessions, and to clearly identify what still needs to be done to maintain their weight appropriately.

You will find many other approaches to the treatment of weight loss, some of which include aversion, while others involve analysis. I have tried any number of them over the years, and this protocol is a distillation of my knowledge of what works in practice. It takes confidence in yourself, the process, and your patients to practise this way, but it is very rewarding.

CHAPTER 13

Obstetrics

The use of clinical hypnosis in obstetrics is attracting more medical research – for example, for use within fertility treatment (Levitas *et al.*, 2006) and as an adjunct to childbirth with hypnobirthing (Wainer, 2000; Phillips-Moore, 2005). This chapter provides an overview of the principal areas within obstetrics where clinical hypnosis can be used practically, taking into consideration time constraints and the specific requirements of the patient and any medical procedures that they may need to undergo.

As this is such a specialist area, I feel that the practitioner who intends to use clinical hypnosis within this field should have additional exposure to training and knowledge of obstetrics itself, specifically to ensure that any work which they do with the patient fits into the medical model, and does not potentially interfere with other treatments that the patient is undergoing (e.g. IVF). I believe that, within this field, clinical hypnosis can be utilised as a truly complementary therapy, supplementing procedures and supporting the individual as they undergo treatment. It is for this reason that myself and Denise Tiran of Expectancy set up a module in clinical hypnosis within midwifery, which is a stand-alone module for obstetric specialists and for clinical hypnotherapists with a particular interest in specialising in this field. The module is the first in this field in the UK to be accepted as part of a BSc university degree in midwifery. The reason I have mentioned this training, and the level of the qualification, is to emphasise that this is an area of clinical hypnosis which needs to be more closely monitored and regulated, precisely because the practitioner is dealing with potentially vulnerable women, who in some cases have a 'try anything' approach to giving birth to a healthy child – and there are, regrettably, some clinical hypnosis practitioners who are prepared to treat these women without a thorough knowledge of what it is they are working with.

In this chapter I shall address the following key areas:

➤ fertility
➤ pregnancy
➤ childbirth
➤ post-birth mental health of the new mother
➤ the new father.

Clinical hypnosis can be effectively utilised at any stage of pregnancy, even during the first trimester. For example, one study (Marc *et al.*, 2008) found that women who were given hypnosis treatment required less sedation during termination of first-trimester pregnancy. The emphasis of the clinical hypnosis treatments at all stages, from treatment for fertility to post-birth mental health of the new mother, is based on the following:

➤ The mental health problems associated with motherhood, and/or stress as a result of attempting to conceive, reduce the likelihood of conception.
➤ The more relaxed a woman feels, the less likely she is to experience pain or problems during birth.
➤ The more control a woman can take of the labour and birth, the less external intervention is required, which is better for both baby and mother.
➤ It is better to identify and deal with any issues relating to parenthood before the birth of the child.

FERTILITY

One point which is well worth mentioning here is that patients rarely present for fertility treatment with clinical hypnosis as a first port of call. More commonly the patient has tried 'everything' to get pregnant, and comes to the process as a 'last ditch attempt.' Obviously, the most significant issue here will be one of stress associated with the patient's belief that this is their 'last chance for a baby before they give up.' This is best addressed first before investigating any other problems that may need to be dealt with. It is essential to recognise that stress alone, without any other underlying problems, can change the internal environment of a woman sufficiently to make it hostile to conception. As the human form has not changed dramatically since the time of our cavemen ancestors, it is fair to assume that the inability to conceive at times of stress (lack of food, harsh weather conditions, etc.) would be an appropriate survival mechanism. I explain this to women who come to me for help with conception. This account of the patient's physical responses offers her an explanation of *why* she has not been able to conceive before. This is particularly helpful because the patient may have started to perceive herself as a failure. Giving an explanation that relieves the patient of immediate responsibility for her inability to conceive will immediately reduce her stress responses, as the problem is no longer viewed as something for which she is at fault. Starting from this premise will allow a more open and appropriate discussion between the patient and the practitioner about how best to proceed. Once a full case history and discussion about objectives have taken place, it is not uncommon for a picture to emerge from the patient that is considerably broader than the initial objective of improving fertility. It serves to remind both the practitioner and the patient that the treatment is for an individual, not for a problem, and is therefore holistic in nature.

CASE HISTORY

Over and above the usual relevant information about the patient that would be obtained in any session, the practitioner will need to take case-specific information.

Not all of this may be relevant to the patient, so the practitioner will need to be selective. Points to cover include the following:

Obstetric history

This will include asking whether the patient has had any children, stillbirths, miscarriages or abortions. This section of the pre-induction session needs to be dealt with sensitively and sympathetically, giving the patient time to talk and, if necessary, to display emotion. It may be appropriate to refer the patient for counselling if it becomes evident that she wishes to talk about this in depth. In terms of evaluating whether to use a clinical hypnosis protocol to do this before proceeding to work directly on the patient's fitness for fertility, I would talk to her and give her the options. If she feels that she would rather work with me on this, using clinical hypnosis as the vehicle, then this is precisely what I would do. Referral on to a counsellor would take place within the context of the treatment, giving the patient the option of coming back for clinical hypnosis when (and if) they feel that they have moved on sufficiently to work specifically on their fertility.

Sexual history

A medical history in relation to fertility is taken. If the patient has had sexual problems (for example, vaginismus), or has experienced trauma or violence in her sexual history, working with these issues may be the key to unlocking her fertility. I would only work with the patient's sexual history if she feels that it has relevance to the issue of fertility, otherwise it can become a somewhat redundant exercise which, in some instances, can reinforce the current pattern of infertility, rather than free the individual to move forward.

Relationship history

Helping the patient to discuss the history of her present relationship, and the current stability of this relationship, can prove very important when selecting the most appropriate treatment base. If the relationship is unstable, and the patient acknowledges that she feels that having a child will improve it, future pacing to a time when a baby has been born, but the dynamics of the relationship itself have not changed, can allow the patient to acknowledge that the relationship needs to change first. In some cases the patient will identify from this process that their partner is not the person whom they wish to be the father of their child, something which they have not consciously recognised until this point in time. It is then for the patient to decide whether their objectives for therapy have changed and, if so, what it is they really need to work on.

Outside the context of the current relationship, it may be appropriate to do some therapeutic work on relationship patterns. If, for example, the patient identifies that they consistently choose a particular 'type' of man, and the relationships themselves follow a regular (and inappropriate) pattern, such as verbal abuse or subjugation, I would help the patient to gain confidence and assertiveness skills *before* progressing to work on the fertility issues. If this is to be done, it is always through discussion with the patient, so that she is clear about what you are aiming to achieve, and why you are taking this particular route. If the patient does not want to go down this road, I will always ask 'What, specifically, do you want to achieve from these sessions?' If the response remains 'To get pregnant, nothing else matters . . .', I will work only on this, but will include within the general ego-strengthening suggestions for the patient to be more confident and assertive generally. I often find that when good rapport and a high level of trust have been established, the patient will generally acknowledge the appropriateness of the suggestions, even if they are not immediately consistent with their current view of the world. If the patient understands the underlying logic and potential benefits of your suggestions, they will take them on board regardless of their initial reactions.

Personal history

When taking the personal history, it is appropriate for the practitioner to ask questions about the changes that the patient envisages will occur once they have become pregnant. In relation to this, issues of weight control and body image, career path and sexuality may arise. If this is the case, they should be discussed in depth, and any issues which the patient believes to be potential stumbling blocks can be addressed within the hypnotherapy. Parts Therapy, particularly where the patient is asked to imagine or describe the part of them that fears change (this can be given a name – for example, the part of them that is concerned that they will fall behind in their career, or the part of them that is afraid to put on weight), and a negotiation can take place between the patient's conscious awareness and objectives, and their unconscious fears and concerns. This is a very effective process, as it will usually result in the patient gaining insight into destructive behaviours that they are currently exhibiting. This then leads to the development of new attitudes towards the self and, in some instances, for the patient to question whether they in fact want to get pregnant at this time.

IVF

If a woman is about to undergo IVF treatment, the most effective work will be done in relation to relaxation, and by teaching the patient self-hypnosis. Issues relating to anxiety and the projection of failure may need to be addressed in the form of a visualisation, with the patient *feeling* the process taking place. In this context, it is safe to assume that the state of mind of a woman at this stage will be one of anxiety, and a desperate need for the process to work. As we all know, the more desperate one becomes, the more anxiety levels increase, and the less receptive the body becomes to anything that could be perceived as an additional stressor. Pregnancy can fall into the latter category, and regardless of how much the patient *wants* a baby, her body may perceive different needs at play. This is why the main emphasis when using clinical hypnosis in an IVF context is relaxation and positive future visualisation. In some instances, the future visualisation can only be done when the patient has dealt with other issues relating to becoming pregnant so it is always relevant to remind the patient that you are treating them therapeutically as an individual, not just as someone who wants to get pregnant. A good case history is crucial.

PREGNANCY

The following are the main areas that can be positively influenced by clinical hypnosis during pregnancy:

➤ improving the quality of sleep
➤ communication with the unborn child
➤ relaxation
➤ preparation for labour
➤ preparation for motherhood
➤ generalised anxiety
➤ hyperemesis gravidarum
➤ dealing with unresolved issues relating to pregnancy, birth and motherhood.

When using clinical hypnosis to treat a pregnant woman, it is advisable to use permissive techniques only. Also, regardless of the patient's primary modality, the inclusion of kinaesthetic suggestions is useful for leading them to become more aware of their body, especially a relaxed body. The more connection the woman develops with herself, the more control she will be able to exercise in terms of the changes that occur during the whole event of pregnancy, birth and motherhood.

Relaxation

Teaching self-hypnosis to a pregnant woman is one of the most useful tools that a clinical hypnosis practitioner can employ (Reid, 2002). Once this has been done, the patient herself can be taught to introduce the types of suggestions that will be most useful to her, whether these involve communicating with her child, further relaxation, reducing anxiety, or preparation for birth and motherhood. Giving the patient as much control as possible in this instance is critical. Making the hypnosis sessions educative rather than primarily therapeutic in nature will allow the patient to maximise her chances of using it successfully for pain relief during labour itself.

Obviously, when there are specific problems, such as prolonged nausea (Simon and Schwartz, 1999), these will be treated in session. Suggestions for warmth, distraction or dissociation can be used.

CHILDBIRTH

Once again, relaxation techniques are essential. From the commencement of the third trimester, techniques that are specifically designed to be used for the labour and birth can be taught. These include:

➤ self-hypnosis
➤ anchors
➤ dissociation techniques
➤ distraction techniques
➤ communication with the child
➤ pain control (analgesia).

Self-hypnosis

The teaching of self-hypnosis for use during labour has a number of functions. It gives the patient a level of control over the experience that they would not otherwise have, it creates a state in which they can dissociate, distract themselves, or access positive anchors, and it also gives them a way of resting and paying useful attention to the signals from their body. All in all it is the most effective and powerful technique, and, when one considers that there is nothing else provided by mainstream medicine, it is all the more worthwhile.

Anchors

Anchors for confidence, relaxation, distraction, pain control or dissociation can be taught to the patient for use both during and out of self-hypnosis. These anchors are taught in the clinical hypnosis session, and are to be reinforced by the patient as they practise. The more they practise, the stronger the effects of the anchors. The easiest type is the technique in which the patient forms a circle with their thumb and first finger, with the finger and thumb tip touching to create the circle. This shape is to be defined in the clinical hypnosis session, re-created during self hypnosis (and at any other time when the patient has access to the positive feelings required), and fired off (i.e. utilised) during labour. It is more effective to have just one anchor, as having several can become confusing. It is for the practitioner to install the anchor which the patient feels will be most useful for them.

Dissociation techniques

During hypnosis sessions in the third trimester, when the patient is directed to turn her thoughts towards the birth, dissociation techniques can be taught which allow the patient to step out of her body if she is experiencing pain or discomfort. This can involve suggestions to take herself for a walk outside of the room, to float herself out of her body, or to remove herself to a specific location by use of a memory (for example, taking herself back to a time when she was relaxing on a beach holiday). Dissociations can also involve moving through time, perhaps forward to when the patient is holding her newborn child. This both focuses attention and allows her to dissociate from her immediate pain experience.

Distraction techniques

Suggestions of any kind that involve changing the emotional state and/or relaxation of muscles are very effective. I find that humour works well in this context, and will often tell the patient the story of 'Birth in the Borneo Longhouse.' This story involves telling the patient what it would be like to give birth there, with all their family around them watching. The only person not present in the room is the prospective father, who is on the roof with a string tied to his genitals. The other end of the string is in the hand of the woman giving birth. Every time she has a contraction, she pulls on the string. Thus the father shares in her experience. This always produces a laugh from my patient. When laughter occurs, the muscles relax, and endorphins are pumped into the system. I remind the patient to think about the story when she is giving birth herself. I have known women who, during labour, pull on an invisible string (a self-created anchor), much to the bemusement of the husband in attendance!

Communication with child

Hypnosis sessions and self-hypnosis are an ideal time for the mother to communicate with her unborn child. She may visualise this in any way that she wishes, and use this time to bond with and also prepare the child for the birth experience, asking her baby to respond appropriately.

Pain control

Research has shown that using hypnotic techniques for labour improves obstetric outcomes, including postnatal depression, a reduction in the length of time spent in the first stage of labour, and a reduction in chemical anaesthesia (Harmon *et al.*, 1990). In France, hypnotic techniques have long been taught to pregnant women for use during labour. It is known there as 'Sophology', and is both well received and accepted within mainstream medicine. Pain control that is introduced into post-hypnotic suggestions includes future orientation to the time when the pain is over, and the 'riding the wave' technique, which involves having the patient go with the pain rather than tensing and fighting against it. Glove anaesthesia can also be taught, effectively allowing the patient to move the pain relief to wherever they need it.

Breech birth

Hypnosis has been effectively demonstrated to be useful for patients who are experiencing breech birth (Mehl, 1994). In this situation it involves the introduction of general suggestions for relaxation, with specific suggestions to reduce stress and anxiety. The baby can be asked questions about why they are presenting this way, allowing the patient to 'negotiate' with the baby and move them to an appropriate presentation.

POST-BIRTH MENTAL HEALTH OF THE NEW MOTHER

Research has demonstrated that the incidence, severity and duration of postnatal depression can be positively influenced by the use of mind–body techniques (MBTs) (Harmon *et al.*, 1990; Mantle, 2002). There is also anecdotal evidence to show that when a woman learns and uses self-hypnosis throughout her pregnancy, the child will be more relaxed not only during the birth, but also once they are born, and will sleep better and generally be a more contented baby. I have seen instances myself where new mothers 'count down' their babies into sleep using the hypnosis induction of 10 to 1 which I have taught them as a relaxation technique during their pregnancy.

When a new mother presents with postnatal depression, it is obviously important to ensure that the GP who diagnosed the condition and then prescribed medication to alleviate the symptoms is informed, and that permission to treat the patient is obtained, if clinical hypnosis is to be used. This ensures that the self-diagnosed get a correct diagnosis, and that any medication prescribed will not interfere with the treatment. The key effects of hypnotherapeutic treatments in patients with postnatal depression are as follows:

➤ alleviation of feelings of depression
➤ a reduction in tiredness by enhancing quality of sleep, and ability to rapidly return to sleep after waking
➤ a reduction in hypersensitivity to perceived criticism
➤ the development of assertiveness skills
➤ a reduction in feelings of inadequacy and/or inability to cope (particularly for the first-time mother)
➤ enhancing the sense of self both as a mother and as an individual
➤ improving the bond between mother and child.

Techniques that are especially effective include the following:

➤ *NLP anchoring* for reducing stress and enabling the patient to cope more effectively in an immediate situation
➤ *visualisation* of coping effectively
➤ a *dissociation* may be useful for those patients who talk about 'a part of me that cannot cope'
➤ *assertiveness techniques*, to enable the patient to feel more positive and able to ask questions and take control
➤ *relaxation techniques*, including learning self-hypnosis to get to sleep and as a way of letting go of anxiety
➤ *future pacing to a time when the patient can cope* – often the patient will describe feeling trapped in the present, and unable to imagine a time when they can cope. By moving the patient forward to a time when they are able to cope, and asking them to describe the scene in detail, this can be translated into a hypnotic script that will encourage them to create an image of how it *will* be when they can manage better. This works as a template which the mind will work on and strengthen during sleep, and the patient will start to work towards unconsciously.
➤ *inner child techniques* – this is especially significant for the new mother who does not have a positive parenting template and therefore has a fear of replicating the inappropriate behaviours and feelings of her own mother. By re-parenting her own inner child, the adult is able to create her own template for motherhood, which is positive and helpful.

WORKING WITH MEN

Up to this point, I have only discussed the therapeutic requirements of women. The needs of the male partner can often be overlooked, and although this is a substantial topic in itself, it is worth including an overview in this chapter. The male partner will most often present for hypnotherapy when he sees the benefits that his partner is gaining from her sessions, and he can be encouraged to visit to reduce stress. Any implication that he may have a problem is most strenuously avoided, as this can only add to the stress of the presenting situation. When I work with men in this context, I ensure that the case history taken is a 'clean' one (i.e. not focusing on the relationship or fertility issue which may be suggested to me by the female partner, whom I will already have seen). Ensuring that this is done will allow the most effective form of therapeutic treatment, and will also help the male partner to feel more secure about the confidentiality of your approach. No information that is obtained from either partner should be allowed to leak through into the other's sessions. If I feel that there may be a danger of this happening, I refer the male patient on to another practitioner (usually male). When working with the male partner of a woman who is experiencing difficulties with fertility, pregnancy or motherhood, one must always ensure that if the male partner is treated, they are treated as an individual first, and not as a component of the woman's treatment or problem. By referring them on to a male practitioner, the rapport that is obtained will be different and often more effective in ensuring a positive therapeutic outcome for both partners. Obviously, I would evaluate this on a case-by-case basis, and allow the patient to drive the decision, rather than making it for them. If I decide to refer them on, I give my reasons for doing so to the patient, so that they know I have their best interests in mind when doing so.

When treating men in this context, it is important to be aware of the following issues.

Relationships and conception

The stability and nature of the relationship between the potential parents may become an issue in conception, and it is valid to consider this for treatment if the relationship is not particularly happy. In this instance, one of the partners may be using parenthood as 'relationship glue' or as the next logical step in a relationship that is failing due to boredom. If the male partner recognises (whether they are consciously aware of this or not) that the relationship itself is not secure, and therefore that having a child will simply hasten the end of the relationship, arguments and the withdrawal of sex can occur. This information will most often emerge while taking the case history with the woman, and the therapist will then encourage her to talk to her partner about this, and, if the partner is willing, to make them aware that a session with the clinical hypnosis practitioner may be helpful in resolving the relationship issues, or at least in opening up a dialogue between the two parties. If the male partner is unwilling to participate in therapy, the therapist will need to work with the woman and explore how she feels about the relationship, and whether she is with the right partner or this is the appropriate time to be thinking about having a child.

Sexual issues

Attitudes of the male partner relating to sex once his partner has given birth may be an issue, and one which is unconsciously preventing him from performing.

Performance issues may occur when the couple undergo IVF or other artificial means of impregnation. For example, the discovery of a low sperm count can undermine the male partner's sense of masculinity, which in turn can affect performance. If the male partner presents for therapy, it will most often be in the context of 'stress.' Any practitioner who is undertaking therapy with an individual in these circumstances must be careful to treat the patient, and, instead of focusing on the problem that they are experiencing, to take time to build up the individual and their resources and confidence before approaching their interaction with the problem or the problem itself.

Fatherhood

A poor template for fatherhood can create fear and anxiety in the prospective father, who may express concerns that they will not be a 'good' father, and even that they may fear turning into their own father. This is particularly distressing if the father in question had alcohol- or violence-related problems, which the patient is concerned about manifesting himself.

Much of the hypnotherapeutic work here will focus on confidence, creating a positive template for fatherhood, and allowing the patient to come to terms with any of his own concerns about his relationship with his father. Relaxation techniques are also important, to help the patient to deal with the stress of change that will occur with the birth of a child.

PARENTHOOD

One final point should be made in relation to parenthood. In general, socio-economic changes will occur as a result of becoming a parent. The family unit may be transformed from two wage-earning adults who have freedom to please themselves, to one wage earner, three mouths to feed, and considerably less freedom and money. In some instances this may be an important concern, and although this may be unexpressed, it can have an impact on the relationship and on whether the couple wish to become parents. I make note of this here simply to highlight the fact that when treating a man, a woman or both partners in relation to fertility and pregnancy, there may be much more surrounding the situation which can influence the outcome than initially meets the eye. The practitioner will always need to bear in mind that they are treating an individual first, and an individual with an objective second. If this is taken into consideration, a successful outcome can always be achieved within therapy, even when the outcome may not be what the patient initially had in mind.

In conclusion, do not underestimate the benefits of self-hypnosis as a tool for relaxation and as a way of effectively reinforcing post-hypnotic suggestions. The hypnosis sessions thus become only a part of this process, with the mother taking progressively more control and doing more of the work herself as she gets closer to the birth of her child.

Conclusion

Clinical hypnosis as a process cannot be neatly categorised. This volume is not comprehensive, and the subject of each chapter could easily take up a whole book on its own. I have attempted to give an overview of the form and content of clinical hypnosis sessions, and to set out some of the variations that are relevant to patients' interactions with their condition. It is these variables that make each session with a patient unique.

As this volume has set out to demonstrate, the practitioner needs to listen and observe, demonstrate rapport, and create confidence in the process before setting out to use the hypnotic state to fully facilitate this change.

These skills can be transferred to any form of communication with another individual, and it is always worthwhile remembering that just as we are observing others, so they are taking note of the things that we say and do. An understanding of these skills will make the individual think more – and often say less.

Appendix III lists the details of websites that you can explore in order to obtain further information about this fascinating subject.

I hope you have enjoyed this volume.

Ursula James
ursulajames@thamesmedicallectures.com

References

Anbar RD (2003) Self-hypnosis for anxiety associated with severe asthma: a case report. *BMC Pediatr.* **3:** 7.

Barabasz AF and Barabasz M (1989) Effects of restricted environmental stimulation: enhancement of hypnotizability for experimental and chronic pain control. *Int J Clin Exp Hypn.* **37:** 217–31.

Berger JM (2002) False memory syndrome and therapist liability to third parties for emotional distress injuries arising from recovered memory therapy: a general prohibition on liability and a limited liability exception. *Spec Law Dig Health Care Law.* **275:** 9–41.

Bob P (2007) Hypnotic abreaction releases chaotic patterns of electrodermal activity during dissociation. *Int J Clin Exp Hypn.* **55:** 435–56.

Buchser E, Burnand B, Sprunger AL *et al.* (1994) Hypnosis and self-hypnosis, administered and taught by nurses, for the reduction of chronic pain: a controlled clinical trial. *Schweiz Med Wochenschr Suppl.* **62:** 77–81.

Buell FA and Biehl JP (1949) The influence of hypnosis on the tremor of Parkinson's disease. *Dis Nerv Syst.* **10:** 20–3.

Cerezuela GP, Tejero P, Choliz M *et al.* (2004) Wertheim's hypothesis on 'highway hypnosis': empirical evidence from a study on motorway and conventional road driving. *Accid Anal Prev.* **36:** 1045–54.

Conn JH (1980) Hypnosis and free will. *J Am Soc Psychosom Dent Med.* **27:** 2–9.

Creswell JD, Way BM, Eisenberger NI *et al.* (2007) Neural correlates of dispositional mindfulness during affect labeling. *Psychosom Med.* **69:** 560–5.

David D, Brown R, Pojoga C *et al.* (2000) The impact of posthypnotic amnesia and directed forgetting on implicit and explicit memory: new insights from a modified process dissociation procedure. *Int J Clin Exp Hypn.* **48:** 267–89.

De Groot HP, Gwynn MI and Spanos NP (1988) The effects of contextual information and gender on the prediction of hypnotic susceptibility. *J Pers Soc Psychol.* **54:** 1049–53.

De Pascalis V, Cacace I and Massicolle F (2008) Focused analgesia in waking and hypnosis: effects on pain, memory, and somatosensory event-related potentials. *Pain.* **134:** 197–208.

Eslinger MR (2000) Hypnosis principles and applications: an adjunct to health care. *CRNA.* **11:** 190–6.

Feldman JB (2009) Expanding hypnotic pain management to the affective dimension of pain. *Am J Clin Hypn.* **51:** 235–54.

Galanter M (1983) Engaged members of the Unification Church. Impact of a charismatic large group on adaptation and behavior. *Arch Gen Psychiatry.* **40:** 1197–202.

Gibson HB and Curran JD (1974) Hypnotic susceptibility and personality: a replication study. *Br J Psychol.* **65:** 283–91.

Glisky ML and Kihlstrom JF (1993) Hypnotizability and facets of openness. *Int J Clin Exp Hypn.* **41:** 112–23.

Goligorsky MS (2001) The concept of cellular 'fight-or-flight' reaction to stress. *Am J Physiol Renal Physiol.* **280:** F551–61.

Grant JA and Rainville P (2005) Hypnosis and meditation: similar experiential changes and shared brain mechanisms. *Med Hypotheses.* **65:** 625–6.

Harmon T M, Hynan MT and Tyre TE (1990) Improved obstetric outcomes using hypnotic analgesia and skill mastery combined with childbirth education. *J Consult Clin Psychol.* **58:** 525–30.

Hilgard ER (1981) The eye roll sign and other scores of the Hypnotic Induction Profile (HIP) as related to the Stanford Hypnotic Susceptibility Scale, Form C (SHSS:C): a critical discussion of a study by Frischholz and others. *Am J Clin Hypn.* **24:** 89–97.

Johnson LS, Dawson SL, Clark JL *et al.* (1983) Self-hypnosis versus hetero-hypnosis: order effects and sex differences in behavioral and experiential impact. *Int J Clin Exp Hypn.* **31:** 139–54.

Kensinger EA and Schacter DL (2007) Remembering the specific visual details of presented objects: neuroimaging evidence for effects of emotion. *Neuropsychologia.* **45:** 2951–62.

King BJ and Council JR (1998) Intentionality during hypnosis: an ironic process analysis. *Int J Clin Exp Hypn.* **46:** 295–313.

Kirsch I (2001) The response set theory of hypnosis: expectancy and physiology. *Am J Clin Hypn.* **44:** 69–73.

Kohen DP and Zajac R (2007) Self-hypnosis training for headaches in children and adolescents. *J Pediatr.* **150:** 635–9.

Lerner Y, Papo D, Zhdanov A *et al.* (2009) Eyes wide shut: amygdala mediates eyes-closed effect on emotional experience with music. *PLoS One.* **4:** e6230.

Levitas E, Parmet A, Lunenfeld E *et al.* (2006) Impact of hypnosis during embryo transfer on the outcome of *in vitro* fertilization–embryo transfer: a case–control study. *Fertil Steril.* **85:** 1404–8.

Loewald HW (1955) Hypnoid state, repression, abreaction and recollection. *J Am Psychoanal Assoc.* **3:** 201–10.

Lynn SJ and Rhue JW (1986) The fantasy-prone person: hypnosis, imagination, and creativity. *J Pers Soc Psychol.* **51:** 404–8.

McMorris T, Swain J, Smith M *et al.* (2006) Heat stress, plasma concentrations of adrenaline, noradrenaline, 5-hydroxytryptamine and cortisol, mood state and cognitive performance. *Int J Psychophysiol.* **61:** 204–15.

McNeilly R (1994) Solution-oriented hypnosis. An effective approach in medical practice. *Aust Fam Physician.* **23:** 1744–6.

Maltz M (2003) *Psycho-cybernetics* (updated edition). Upper Saddle River, NJ: Prentice Hall Press.

Mantle F (2002) The role of alternative medicine in treating postnatal depression. *Complement Ther Nurs Midwifery.* **8:** 197–203.

Marc I, Rainville P, Masse B *et al.* (2008) Hypnotic analgesia intervention during first-trimester pregnancy termination: an open randomized trial. *Am J Obstet Gynecol.* **199:** 469 e1–9.

Matheson G, Shue KL and Bart C (1989) A validation study of a short-form hypnotic-experience questionnaire and its relationship to hypnotizability. *Am J Clin Hypn.* **32:** 17–26.

Mehl LE (1994) Hypnosis and conversion of the breech to the vertex presentation. *Arch Fam Med.* **3:** 881–7.

Mercer SW, Reilly D and Watt GC (2002) The importance of empathy in the enablement of patients attending the Glasgow Homoeopathic Hospital. *Br J Gen Pract.* **52:** 901–5.

Moss BF and Magaro PA (1989) Personality types and hetero- versus auto-hypnosis. *J Pers Soc Psychol.* **57:** 532–8.

Nash MR, Drake SD, Wiley S *et al.* (1986) Accuracy of recall by hypnotically age-regressed subjects. *J Abnorm Psychol.* **95:** 298–300.

Pekala RJ (2002) Operationalizing trance II: clinical application using a psychophenomenological approach. *Am J Clin Hypn.* **44:** 241–55.

Pekala RJ, Kumar VK, Maurer R *et al.* (2006) 'How deeply hypnotized did I get?' Predicting self-reported hypnotic depth from a phenomenological assessment instrument. *Int J Clin Exp Hypn.* **54:** 316–39.

Phillips-Moore J (2005) HypnoBirthing. *Aust J Holist Nurs.* **12:** 41–2.

Piccione C, Hilgard ER and Zimbardo PG (1989) On the degree of stability of measured hypnotizability over a 25-year period. *J Pers Soc Psychol.* **56:** 289–95.

Pyun YD and Kim YJ (2009) Experimental production of past-life memories in hypnosis. *Int J Clin Exp Hypn.* **57:** 269–78.

Rainville P, Hofbauer RK, Bushnell MC *et al.* (2002) Hypnosis modulates activity in brain structures involved in the regulation of consciousness. *J Cogn Neurosci.* **14:** 887–901.

Reid J (2002) Self-hypnosis in midwifery. *Pract Midwife.* **5:** 14–16.

Ruch JC, Morgan AH and Hilgard ER (1974) Measuring hypnotic responsiveness: a comparison of the Barber Suggestibility Scale and the Stanford Hypnotic Susceptibility Scale, Form A. *Int J Clin Exp Hypn.* **22:** 365–76.

Schubert C and Schussler G (2009) [Psychoneuroimmunology: an update] [Article in German]. *Z Psychosom Med Psychother.* **55:** 3–26.

Shenefelt PD (2003) Hypnosis-facilitated relaxation using self-guided imagery during dermatologic procedures. *Am J Clin Hypn.* **45:** 225–32.

Shor RE and Orne EC (1963) Norms on the Harvard Group Scale of Hypnotic Susceptibility, Form A. *Int J Clin Exp Hypn.* **11:** 39–47.

Simon EP and Schwartz J (1999) Medical hypnosis for hyperemesis gravidarum. *Birth.* **26:** 248–54.

Taggart P, Sutton P, Redfern C *et al.* (2005) The effect of mental stress on the non-dipolar components of the T wave: modulation by hypnosis. *Psychosom Med.* **67:** 376–83.

Tellegen A and Atkinson G (1974) Openness to absorbing and self-altering experiences ('absorption'), a trait related to hypnotic susceptibility. *J Abnorm Psychol.* **83:** 268–77.

Wagstaff GF (1981) *Hypnosis, Compliance, and Belief.* New York: St Martin's Press.

Wain HJ, Amen D and Jabbari B (1990) The effects of hypnosis on a parkinsonian tremor: case report with polygraph/EEG recordings. *Am J Clin Hypn.* **33:** 94–8.

Wainer N (2000) HypnoBirthing. A radical change on our perspective of pain in childbirth. *Midwifery Today Int Midwife.* **55:** 36–8.

West ED (1967) Systematic desensitisation for phobias. *Lancet.* **1:** 897–8.

Whitehouse WG, Dinges DF, Orne EC *et al.* (1996) Psychosocial and immune effects of self-hypnosis training for stress management throughout the first semester of medical school. *Psychosom Med.* **58:** 249–63.

Wilson SC and Barber TX (1978) The Creative Imagination Scale as a measure of hypnotic responsiveness: applications to experimental and clinical hypnosis. *Am J Clin Hypn.* **20:** 235–49.

Woody EZ and Szechtman H (2003) How can brain activity and hypnosis inform each other? *Int J Clin Exp Hypn.* **51:** 232–55.

Yanovski A and Bricklin B (1967) Spontaneous abreaction during major surgery under hypnosis. *Psychiatr Q.* **41:** 496–524.

Appendix I: A brief history

This list is not a complete account of all who have used or studied hypnosis or hypnotic phenomena. In this section, only specific events and individuals are mentioned whose innovations and contributions changed the perception or use of clinical hypnosis, or are relevant to the medical applications of this tool.

BEFORE MESMER

From ancient Egypt through to Roman times and beyond, the use of suggestions made by an authority figure while the recipient was in a sleep-like state has been recorded. In the healing temples of Aesculapius, the Greek God of Medicine, the priests would walk among the patients as they slept, giving suggestions of health and well-being, which would be interpreted as the gods speaking to them in their dreams.

In many cultures throughout the world, shamans, wise men and healers use the power of words and ritual from an authority figure, associated with the expectations of their followers, to 'heal.' The terms 'cure' and 'healing' are not in the vocabulary of clinical hypnosis, although there are similarities and overlapping experiences even in mainstream medicine, where, for example, words heard by a patient in surgery can be related back postoperatively.

FATHER GASSNER

The first name in modern history associated with the use of a hypnotic state is the Catholic priest, Father Gassner. He theorised that patients who suffered ailments with no obvious origin were possessed by the devil and needed to undergo a ritual in order to be freed. This ritual took the form of being touched by a crucifix, and the patient would then fall in a faint-like state, when suggestions for casting out the devils and resuming their normal behaviour would be made. This sleep was termed 'death', from which the power of Christ through Father Gassner would help them to be 'reborn' cured from their ailment. Father Gassner would allow observers to watch this ritual, among them, Franz Anton Mesmer.

MESMER, FRANZ ANTON (1734–1815) AND ANIMAL MAGNETISM

Mesmer theorised that disease was the direct result of an imbalance of a magnetic fluid. This could be influenced by a process of redistributing this universal fluid, known as 'animal magnetism.' During this process a 'crisis' was suggested to the patient, wherein they experienced pseudo-epileptic seizures and a remission of the neurotic symptom. The 1784 French Royal Commission studied these events and came to the general conclusion that the results were attributable to the suggestions and imagination of the patient, rather than to any magnetic force. Mesmer's theories were then discredited.

PUYSEGUR, MARQUIS DE (1751–1825)

One of Mesmer's students, de Puysegur, continued his work. He no longer suggested the 'crisis' that was so central to Mesmer's process, and it no longer occurred. He discovered that patients fell into a sleep-like state (somnambulism) in which they experienced amnesia of trance events and became highly responsive to suggestions. Puysegur concentrated on certain aspects of this suggestive state, namely the focus of attention, the heightened acceptance of suggestions, and the amnesiac state of hypnotic events as experienced by subjects.

ABBE DE FARIA (1746–1819)

De Faria gave demonstrations of animal hypnosis where hypnotic phenomena such as hallucinations were observed.

BRAID, JAMES (1795–1860)

Braid coined the term 'neurypnosis', which soon became shortened to 'hypnosis.' He initially theorised that the somnambulism discovered by de Puysegur was caused by paralysis of the nerve centres. Braid went on to observe that hypnotic trance could be induced by the fixation of attention on a fixed object (for example, a watch). He also demonstrated that patients could be re-hypnotised by a single stimulus (for example, a word). He later concluded that hypnosis was caused by focusing the attention on one idea (monoideism) rather than a physiological process. Pavlov later expanded on these theories of neural inhibition in his concept of sleep states as a form of progressive cortical inhibition.

ELLIOTSON, JOHN (1791–1868)

Elliotson believed that hypnosis should be thoroughly researched, and that it was the responsibility of the medical profession to conduct that research. In 1846, he founded the first hypnosis journal, *Zoist*, which published research on the use of hypnosis with a wide range of medical conditions. When he chose hypnosis as his subject for the Harveian Oration in 1846, he was discharged from University College Hospital as a result.

ESDAILE, JAMES (1808–1859)

Esdaile specialised in hypno-anaesthesia (mesmeric sleep), and performed hundreds of operations in India using hypnosis as the only anaesthetic. When he was placed in charge of a hospital near Calcutta, he continued his research into the use of hypnosis in surgery, only to be overtaken by events when the anaesthetic properties of ether and chloroform were discovered in 1853. He published a number of volumes, among them *Hypnosis in Medicine and Surgery* (originally entitled *Mesmerism in India*). In 1891 the British Medical Association reported that 'as a therapeutic agent, hypnotism is frequently effective in relieving pain, procuring sleep and alleviating many functional ailments.' This is considered to be a direct result of Esdaile's work in the field.

CHARCOT, JEAN-MARTIN (1825–1893)

Charcot was a neurologist at the Salpetriere neurological clinic, who theorised that hypnosis and hysteria were both symptomatic of disorders in the central nervous system. He believed hypnosis to be a pathological state that weakened the mind and could only be experienced by hysterics. He concluded that hypnosis was an induced seizure when his hysteric patients showed epileptic-like symptoms when they were in a trance. Renowned for his work in various aspects of medicine, his reputation was undermined when this theory was disproved by the work of Liébeault and Bernheim.

LIÉBEAULT, AMBROISE-AUGUSTE (1823–1904)

A student of Charcot, this physician focused on the importance of the use of suggestions in creating a hypnotic state, and was the first to formally observe the subjective nature of hypnotic phenomena. He concentrated on rapid hypnotic techniques (such as the use of the word 'sleep', with a hand pass to induce trance), and did not consider deep trance states to be a requirement for therapeutic change.

BERNHEIM, HIPPOLYTE (1825–1893)

Professor of Medicine at the University of Nancy, and a student of Liébeault, Bernheim also concentrated on the importance of the use of suggestions in creating a hypnotic state. He theorised that patient expectation of trance events would influence their suggestibility, and that hypnosis was part of ideo-motor action influenced by suggestion. This school of thought focused on hypnosis as a psychological process where suggestions were central, and the hypnotic ritual element was minimised. Bernheim's major contribution to the history of hypnosis was in publicising the use of hypnosis to a wider audience.

BREUER, JOSEF (1842–1925)

Breuer was the first physician to formally use hypnosis to treat conditions other than by pain alleviation. Breuer's work initially attracted Freud to the use of hypnotic techniques. This is documented in the case of Anna O, which led to a change in emphasis in the use of hypnosis from direct suggestions to alleviate symptoms, to the use of hypnosis to uncover the origin or cause of the symptom (hypno-analysis).

JANET, PIERRE (1859–1947) AND FREUD, SIGMUND (1856–1939)

Janet and Freud worked together on observing the effects of hypnosis, and from this research Freud went on to create 'free association.' This was based on observing the random, dream-like quality of comments made by hysterical patients as they experienced the hypnotic state, or post-hypnotically. Freud theorised that the hypnotic state was not essential to the recovery of the patient, whereas Janet went on to work with the framework of the 'dissociated self' as a therapeutic technique within hypnosis.

BRAMWELL, JOHN MILNE (1852–1925)

Author of *Hypnotism: Its History, Practice and Theory*, Bramwell is best known for his work with hypnosis in medicine and surgery, having learned of hypnosis through the work of James Esdaile.

COUÉ, ÉMILE (1857–1926)

The pioneer of positive self-suggestion as a way of achieving well-being and mental health, Coué is best known for his phrase 'Every day in every way I am getting better and better.'

MOLL, ALBERT (1862–1939)

A contemporary of Bramwell, Moll wrote *Hypnotism* in 1889. He explored the legal aspects of using hypnosis, how the waking state differs from a hypnotic state, and made the first reference to 'waking hypnosis.'

WORLD WAR ONE

The First World War had an impact on the way in which hypnosis, psychiatric definitions of conditions and psychiatric treatment were viewed and conducted.

As soldiers began to return from the trenches displaying symptoms that became known as 'battle fatigue' – which have more recently been termed post-traumatic stress disorder (PTSD) – the classification of mental illness and treatment had to be rapidly reappraised. One of the results of this reappraisal was the development of a regression technique (hypno-analysis) by Dr Hadfield in the UK to uncover these traumatic memories in order to produce a cathartic outcome. The psychiatric profession became interested in the use of hypnosis at this time because of the potential for rapid improvement of psychiatric cases. Once again, before thorough research could be undertaken, the use of pharmacological agents became the major treatment of choice.

AFTER WORLD WAR TWO

It was not until 1955 that the British Medical Association officially recommended that medical schools should add hypnosis to their curriculum. In 1958, hypnosis was first taught to practitioners in France as part of their medical education.

ERICKSON, MILTON (1901–1980)

An American physician, known as the 'father of modern-day hypnosis', Erickson conducted numerous clinical and experimental studies that evaluated the nature of trance, trance logic, the use of specific language, the use of metaphor, the role of the patient in creating hypnotic states, and hypnosis as an inner-directed altered state of consciousness. He is best known for the use of indirect suggestions and communication as a means of therapeutic strategy. Within this, Erickson utilised the concept of unconscious search processes whereby the mind seeks the answer to a question from within. On that basis, the individual created the problem, so they already have some idea about how to resolve it.

His work led to a number of developments, some of which focused on one specific aspect of his work. Examples include:

➤ hypnotic theories (Ernest Rossi)
➤ strategic models of therapy in hypnosis (Jay Haley)
➤ neurolinguistic programming (patterns of language and communication) (Richard Bandler and John Grinder).

With neo-Ericksonian approaches the general emphasis is on:

➤ the patient's ability to access appropriate methodologies for change by creating an appropriate internal environment
➤ the use of indirect suggestions.

WHITE, ROBERT (1904–2001)

In *A Preface to the Theory of Hypnotism*, White put forward the theory that hypnotic experience and therapeutic change require the patient to be creative. Therefore, he argued, hypnosis was more closely related to goal-driven processes than purely neurological or physical events. Sarbinin expanded on this theory of hypnosis to encompass the event as a social encounter involving role play.

RESEARCH AND DEVELOPMENT

Research into the medical applications of hypnosis really began in the 1950s and 1960s with individuals such as TX Barber, ER Hilgard, MT Orne, TR Sarbinin, J Hartland and D Elman. Since then, clinical hypnosis has been introduced into medical training programmes in the USA, France and Germany. It has yet to be brought into mainstream medical education in the UK, despite the British Medical Association recommendation of 1955 that it should be taught. The University of Oxford Medical School was the first medical school in the UK to offer a clinical hypnosis module as a special study option within its undergraduate programme in

2002, taught by the author, and she has since introduced it to most of the medical schools in the UK.

MODERN HYPNOSIS

The modern uses of hypnosis have themselves become as polarised as the figures from its history. The Theosophical Society, charismatic healing, stage hypnosis and advertising all use elements that stem directly from Mesmer.

Appendix II: Glossary of terms

Reproduced with kind permission of its author, Tom Connelly, Secretary of the British Society of Clinical Hypnosis.

A

Aesthesiogenic
Referring to sensations of a sensory nature produced by suggestion.

Agnosia
Condition in which the patient is unable to correctly interpret sensory impressions.

Alexia
Inability to recognise the written word as words. This condition is often the result of a brain lesion, but can be caused by suggestion.

Amnesia
The loss of memory (partial or total), often caused by shock or trauma. It can be due to physical causes, or it may be caused by suggestion. It sometimes occurs spontaneously after arousal from hypnosis.

Anaesthesia
Loss of sensation and sensitivity, usually due to a chemical agent (as with surgery), but also an important phenomenon of deep hypnosis. Hypnosis can be used as an anaesthetic, and there are many instances of its usage on record.

Analgesia
Reduction or loss of the sensation of pain, which can be achieved through hypnosis.

Anchorages
Frames of reference that people use to make further judgements.

Anchoring
The technique of associating several 'keys' with one fixed point of reference, with the idea of using those keys to later evoke that fixed reference. It is a form of conditioning by association of ideas. Used in neurolinguistic programming and clinical hypnosis.

Animal magnetism
A term coined by Franz Anton Mesmer (1734–1815), who theorised that the effects of 'hypnotism' (which was later to be called 'Mesmerism' after him, and before that time was known as 'Charming') were due to a fluid

magnetic medium that could be passed from person to person.

Aphasia
Loss of the ability to speak, usually due to non-physical causes, and typically a symptom of hysteria. It can also be produced by hypnosis (without the presence of hysteria), and can be caused by lesions of the brain (cortical).

Aphemia
Inability to speak certain words.

Atavistic theory
The theory proposed by Ainslie Meares MD to explain the phenomenon of hypnosis. He posited that in hypnosis the higher centres of the brain are systematically closed down and access is gained to parts of the brain that are primitive and pre-rational. Thus hypnosis could be explained as a form of regression to pre-critical functioning.

Attention
The ability to sustain one's awareness by focusing it on a particular thing.

Autogenic
Relating to things that originate within the self.

Auto-hypnosis
The process whereby a patient is able to place himself in a state of hypnosis.

Autonomic
Self-directed, independent.

Autonomic nervous system
The part of the nervous system that is responsible for many of the body's functions, particularly those of the glands, the smooth muscles, respiration and circulation. It is located along the spine and cerebrospinal system and is completely efferent in function. It is reactive and responsible for the 'fight or flight' response.

Auto-suggestion
Any suggestion that originates from within the self.

Aversion
A strong dislike of something.

Aversion therapy
A form of deconditioning by associating something unpleasant with a particular behaviour pattern that one is trying to eradicate. Typical of behaviour therapy, it is sometimes used in hypnosis (for example, to associate a foul thing, such as dog excrement or vomit, with the act or taste of smoking, thus helping to decondition and extinguish the habit).

B

Behaviour therapy
A means of modifying behaviour by examining the symptoms of a particular problem, and then employing various conditioning techniques to modify or remove these symptoms (for example, flooding, reciprocal inhibition, aversion therapy, systematic desensitisation, massed practice, etc.).

Biofeedback
The use of electronic apparatus to give specific signals to indicate changes in the body. By using this 'feedback' of information, patients can learn to affect the normally autonomic processes such as heart rate and blood pressure.

Biofeedback can be used in hypnosis to teach tense patients how to relax.

Birth trauma

Trauma and anxiety caused by the rigours of the birth process. It is a possible cause of some free-floating anxiety. Re-birthing (developed by Leonard Orr) is designed to reconnect and release the patient from the effects of this trauma. In hypnosis the patient would be regressed to this birth time, with similar effects.

C

Case history

Details of the patient's life circumstances in general, and specific information about their presenting problem. Usually taken before treatment commences, it can provide important pointers to the cause and cure of the problem. Never underestimate the value of a detailed case history.

Catalepsy

A condition observed in some forms of mental illness, and also a phenomenon obtainable by hypnosis, where a patient's limb or limbs become rigid and can be placed in any position, where they will remain.

Catharsis

This word literally means 'purging', and describes the process of releasing repressed or pent-up emotional energy. This is usually brought about by 'reliving', re-experiencing, acting out or talking out the memories of causal events.

Censor

According to psychoanalysis, this is a psychological 'mechanism' that acts as a kind of filter or barrier to prevent repressed material or impulses from coming into consciousness.

Charming

Pre-Mesmer hypnosis; also animal hypnosis (snake charming, etc.).

Chevreul's pendulum

A simple method of determining or increasing a patient's suggestibility. A small pendulum is held over paper on which a cross (consisting of two intersecting lines) is drawn. The patient then begins to swing the pendulum along one of the lines while the hypnotist suggests that it will begin to gradually move from its path until it is swinging along the path of the other line.

Classical conditioning

The process of associating a stimulus with a response.

Clinical hypnosis

The process of carrying out therapy using hypnosis.

Closure

The completion of a psychological process. Developed in Gestalt psychology.

Complex

A psychological matrix of related emotional material. The term originated with Jung.

Compulsion

A state in which a patient feels an irresistible urge to carry out an act, whether this is a thought or a pattern of behaviour, even against his will (re: compulsive behaviour).

Concentration

The fixing of attention in one place or on one thing.

Conditioned reflex

The process whereby an action is carried out in response to a trigger because the action and the trigger (stimulus) have become associated (conditioned). This term originated with Ivan P Pavlov.

Contrasuggestibility

A rare but curious tendency of some patients to respond to a suggestion by acting out the opposite of its intention.

Counter-suggestion

A suggestion that is given in order to neutralise a previous suggestion or belief.

Critical faculty

The ability to make a decision about the validity of a particular thing depends upon the exercise of the critical faculty. It is associated with the conscious mind and the left hemisphere of the brain. Absence of the critical faculty means that all 'proposals' are accepted as valid, and as such this is the temporary goal of hypnosis. Dreams are a good example of a state of the mind in which the critical faculty is in abeyance, as the most improbable things can take place in them but they seem perfectly realistic at the time.

D

Deepening

Once the trance state has been induced it can then be deepened. This usually takes the form of a simple countdown from ten to one (along with suitably relaxing suggestions), or perhaps some form of guided imagery, such as descending a long flight of stairs.

Defence mechanism

Usually associated with the 'censor', this is a psychological strategy to prevent painful, repressed or unpleasant material from coming to consciousness, where it might have to be faced and dealt with.

Dehypnotisation

The process of bringing the hypnotic state to an end and waking the patient. It is usually arranged to happen at a particular signal, such as the count of one to five. Always remember to remove or nullify suggestions that you do not intend to remain.

Dental hypnosis

Typically hypnosis that is used to minimise the pain of dental surgery or to overcome a patient's morbid fear of dentistry.

Depersonalisation

A psychological condition that is common to many mental illnesses but which can also be brought about in deep hypnosis when amnesia deprives the patient of their immediate personal identity.

Desensitisation (systematic)

A therapeutic method developed in behaviour therapy (by Joseph Wolpe), whereby the patient is gradually exposed to the source of their anxiety while engaging in anxiety-inhibiting behaviour, such as deep muscle relaxation, thereby affecting deconditioning. Hypnosis can be combined to good effect with systematic desensitisation to form the therapy of hypno-desensitisation.

Diagnosis

The process of discerning the nature of an ailment.

Direct suggestion
An openly stated hypnotic command that is direct, authoritative and without guile. Its meaning can be taken at face value, in contrast to indirect suggestion.

Dominant effect (the law of)
The concept that a strong emotion will always displace a weaker one (the rule being that only one emotional state can exist in experience at any one time). If you evoke and connect emotion to your suggestions, they will be much more effective. Also, to move a feeling or emotion out of experience, evoke a stronger one. It is difficult to feel anxious when one is angry or happy.

E

Echolalia
Also known as 'echophrasia', the automatic repetition, parrot fashion, by a hypnotised subject of the words of the hypnotist (even when the words make no sense or are in a foreign language).

Ego
Freud proposed that the Ego was the part of the mind that directly interfaced with reality, balancing the urges of the Id and the demands of the Superego. More commonly used to refer to the patient's sense of self.

Egocentric
Acting as if the world revolves around the self and the self is the centre of the world.

Eidetic
Referring to eidetic memory and eidetic imagery, commonly known as 'photographic memory.' This can be induced in deep hypnosis, to the point where (with fantasy) it becomes hallucination.

Engram
The name given to the theory that memory is stored as 'traces' or 'images' in the brain. Thus memories are stored in engrams.

Epinosic
The psychoanalytical term for secondary gain.

Erethism
Extreme sensitivity of a part of the body. It may have an organic cause or it can be induced by hypnosis.

Erotophobia
Irrational fear of sexual stimuli or arousal.

Expectation
An important factor to take into account before beginning hypnosis. If the patient expects to be successfully hypnotised, they probably will be. In pre-induction talks always take the time to ensure that the patient has a realistic idea of what the hypnotic state will be like and what its likely outcome will be.

Extinction
The process of deconditioning a reflex, more commonly known as 'breaking a habit.' The condition is said to be made extinct.

Extrovert
A term originally coined by Jung which has passed into popular parlance to describe an outgoing personality type (as opposed to Introvert).

Eye closure
The point in hypnotic induction when

the subject can no longer keep their eyes open. At this point the hypnotist has achieved eye closure.

Eye fixation
The fixing of the subject's gaze on a point (to narrow and focus their attention).

Eyelid catalepsy
A good test of receptivity to suggestion and eyelid relaxation. The subject is told after eye closure that their eyelids are so relaxed that they cannot open them (sometimes the subject is also asked to look upwards as if at a point on their forehead). When this is shown to be the case, eyelid catalepsy has been achieved.

F
Fascination
The process of bringing about a hypnotic state by fixing the gaze on a point (typically a small shiny object). Also animal hypnosis.

Fight or flight response
The two basic choices (supervised by the autonomic nervous system) that are available in response to an alarming development. These instinctive choices were once necessary for our survival in an early predatory environment, but are largely obsolete in the modern civilised world. They remain as options that can rarely be taken, and severe stress can result from these natural impulses being thwarted.

Filter theory
The theory that the hypnotic state is a result of the mind's attention becoming increasingly selective and narrow in its focus. Whether this is fixation on an external object, on the sound of the

practitioner's voice or on the process of relaxation, the subject can eventually filter out almost everything, including the critical faculty. The mind becomes absorbed in the 'tension' of attention.

Fixation
In hypnosis, focusing of the attention on a single point. In psychoanalysis, the arresting of development at a particular stage.

Fractionation
In hypnosis, a method of induction (Vogt's fractionation method) where the subject is partially relaxed and then roused and asked to recount the sensations experienced. The hypnosis/relaxation then continues again, often with the practitioner 'feeding back' the recounted experience and leading the patient still deeper. The patient is then roused again and their experiences sought, before the hypnosis resumes once more. The process continues until a deep trance state is obtained.

Free association
A technique originating in psychoanalysis, which is now commonly used in many therapies where the intention is to access memories and ideas that are not available to conscious recollection. Stimulus words are given, to which the patient responds with the first word that is evoked. The technique is sometimes used in hypno-analysis.

Functional disorder
A disorder that affects the physical body but which has a psychological origin.

Fusion
In hypnotic practice, the process of

joining two or more normally disparate concepts, feelings or even memories of experience to form a new experience. To take a simple example, if a patient feels anxiety at the sight of a cat but can clearly remember the feeling of happiness at receiving a special gift, ideo-fusion can be used in hypnosis to connect the image of a cat to the feeling of pleasure at receiving a gift, by having the patient summon both image and sensation at the same time.

G

Galvanometer

A device that measures the galvanic skin response. This response is a small change in the electrical conductivity of the skin, due in part to the presence of stress, which is used as the basis of lie detection technology. it is used by some hypno-analysts to detect areas of conflict and stress as the patient recounts their personal history.

Generalisation

A psychological process, often uncovered by hypnosis, that lies at the root of many phobias and neuroses. It is part of the normal learning function, but can lead to error due to unchecked extrapolation. To take a simple example, if a person was tormented as a child by a bully with red hair, this may lead to the unconscious generalisation that all people with red hair are tormentors. Therefore that individual might feel anxiety in the presence of a red-haired person, even if they have never met them before. The problem can develop even further as the colour red itself develops into a stimulus for anxiety, even though it is no longer connected to a person, but to some other object.

Glossolalia

The 'babbling' or speech of a person in some unknown tongue, usually while believing that perfect sense is being made. It can be a symptom of religious hysteria and mental disorder, and can also be made to occur by suggestion in deep hypnosis.

Gnosis

(From the Greek word for knowledge.) In clinical hypnosis, the uncovering of a piece of information or personal experience that enables a dynamic re-evaluation, leading to rapid improvement or cessation of presenting problems. Axial information.

Group hypnosis

The phenomenon whereby hypnosis of large groups of people often results in a greater level of success, perhaps because the members of the group 'feed back' from each other. Mass hypnosis is a recognised phenomenon. Group hypnosis is not normally used in therapy, which needs to be tailored to specific patients, but it is used at religious and political gatherings to get simple ideas accepted at a group level.

H

Hallucination

An experience of one or more senses that occurs without an external stimulus. The cause of the sensory activation is internal. Hallucination is common in psychosis and drug misuse, and it can be evoked in the deeper states of hypnosis and also by direct electrical stimulation of the brain. Positive hallucination describes the process of experiencing something that is not actually present. Negative hallucination describes the process of not experiencing something that is present.

Hand clasp test

A test of susceptibility that is common in stage hypnosis but little used in therapy. The subject is asked to clasp their hands together by interlocking the fingers. The hypnotist might then make suggestions that the hands are sticking together more and more tightly. Eventually the subject is told categorically that their hands are locked together and that they will not be able to separate them until the hypnotist gives that instruction. If the subject is unable to part their hands, or has some difficulty in this act, they are judged to be susceptible to hypnotic suggestion at that time.

Hetero-hypnosis

The process whereby a hypnotist hypnotises a subject or subjects (as opposed to self-hypnosis).

Hidden observer

A phenomenon occasionally experienced in hypnosis in which a part of the mind seems to watch the proceedings in a detached and passive way, even though the rest of the body and personality might be engaged in carrying out some hypnotic suggestion.

Hyperaesthesia

Vivification of the senses, which can be achieved by hypnosis.

Hyperamnesia

In direct contrast to amnesia, which is the partial or total inability to recall memories, hyperamnesia is an increase in the ability to remember.

Hypersuggestibility

A phenomenon of deep hypnosis characterised by an increase in suggestibility.

Hypno-analysis

The process of examining the personal history of a patient using regression, which is facilitated by hypnosis.

Hypnogenic

Referring to something that produces the hypnotic state.

Hypnogogic

Referring to a brief hypnotic state that is experienced during the transition to natural sleep.

Hypnoplasty

A similar process to automatic writing under hypnosis, but clay or plasticine is used by the patient to make images or objects.

Hypnopompic

Referring to a brief hypnotic state that is experienced during the transition between natural sleep and wakefulness.

Hypnosis

The process of obtaining a special condition of cooperation, acceptance and partial critical abeyance brought about through a combination of induction, motivation, expectation and trust. It results in a hypnotic state.

Hypnotic

Referring to a state that is characteristic of the light hypnotic state, or to the process of obtaining a hypnotic state.

Hypnotic trance

See 'Trance.'

I

Ideo-motor response
Literally a physical response to an idea. It is used in hypnosis for signalling. Typically the index fingers of each hand are designated 'yes' and 'no' values, and the control of these fingers is passed to the hypnotised patient's subconscious mind, which then responds to questions by moving the 'Yes' or 'No' finger.

Implosion therapy
Also known as 'flooding', a practice that originated from behaviour therapy. The patient is exposed to the source of anxiety (for example) without aversive consequences, until the fear eventually subsides.

Impotence
The inability to have an erection. In cases where this problem has a psychological origin it can be treated successfully with hypnosis.

Induction
Hypnotic induction is the process used in the transition of the subject from normal waking consciousness into the 'hypnotic state.'

Introvert
A term originally coined by Jung which has passed into popular parlance to describe an inwardly focused personality type (as opposed to Extrovert).

J

James, William
Pioneering American psychologist (1842–1910), and author of *The Principles of Psychology*, which helped to establish psychology as a science and influence many of the seminal thinkers of that period.

Jehovah complex
Megalomania; identification with God or a supreme being.

Jung, Carl Gustav
Swiss psychiatrist (1875–1961), who collaborated with Sigmund Freud (1907–1912) to expand the theory of psychoanalysis. In 1912 he broke from Freud to develop his own significant branch of psychoanalysis, which became known as analytical psychology.

K

Kent–Rosanoff list
A list of words for use in free association which the authors have thoroughly tested and analysed, especially the frequency of various responses. Thus the results of a free association session with the words on the list can be compared with previous results (taken from people in different known psychological states). This list is not normally used in clinical hypnosis, but may have some application in hypno-analysis.

Kinaesthetic memory
Physical memory of bodily states, positions, movements and sensations. It is frequently used in hypnosis, especially during induction when bodily states are evoked by suggestion.

L

Lachrymal glands
The small glands that are responsible for tear production. They often become active as hypnosis deepens.

Latent time
The period of time that elapses between stimulus and response. It often becomes extended as hypnosis deepens.

Lethargy
An early term coined by JM Charcot to describe the light or early stage of hypnosis.

Levitation
The phenomenon whereby a limb is caused to rise by suggestion. It is often used in hypnotic induction and deepening, and is useful where the ensuing therapy employs partial dissociation or glove anaesthesia.

Liminal
Referring to a threshold.

Liminal sensitivity
The threshold of sensation; the minimum stimulus required to cause sensation. (Hence 'subliminal' means beneath the threshold of sensation.)

Locus of control
The place from which a person believes the controlling influence in their life emanates. People with an internal locus of control feel that they control their life from within themselves and are responsible for everything that happens to them. People with an external locus of control feel that their life is governed by forces external to them over which they have no real influence.

M

Magnetism
See 'Animal magnetism.'

Mass hypnosis
The process whereby a large group of people simultaneously experience a state of heightened suggestibility and become open to the experience of hypnotic phenomena.

Massed practice
A technique borrowed from behaviour therapy, where a patient is encouraged, either in or out of hypnosis, to deliberately repeat their symptom(s) over and over again. A typical use of this approach might be for a facial tick. The unconscious stimulus becomes exhausted (extinct) as a result of the conscious repetition.

Memory manipulation
Under hypnosis, the enhancement, removal or even changing of memories. This facility of hypnosis is often used in therapy.

Mesmerism
The type of 'hypnosis' that was practised by Mesmer and his followers. It was typically theatrical and involved the use of 'hypnotic passes', where the hands are moved along the shape of the body as if combing some invisible medium. It is still practised today in eastern countries and in parts of Russia, and is experiencing something of a revival in some parts of America, mainly due to immigrants bringing these skills with them and the growing 'new age' belief in spiritual healing.

Monoideism
A state of fixation on a single thought or topic. It is encountered in hypnosis as concentration increases. The term was coined by James Braid.

Mythomania
Imaginary rationalisation of acts and

exaggerations on suggested themes, often encountered in deep hypnosis.

N

Nancy School
An early French school of psychotherapy founded in 1866 by AA Liébeault (in the city of Nancy). Hypnosis played a major part in the treatment methodology, and much research was conducted into this subject, particularly by HM Bernheim.

Negative hallucination
Not seeing something that is actually there. Often used in stage hypnosis.

Negativism
A form of resistance to suggestions. It can be so strong that the opposite course of action to that suggested is taken (active negativism). Simply refusing to accept suggestions is termed 'passive negativism.'

Nervous sleep
The term coined by James Braid to describe hypnosis.

Neurosis
A functional problem of entirely psychogenic origin, which is often manifested as maladaptive habit(s). It is usually treatable by clinical hypnosis.

Nightmare
A dream that arouses great fear and alarm.

O

Obsession
A persistently recurring idea that is compelling and difficult to put out of one's mind.

Obsessive-compulsive disorder
A condition in which the patient feels compelled to carry out a persistently recurring idea. This can take many forms, such as excessive hand washing (sometimes the patient feels the need to wash their hands more than 100 times per day) or excessive checking of door locks or clothing, etc. It is treatable with hypnosis.

Oedipus complex
A term coined by Sigmund Freud (from the Greek myth) to describe the state in which a young male is sexually attracted to his mother, causing jealousy of the father, and resulting in a feeling of conflict and guilt. In the Greek myth, Oedipus killed his father and unknowingly married his mother.

Oneirosis
An early term for a stage of light hypnosis, similar to the hypnogogic state, and characterised by visual imagery. It is derived from the Greek word *oneiros*, meaning 'dreams.'

One-trial learning
A single occurrence or event that has such a powerful effect on the patient that it modifies their behaviour from then onward. For example, a person who becomes violently ill as a result of drinking too much whisky might be unable to drink whisky thereafter.

Operant conditioning
A form of learning identified in behaviourism (BF Skinner), in which the behaviour of a person or animal is modified by positive or negative reinforcement (such as praise or punishment).

Operator
A term that is occasionally used to refer to the hypnotist.

Overcompensation
Conscious or unconscious behaviour that is designed to make amends for (or disguise) some (real or imagined) shortcoming.

P

Painless surgery
Surgery in which hypnosis is used as the only anaesthetic.

Paradoxical sleep
Another name for rapid eye movement (REM) sleep.

Paramnesia
Distorted memories (rather than lost memories, as with amnesia).

Pavlov, Ivan P
Russian physiologist (1849–1936) who won a Nobel Prize in 1904 for his work on the digestive system. He became well known for his experiments on conditioning.

Peripheral nervous system
That part of the total nervous system which connects the sensory systems of the body to the central nervous system (brain and spinal cord).

Perls, Fritz
German psychologist (1893–1970), originally a psychoanalyst, he went on to develop Gestalt therapy.

Phobia
An intense fear or morbid dread of a specific object or situation. Phobias are treatable with hypnosis.

Photoma
Optical hallucination consisting of sparks or points of light. It is sometimes reported in hypnosis.

Placebo
A substance, usually prescribed, that is given to a patient with the intention of producing beneficial results by utilising the patient's belief that he has been given useful medicine. The placebo does not have any medical potency of a chemical nature, and relies for its effect on suggestion. It is sometimes given as part of an experiment to determine the effectiveness of a new drug, where the group that is given the placebo serves as the control. It is recognised by medical authorities that as much as 30% of the effectiveness of any particular drug is due to the placebo effect.

Post-hypnotic
Referring to something that takes place after hypnosis. For example, post-hypnotic suggestions are those given by the hypnotist to the subject to be carried out later, after the hypnotic session has been terminated.

Postural sway test
A simple test of hypnotic susceptibility. The subject is asked to stand erect with their feet together and eyes closed. They are then asked to recall a time as a child when they swung back and forth on a swing. If the subject has good powers of imagination and concentration, they will begin to swing perceptibly back and forth.

Prestige
The esteem in which a patient holds their hypnotist's abilities. Prestige is

valuable to the hypnotist, who should always seek to maintain a smart, professional image in order to encourage and maintain a sense of prestige.

Psychoanalysis

A theory developed by Sigmund Freud and his followers, based on the idea that neurotic and maladaptive behaviour is caused by emotional and instinctive energies that become repressed in the patient's unconscious. Therapy takes place when these repressed elements are brought to consciousness and catharsis occurs. Psychoanalysis usually involves an extensive case history being taken, along with dream analysis.

Psychodrama

A technique of working with a group, originally devised by JL Moreno, in which members of the gathering 'act out' their problems as if in real life.

Psychogenic

Of psychological origin.

Psychosomatic

Referring to effects in the body that originate in the mind.

Q

Quantum psychology

A fusion of Eastern philosophy, Western psychology and quantum physics.

Questioning

A method of giving suggestions via the medium of structured questions. This takes advantage of the latent affirmative response. For example, the question 'Would you like to be more confident?' elicits a conscious and/or unconscious 'Yes', which affirms the content of the suggestion at an unconscious level. The straightforward statement 'You are going to feel more confident' may be denied by the immediate experience of the patient, even though the critical faculty is diminished.

R

Rapport

The feeling of trust, cooperation and acceptance that can exist between hypnotist and subject. Once rapport has been established, susceptibility to suggestion increases greatly.

Rationalisation

From a psychological point of view, the process of explaining an action in terms of its reasonableness. Usually this is an action that the patient is not particularly proud of, but the aim is to diminish feelings of guilt by showing that the act follows natural logic. From a hypnosis point of view, rationalisation occurs when a subject seeks to explain their actions in hypnosis or post-hypnotic suggestion in a 'reasonable fashion.' For example, a subject might be hypnotised and told that every time the hypnotist claps his hands the subject will remove his jacket. This suggestion can be tested several times, and each time the subject will remove his jacket, but when asked why he keeps doing this he will rationalise and say something like 'It keeps getting warm in here' or 'I don't feel comfortable wearing it.'

Reciprocal inhibition

A term from behaviour therapy, which is included here because of its use within hypno-desensitisation. Reciprocal inhibition takes place when an anxiety-inducing stimulus is made to occur at the same time as an anxiety-inhibiting response (such as deep relaxation). The anxiety-inducing stimulus will then begin to lose its ability to evoke anxiety. For example, if a patient is made to relax completely while experiencing a situation that would normally make them anxious or that would provoke a phobic reaction, the ability of that situation to cause a reaction will be diminished.

Rehearsal
The method of obtaining psychological experience by practising events in imagination as if they were actually occurring. It is useful for goal orientation.

Relaxation
Removal of the state of readiness of the body's muscles (i.e. of the will to move them). It thus involves a lack of tension, leading to a comfortable stillness.

REM sleep
Rapid eye movement sleep, characteristic of the dream state.

Repression
One of the earliest concepts of psychoanalysis, the theory that a psychic function exists which seeks to prevent certain emotionally charged memories from coming to consciousness by keeping them deep in the unconscious mind. It is claimed that these 'repressed memories' are the dynamic source of neurosis and maladapted behaviour. Whether such a repressing function exists is open to debate. Nevertheless, the mind does seem to work as if it does. Experience has demonstrated that unearthing and expressing the energy of these 'imprisoned' memories can lead to the relief of symptoms.

Resistance
In hypnosis this refers to the opposition that is sometimes faced by hypnotists when trying to induce hypnosis in a subject. This is usually unconscious resistance due to deep-rooted fear or distrust, so it can occur even when the subject consciously desires to be hypnotised. The hypnotist will need to establish strong rapport and work on the fear first. Every normally functioning person can be hypnotised.

Reticular activating system (RAS)
The part of the brain that controls wakefulness and sleep.

Retrograde amnesia
Inability to recall memories before a certain event. For example, a person might not be able to remember anything that happened before an accident, but can remember everything that has happened since then.

Reverie
The drifting of the mind into daydreams or fantasy.

Revivification
Literally, bringing back to life or reanimation. This term refers to regression experience where the subject fully re-experiences that time and adopts all of the characteristics of the period. For example, a subject who has been regressed to the age of five and who is revivifying will have no memory of anything after that age, and will speak, act and think like a five-year-old.

S

Salpetriere School of Hypnosis
A school of psychopathology operated

by JM Charcot, whose views on hypnosis influenced Sigmund Freud. Charcot believed that hypnosis was due to a form of hysteria.

Schizophrenia

A serious mental disorder that affects the sufferer's ability to deal with reality. It is usually ascribed to dissociation, or splitting of consciousness.

Script

In hypnosis this term is usually used to describe a pre-prepared induction or deepener.

Secondary gain

Every cloud has a silver lining! Nobody really wants a problem, but sometimes a problem can have a small advantage attached to it, and it is this advantage that is described by the term 'secondary gain.' For example, no one wants a painful headache, but it may have the secondary gain of getting the sufferer some attention.

Selective amnesia

Inability to recall memories about a specific object or event. It is often used as a demonstration of hypnotic phenomena. For example, a subject might be told to forget a number between one and five, and then asked to count the fingers on his hand!

Selective attention

The natural ability of people to select which incoming information they will consciously receive. We perceive much more than we realise, but something within us decides what is important to notice. Normally an unconscious process, selective attention can be temporarily explored consciously. The manipulation of selective attention is thought to be important in achieving a hypnotic state.

Self-hypnosis

The process whereby a person enters a hypnotic state under their own guidance, without using an external hypnotist. It is also known as 'auto-hypnosis.'

Signalling

Usually referred to as ideo-motor response (IMR) signalling, the use of a small bodily movement for communication.

State-dependent memory

Any memory that is dependent upon the replication of certain physiological 'contexts' before it can be recalled. For example, an event that takes place while the subject is highly intoxicated or in a state of extreme emotion might be forgotten upon return to normality, and can only be recalled when the abnormal state is re-experienced. To a certain extent all memory can be said to be state dependent but, fortunately for most people, 'normal consciousness' is a steady state.

Subconscious

Mental processes that are not normally conscious, separate from consciousness. The word 'subconscious' is often used loosely and interchangeably with 'unconscious.'

Subliminal

Below the threshold of sensory awareness.

Suggestibility

The extent to which a person will accept a proposal as being fact.

Suggestion

A proposal that is made to a person as fact, usually just before or during the hypnotic state. Its purpose is usually to obtain a deeper hypnotic state, increase suggestibility or obtain some therapeutic change.

T

Tactile induction

A method of inducing hypnosis by gently stroking the subject's body, usually the forehead, although almost any part of the body can be used. It is not often used in therapy these days, and has its roots in Mesmerism and animal hypnosis (trout tickling!).

Trance induction

The process of bringing about a 'hypnotic' state, either in oneself (self-hypnosis) or in another person (hetero-hypnosis).

Transference

A word that has its origins in psychoanalysis, and which refers to the way that patients sometimes 'project' unconscious associations on to the practitioner. For example, a patient may project emotional attachments that they cannot feel for a parent on to the practitioner. Transference is not usually a problem unless therapy is protracted.

Trauma

Shock to a person, which may be physical or psychological, or both. It can have effects that persist beyond the immediate healing process.

U

Unconditioned response

An original or normal reflex response to a stimulus, as opposed to a 'conditioned response', which is learned behaviour. For example, a dog will normally salivate when it sees food, so this is an unconditioned response. However, with training the dog can be made to salivate in response to a bell ringing, so this is a conditioned response.

Unconscious mind

A collective term which covers all of the mental processes that are operating outside of immediate consciousness awareness. This has described in terms of an iceberg metaphor, where consciousness is represented by the one-eighth of the berg that projects above the waterline. The seven-eighths of the berg below the waterline represent the unconscious mind. Another analogy is the eating process, where eating represents the conscious processes, while digestion is unconscious. There are areas where conscious and unconscious processes overlap – for example, breathing. Most of the time we are unaware (unconscious) of our breathing, especially during sleep, but it is possible to consciously intercede and modify our breathing patterns. So it can be seen that we have unconscious processes that are so 'deep' that we are never consciously aware of them, whereas other unconscious processes are only unconscious because they are not 'in' consciousness, or temporarily forgotten.

A good example of an unconscious process as something that continues even though we are no longer consciously aware of it is afforded by the memory. You will no doubt have had the experience of trying to remember a particular name or fact but found that you were unable to do so. So you carry on with your everyday business, during which you might think, or be consciously aware, of many other things, when suddenly the name or fact 'pops' into your mind (consciousness), 'proving' that a process has taken place (unconscious search) beyond your conscious awareness (unconscious).

It is not clear which faculty decides whether a process will be unconscious or consciously available to us, but it does seem that a 'need to know' rule applies.

Processes that we no longer need to know about (because they are not a danger to us, or we have become so conditioned to them that the process can be carried out unconsciously) do gradually pass into the unconscious. Yet it seems that some non-conscious faculty or element is always vigilant. This is evident at a large gathering where you are struggling to make yourself heard and all you might consciously hear is a babble of background noise from the crowd, but if someone mentions your name you will suddenly become very conscious of it. Similarly, a mother (until she has become conditioned otherwise) will awaken from deep sleep if her baby murmurs or moves.

Perhaps the most important fact from a psychological or hypnotherapeutic point of view is that the unconscious mind is the repository of memory. Thus therapy is usually a matter of investigating, modifying or bringing into consciousness some causal dynamic (usually trauma or false learning) that has become buried in the unconscious mind.

Psychoanalytical theory posits that there is some form of psychic filter which keeps memories that cannot be faced because they are connected with unpleasant events away from consciousness (repressed) – hence the difficulty involved in recovering them. It may be that there is no such 'filter', but repression is simply a continuation of the mind's natural process of 'deconditioning' memories that are not often used.

If you require a particular fact (memory) every day, it will become conditioned to appearing in consciousness and will be readily available for recall. In other words, it is valued as important. A traumatic event is unpleasant, and unless repeatedly bringing it to consciousness has benefits, it will naturally be 'forgotten' or deconditioned from consciousness.

Then there is the 'state-dependent' theory, which works on the theory that memories do not exist in isolation but are a composite of external and internal states. According to this theory, memories are recoverable while the patient is in, or near to, the external or internal state that they were in during the original learning experience. As an extreme example, a person who was highly intoxicated the previous night might have no memory of events that took place then, but if the patient returns to the intoxicated state the memories can then become available. Similarly, dreams are easily forgotten upon awakening (because the state has changed from sleep to wakefulness), and one way to retrieve them is to return the body to exactly the same position that it was in on awakening. From this theory it can be seen that memories might not actually be screened by a filter, but may be unavailable because of the difference between the physical and mental state at the present moment and the time at which the event occurred. Is there a simpler answer? The unconscious could be said to be everything that we are, but which we are not aware of.

V

Visualisation

The process of creating images with the imagination. It is very useful for goal achievement and artificial experience through rehearsal.

Visual predilection

Psychological research conducted in the 1950s showed that unconscious eye movements often gave evidence of categories of mental processes or neurological activities. Studies of these findings by Richard Bandler and John Grinder eventually developed to become part of the technical knowledge of neurolinguistic programming (NLP). It was recognised that people generally fall into one of three groups of cognitive emphasis: visual, auditory or kinaesthetic. That is, for some people their mental experience is largely visual, for others it is mainly auditory, and for yet others it is largely kinaesthetic. These different types may be recognised by observing eye cues in response to questions.

W

Waking hypnosis

A state of rapport that allows suggestions to be effectively given to the subject, without the need for formal trance induction.

Y

Yes set

A technique outlined by Milton Erickson, where the conversation between the practitioner and the patient is intentionally structured in such a way that the patient must respond with the word 'yes' (in other words, obtaining a positive rather than a negative response). This sets a positive mood for interaction and begins the reframing process.

It is also possible to use the momentum of the repetitive response to have someone agree to something without full consideration. Sales people often utilise this technique by asking a series of innocuous questions to which the answer can only be 'yes', followed quickly by, for example, 'So you want to buy this then?', to which the unwary will often answer 'yes' without giving the matter due thought.

Appendix III: Useful contacts and website addresses

THAMES MEDICAL LECTURES (WWW.THAMESMEDICALLECTURES.COM)
Hypnosis training for healthcare professionals
A not-for-profit organisation set up by the author to promote excellence in medical education. It provides medical school training courses in clinical hypnosis, language and communication, stress management and goal setting, as well as special study modules in UK medical schools.

EXPECTANCY (WWW.EXPECTANCY.CO.UK)
Training courses in hypnosis for pregnancy and childbirth
University-accredited training courses for midwives, obstetric specialists and hypnotherapists in the use of clinical hypnosis techniques for pregnancy and childbirth.

FIRST WAY FORWARD (WWW.FIRSTWAYFORWARD.COM)
CDs suitable for children
www.firstwayforward.com/childcds.html

URSULA JAMES WEBSITE (WWW.URSULAJAMES.COM)
Hypnosis training, books, CDs and MP3s
Clinical hypnosis CDs on subjects such as smoking cessation, weight loss, motivation, pain control, better sleep, health and well-being, and more. Contact details for arranging consultations with the author or members of her team can also be found on the website, as can information about training courses for clinical hypnosis practitioners.

STOP SMOKING CLINIC (WWW.STOPSMOKINGCLINIC.CO.UK)
Smoking cessation
The author's smoking cessation clinic, based in central London.

INTERNATIONAL JOURNAL OF CLINICAL AND EXPERIMENTAL HYPNOSIS (WWW.IJCEH.COM)

Peer-reviewed journal of clinical hypnosis

For over 50 years, the International Journal of Clinical and Experimental Hypnosis (IJCEH) has been the leading voice in hypnosis for researchers, scholars and clinicians in psychiatry, psychology, social work, dentistry and medical specialties. In fact, the *IJCEH* has been consistently ranked as one of the most influential publications in these respective fields, according to citation impact statistics (Source: SSCI Journal Citation Report).

BRITISH SOCIETY OF CLINICAL HYPNOSIS (WWW.BSCH.ORG.UK)

Clinical hypnosis association

An organisation dedicated to establishing high standards of ethical practice within hypnotherapy. The website contains a continually updated and fully searchable database of skilled hypnotherapists. The author was Vice President from 2000 to 2005.

DR MICHAEL YAPKO (WWW.YAPKO.COM)

Depression specialist

Dr Yapko is one of the modern innovators in clinical hypnotherapy. He writes and teaches widely, and is a recognised specialist in the use of hypnosis to treat depression.

MILTON ERICKSON FOUNDATION (WWW.ERICKSON-FOUNDATION.ORG)

Ericksonian hypnosis establishment

Dr Milton Erickson has become something of a legendary figure in modern hypnotherapy. He pioneered the use of 'indirect' hypnotic techniques during the latter half of the twentieth century, and introduced many paradoxical techniques which have been expanded upon since that time.

ONLINE HYPNOSIS JOURNAL (WWW.HYPNOGENESIS.COM)

Hypnosis magazine

A body of articles about hypnosis and hypnotherapy contributed by hypnotherapists from around the world, the main objective being to demystify the subject and broaden its interest to the general public.

ROYAL COLLEGE OF PSYCHIATRISTS (WWW.RCPSYCH.AC.UK)

Psychiatrists

This website provides information about a wide range of disorders.

BRITISH SOCIETY OF CLINICAL AND ACADEMIC HYPNOSIS (BSCAH) (WWW.BSCAH.COM)

This is a national organisation of doctors, dentists and psychologists, and it incorporates the British Society of Medical and Dental Hypnosis (BSMDH) and the British Society of Experimental and Clinical Hypnosis (BSECH). Membership is also open to those deemed by the council of the BSCAH to have sufficient qualifications and to be engaged in clinical practice or research.

ROYAL SOCIETY OF MEDICINE (RSM) (WWW.RSM.AC.UK/ACADEM/ SMTH_P.PHP)

The RSM has a Hypnosis and Psychosomatic Medicine section for medical practitioners and healthcare professionals with an interest in the subject.

EVIDENCE IN HEALTH AND SOCIAL CARE (WWW.EVIDENCE.NHS.UK)

The principal aim of the NHS Evidence service is to provide easy access to a comprehensive evidence base for everyone in health and social care who takes decisions about treatments or the use of resources – including clinicians, public health professionals, commissioners and service managers – thus improving health and patient care. This website contains information about research into clinical hypnosis and medicine.

Index